HODDER GCSE HISTORY FOR EDEXCEL

MEDICINE THROUGH TIME
c.1250–present

Ian Dawson

In order to ensure that this resource offers high-quality support for the associated Pearson qualification, it has been through a review process by the awarding body. This process confirms that this resource fully covers the teaching and learning content of the specification or part of a specification at which it is aimed. It also confirms that it demonstrates an appropriate balance between the development of subject skills, knowledge and understanding, in addition to preparation for assessment.

Endorsement does not cover any guidance on assessment activities or processes (e.g. practice questions or advice on how to answer assessment questions), included in the resource nor does it prescribe any particular approach to the teaching or delivery of a related course.

While the publishers have made every attempt to ensure that advice on the qualification and its assessment is accurate, the official specification and associated assessment guidance materials are the only authoritative source of information and should always be referred to for definitive guidance.

Pearson examiners have not contributed to any sections in this resource relevant to examination papers for which they have responsibility.

Examiners will not use endorsed resources as a source of material for any assessment set by Pearson.

Endorsement of a resource does not mean that the resource is required to achieve this Pearson qualification, nor does it mean that it is the only suitable material available to support the qualification, and any resource lists produced by the awarding body shall include this and other appropriate resources.

CONTENTS

1 Medicine in Britain – The Big Story from c.1250 to the present

You are about to study 800 years of medical history. That's a lot of history! What's even more astonishing is that by page 9 you will be able to tell – in outline – the whole story of medicine since 1250. Once you have that outline in your mind you will start building up more detailed knowledge but, first, what are the questions at the heart of this Thematic Study?

1.1 The History of Medicine – the big questions

The History of Medicine is about some of the most important questions in the whole of history. Today we live far longer than our ancestors did. We are healthier and have more chance of surviving major illnesses. We are incredibly lucky to be living now and not 500 or even 100 years ago. **So why has medicine – and our health – changed so much over the centuries? Why do we live, on average, so much longer than our ancestors?**

There will be many other enjoyably puzzling questions too – about the **changes** in medicine and the **continuities**, the things that have stayed the same. There'll also be plenty of intriguing questions about **why** there have been changes and continuities.

ASKING GOOD QUESTIONS ?

One of the skills we want you to develop is the ability to ask your own good history questions.

a) What questions do you want to ask about the shape of the graphs below?

b) What answers can you suggest to your own questions?

Use the question starters below as prompts for your questions. Think back to what you learned in Key Stage 3 about different periods of history to suggest answers.

Why ...?   How ...?   What ...?   Who ...?   Was it really ...?   What happened ...?

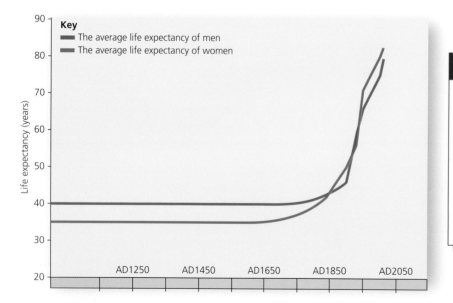

Key
■ The average life expectancy of men
■ The average life expectancy of women

AVERAGE LIFE EXPECTANCY

The graph shows the average life expectancy of men and women over the last 800 years. Average life expectancy is the average age that people can expect to live to when they are born. Of course, many people have always lived longer than the average. For example, in the Middle Ages there were people who lived into their 70s and 80s even though the average life was much shorter.

1.2 Becoming a master of chronology

Lots of things you learned in Key Stage 3 history lessons are going to be exceedingly useful in your GCSE course. One example is your knowledge of chronology – the names and sequence of the different historical periods. As you are going to study such a long span of time you will have to talk and write confidently about a variety of historical periods. We will say more about this on pages 4–5 but, to begin with, can you answer the questions below?

IDENTIFYING HISTORICAL PERIODS

1. Place the four historical periods below in chronological order.

   The Industrial Revolution   The twentieth century
   The Middle Ages   The Renaissance

2. Which picture on this page comes from each chronological period? Give one reason for each choice.

3. Roughly which dates does each period cover?

4. a) What seems to be happening in each picture?
   b) What can you work out from each picture about medicine at that time?

   For example they could tell you about:
   – ideas about what causes disease and illness
   – methods of preventing disease and illness
   – methods of treating the sick
   – who cared for the sick.

A

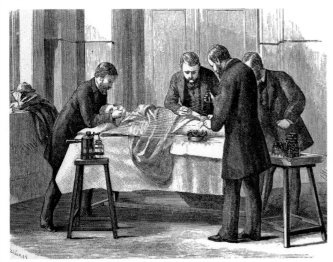

B

C

D

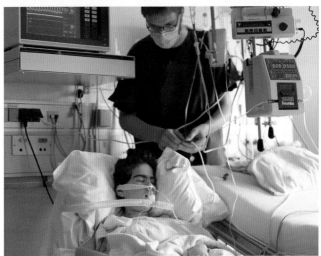

Getting better at history – why we are making learning visible

We'll come back to chronology in a moment, because it's an excellent and important example of a much bigger topic – what do you have to do to get better at history?

In this part of your GCSE course the answer sounds straightforward – you have to build up your knowledge and understanding of the History of Medicine. However, it won't always be straightforward. You will keep meeting new information and sometimes you are going to feel puzzled, maybe even totally confused!

What do you do when you feel puzzled and confused? You have two choices:

> Muddle on, try to ignore or hide the problem and don't tell your teacher. You may lose confidence and stop working hard. The result – you make mistakes in your exams and do badly.

Choice A

> Think about why you're puzzled and **identify** the problem. Then admit there's something you don't understand and tell your teacher. The result – your teacher helps you sort out the problem, your confidence increases and you do well in your exams.

Choice B

Visible learning

It's OK to get things wrong. We all do. And often the things we get wrong and then correct are the things we remember best because we've had to think harder about them. Saying 'I don't understand' is the first step towards getting it right.

Throughout this book we will identify common mistakes that students make and make them visible so that you can see them. Then you have a much better chance of avoiding those mistakes yourself.

Choice B is a lot smarter than Choice A! With Choice B you are taking responsibility for your own learning and your own success. It may sound strange but one crucial way to get better at history is to admit when you're confused and getting things wrong – then you can start to put things right.

We emphasised one very important word in Choice B – **identify**. You cannot get better at history unless you and your teacher identify exactly what you don't know and understand. To put that another way, you have to make that problem **visible** before you can put it right.

The importance of getting the chronology right

One of those very common and very important mistakes – an issue that confuses students **every year** – is chronology. It's so important that we decided it had to be made visible at the very beginning of this book. If you get the chronology wrong you will end up writing about completely the wrong things in an exam. There are plenty of examples of students being asked about developments in one period but writing about an entirely different period because they have confused the name or dates of the period. For example, lots of students have been asked in the exam about changes in medicine in the nineteenth century and written about events between 1900 and 1999. That's a big mistake and a lot of marks to lose.

Why is the chronology confusing? It's because the history of medicine covers 800 years and so includes a number of different periods of history. What you need to do is:

- get the periods of history in the right sequence
- know the approximate dates and centuries of the periods
- know that some periods have more than one name.

So the purpose of the activities is to help you **identify** (that word again!) what you know, what you get wrong and what confuses you. That makes those mistakes **visible** and you can put them right as soon as possible.

CHRONOLOGY

1. Why is it important to identify the things you don't understand and make them visible?

2. Is 1784 in the seventeenth or eighteenth century and can you explain why?

3. The tabards below are in the wrong sequence. What is the correct chronological sequence?

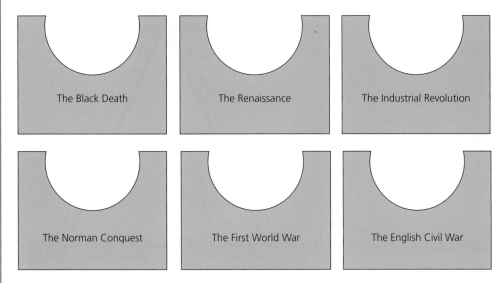

The Black Death

The Renaissance

The Industrial Revolution

The Norman Conquest

The First World War

The English Civil War

4. Look at the two boxes below – Period A and Period B.
   a) One name in each box is the odd one out. Explain which is the odd one out in each box – and why.
   b) The three remaining names in each box are given to roughly the same historical period – but they mean slightly different things. Explain the differences between them. You can use dates to help you and check the timeline below if it helps.

Period A

Tudors and Stuarts	The Renaissance	The age of the Black Death	Early Modern period

Period B

The Victorian age	The twentieth century	The Industrial Revolution	The nineteenth century

11th	**12th**	**13th**	**14th**	**15th**	**16th**	**17th**	**18th**	**19th**	**20th**
1100–99				1400–99			1700–99		

1.3 The Big Story of Medicine

On these two pages you can read the whole History of Medicine since 1250! Starting the book with this Big Story helps solve another problem some students have. They know the details of individual events but they cannot 'see' the whole story – the overall pattern of changes and continuities in the History of Medicine. This is a serious problem when you need to write about long-term changes and continuities in your exam.

The four cards outline this Big Story. Each card has the same sub-headings – and these sub-headings are similar to those in the triangle. **This triangle is hugely important** because it shows the link between what people thought caused disease and illness and how they tried to treat and prevent them. Ideas about cause are at the top of the triangle because they are the most important part of medical history. Those ideas dictate the methods people used to treat and prevent sickness. **Make sure you understand that last sentence before moving on – it's crucial!**

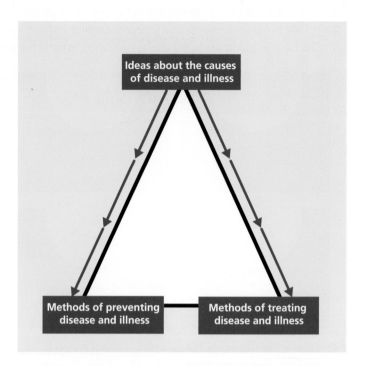

Ideas about the causes of disease and illness

Methods of preventing disease and illness

Methods of treating disease and illness

TELLING THE BIG STORY OF MEDICINE ?

1. Read the four cards to get a first impression of the overall story.
2. Explain why the symbol on each card is important.
3. Use a new sheet of paper for **each** of the four periods. Note down the major features of medicine in each period under these three headings:
    –   Understanding of the causes of disease and illness
    –   Methods of treating disease and illness
    –   Methods of preventing disease and illness
4. Across the top of each page write down two or three short phrases that sum up medicine in that period. Use at least one of the following words in your phrases for each period:

    change   continuity   turning point   progress
5. **This is the core activity on this page.** You have up to two minutes to tell the outline story of medicine. Work in a group of three to plan and tell your story.
6. After you have told your story – write it down. This is important to help it stick in your brain. Think about how to make it memorable by:
    –   using headings
    –   using colours to identify changes and continuities
    –   adding drawings.

MEDICINE IN MEDIEVAL ENGLAND C.1250–C.1500

Ideas about the causes of disease and illness

If you were sick, you might have thought God had sent the illness to punish you for your sins or that you had breathed in bad air. Specialist doctors called **physicians** treated the rich. They would blame your sickness on the **four Humours** (liquids) in your body being out of balance. This Theory of the Four Humours had been developed by Hippocrates and Galen, who were doctors in Ancient Greece, and people still believed their ideas many centuries after they died.

Methods of prevention and treatment

You could pray to God, asking him to forgive you and make you well. You could also take **herbal remedies** (made from plants) which had helped friends or relatives with the same illness. If you saw a physician he checked the colour, smell and taste of your urine to see if your Humours were out of balance. Then he balanced your Humours by **bleeding** (taking blood from your body) or making you vomit. He might also suggest exercise and a different diet.

Some **remedies** helped people recover but nothing stopped the Black Death, a **plague** that arrived in 1348. It killed nearly half the population. People worked hard to keep streets and water supplies clean, but could not stop plague spreading.

THE MEDICAL RENAISSANCE C.1500–C.1700

Ideas about the causes of disease and illness

When you were sick you believed that God or bad air was the cause or that your Humours were out of balance.

Methods of prevention and treatment

Prayer and herbal remedies remained common treatments. Physicians still followed the ideas of Hippocrates and Galen, so bleeding the sick to balance their Humours was a common remedy. **Barber-surgeons** carried out simple operations on the outside of the body but internal surgery was impossible without effective **anaesthetics**.

There were new discoveries. Andreas Vesalius improved knowledge of **anatomy** (the structure of the body) by **dissecting** dead bodies. William Harvey discovered that the blood circulates round the body. Knowledge of these discoveries spread quickly because books were now printed instead of written by hand.

These discoveries built up accurate medical knowledge but they did not cure anyone of their illnesses! In 1665 there was a terrible outbreak of plague in London but, just as in 1348, no one could stop it. They cleaned the streets, cleansed the air and **quarantined** the sick but still they died.

MEDICINE C.1700–C.1900

Ideas about the causes of disease and illness

In 1861 Louis Pasteur published his **germ theory** which said that **bacteria (germs)** cause diseases. He carried out experiments to prove his theory was correct. Some people still believed that bad air caused disease because they spread rapidly in the dirty, smelly industrial towns.

Methods of prevention and treatment

There were breakthroughs before Pasteur's germ theory. In 1798 Edward Jenner used **vaccination** to prevent people catching **smallpox** which killed thousands every year. However, this 'one-off' discovery did not lead to others.

Pasteur's theory did lead to other discoveries such as vaccines to prevent killer diseases. Germ theory also led to the development of **antiseptics** to prevent **infection** during surgery and helped persuade governments to pass laws to provide sewers and clean water.

Not everything changed. People still used herbal remedies, some of which did help the sick. People still had to pay to see a doctor and nearly one in five babies died before their first birthday. However, life expectancy was beginning to rise. By 1900 people on average had a life expectancy nearer to 50 than 40.

MEDICINE IN MODERN BRITAIN C.1900 TO THE PRESENT

Ideas about the causes of disease and illness

In the 1950s scientists discovered the existence of **DNA**, the 'building blocks' of the human body. This led to much more research which identified the individual **genes** that cause some illnesses.

Methods of prevention and treatment

Developments in science and technology greatly improved surgery, for example by identifying blood groups which made blood **transfusions** effective. The discovery and development of chemical drugs and then **antibiotics** in the 1940s have saved millions of lives. In 1942 the Beveridge Report created the plan for the National Health Service (NHS), which began in 1948. For the first time the NHS provided everyone with free treatment from a doctor, so people were more likely to get help before an illness became serious.

DNA

More recently, discoveries about DNA and genes have led to the possibility of preventing diseases which people are born with. This may turn out to be the biggest medical breakthrough of all. The result of these developments is that people born today will, on average, live at least twice as long as people born in 1800.

This is a simple outline. It is not the complete story. You will learn more important details later in the book.

1.4 Why changes happened – and didn't happen

The Big Story on pages 6–7 described the changes and continuities in medical history but it did not say much to **explain** those changes and continuities. This page introduces the **factors** that explain the continuities and changes in medical history.

Each factor is shown as a 'factor diamond' below. You will see and work with these diamonds throughout the book, because explaining why medicine has changed at some times or stayed the same at others is central to understanding its history. It's also central to your exams!

> **Factors**
> Factors are the reasons why medicine changed or stayed the same in each period of history.

In the diagram below there are two groups of factors:

a) The factors to the sides of the triangle have had the most regular impact on medicine, affecting its development throughout history.

b) The factors below the triangle have been important in particular periods of history but not so consistently through time as the factors to the sides the triangle.

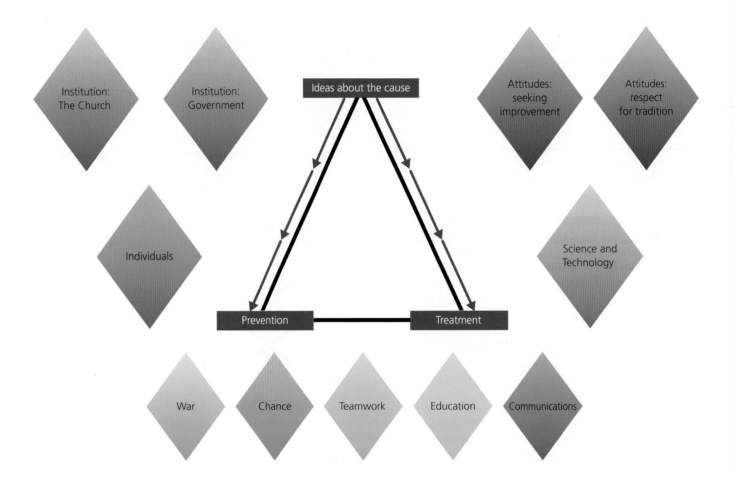

> Only factors relevant to the question being asked or the period are included in the specific enquiries in each chapter.

THINKING ABOUT FACTORS

1. It's time to make good use of your Key Stage 3 history knowledge again.
   a) Work with a partner and choose two of the factors on the right.
   b) For each factor, decide when you think it had most effect on medicine.

   Choose from the four periods identified on pages 6–7:
   – the Middle Ages c.1250–c.1500
   – the Medical Renaissance c.1500–c.1700
   – the eighteenth and nineteenth centuries c.1700–c.1900
   – c.1900 to the present.

   A good way to do this is as follows:
   – Brainstorm what you know about each period (not just the medical history). For example, who governed the country? Was there a great deal of change?
   – Make sure you are clear about the pattern of medical development in each period (see pages 6–7), especially whether each period saw little or lots of change.
   – Now suggest when each of your factors probably had the most impact and whether they helped medicine change or prevented medicine changing.
   – Finally explain why you have chosen that period.

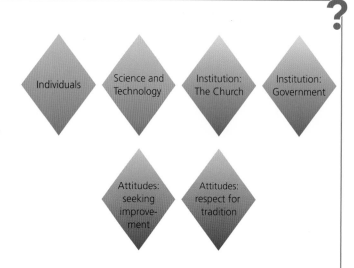

2. Look at the three key moments in medical history below. Which factors are influencing the people or events described in each one? (Don't worry if you're not certain – you will find out exactly why each one took place later in the course.)

1. 1628 – William Harvey's great discovery

In the 1620s William Harvey carried out experiments to prove that blood circulates around the body. However, it was 50 years or more before teachers at universities began to teach their students about Harvey's discovery. Most doctors believed that Harvey's idea must be wrong because he was contradicting the work of Galen, the great Roman doctor. Doctors believed that Galen had discovered everything important about medicine and had written it all in his books. They still believed Galen was right and Harvey must be wrong.

2. 1875 – The Public Health Act

In 1875 the government passed a new law, the Public Health Act, which said that it was compulsory for local councils to improve sewers and drainage and provide clean water supplies. In 1848 an earlier Act said councils could improve these things but did not force them to do so. Then, in 1861, Pasteur published his germ theory, proving that bacteria in dirt and water caused diseases. Then, in 1867, a Reform Act gave many working men (the people who lived in the dirtiest conditions) the vote for the first time. These new voters were most likely to vote for the politicians who would do most to improve their living conditions.

3. 1928 – The discovery of penicillin

In 1928 a scientist called Alexander Fleming noticed that the mould in a dish in his laboratory was killing bacteria in the dish. The mould was **penicillin**. Fleming wrote articles about penicillin but nobody developed the idea. It was only during the Second World War that others scientists followed up Fleming's work and began to give penicillin to dangerously ill patients. When the American and British governments realised that it could cure soldiers with infected wounds they invested huge amounts of money into mass-producing penicillin, the first antibiotic medicine.

1.5 Language is power!

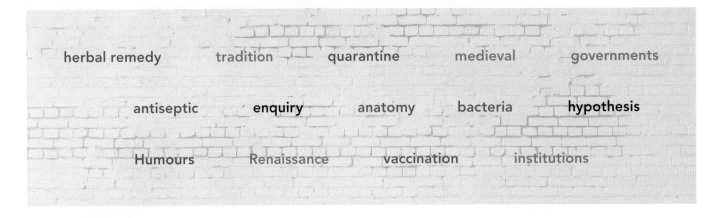

herbal remedy   tradition   quarantine   medieval   governments

antiseptic   enquiry   anatomy   bacteria   hypothesis

Humours   Renaissance   vaccination   institutions

> These are not the only words for your word wall. You will find more later in the book and more explanation about using these words effectively.

Glossary words
When you see a box like this on a page it contains an explanation of what a word means. You can also look up words shown in red in the glossary on pages 163–64.

Lots of classrooms have word walls. So what's the idea? Why have history teachers been filling their walls with words?

There are three good reasons:

1. To help you understand the meaning of technical words and phrases that are part of the History of Medicine.
2. To help you communicate clearly and precisely so you say exactly what you mean. This definitely helps you do well in your exams.
3. To help you spell these important words correctly. Marks are lost in exams for poor spelling.

Do not leave all the work to your teacher! You have a much better chance of doing well in your exams if you take responsibility for your own learning. You need to identify words:

- whose meaning you are not sure of
- you can't spell correctly every time

and make sure you find out their meaning and spelling. One way to do this is to create your own word wall, maybe on a large piece of A3 paper, and add new words to it as you go through your course. Enjoy learning new words and create a sense of achievement for yourself by showing them off and using them correctly!

THE WORD WALL CHALLENGE

1. There are four groups of words on the wall, each in a different colour. What are the four groups?
2. You need to be able to use the words in the word wall in sentences and paragraphs as well as knowing their meaning. Here is a challenge that will develop your ability to use these words effectively:

   Write a paragraph of about 100 words using as many of the words in the wall above as you can – and use words in at least three of the colour groups. Underline the words from the wall that you use in your paragraph. Here's a sentence to get you started:

   When I began my <u>enquiry</u> into the History of Medicine I discovered that <u>herbal remedies</u> have been used for many centuries. Another long-lasting idea …

The headline news in this chapter is 'No important breakthroughs in medicine!' Does the lack of breakthroughs mean that people in the Middle Ages were not very clever? No, that's certainly not true – which makes the lack of breakthroughs puzzling. The answers lie in the illustration below. If you can't make sense of it now, you will by the end of this chapter.

2.1 Understanding the Middle Ages

What can you work out from these illustrations about medicine in the Middle Ages?

UNDERSTANDING THE MIDDLE AGES

To understand medieval medicine you need to understand medieval life and thinking. These questions will diagnose any misunderstandings you have.

1. True or False?
   a) People did not wash or try to keep clean.
   b) You could be fined for throwing rubbish in the street.
   c) People believed that God sent diseases.

2. How influential was the Christian Church?
   a) Very.
   b) Fairly.
   c) Not at all.

3. Who controlled education?
   a) The king and his council.
   b) The bishops and local priests.
   c) The schools.

4. What were the king's two chief duties?
   a) Defending the country.
   b) Improving people's health.
   c) Keeping law and order.

5. How did ideas spread?
   a) Through printed books.
   b) Through handwritten books.
   c) By people talking to each other.

6. Which of these statements best fits people's attitudes?
   a) We must respect traditional ideas, especially what is written in the Bible.
   b) We must seek out new ideas. It is important to challenge old ideas.

Medieval attitudes – the example of Hippocrates and Galen

One vital thing to understand about the Middle Ages is that people respected traditional ideas. Doctors therefore followed the ideas of Hippocrates who had lived over 1500 years earlier in Greece. Claudius Galen was also Greek but worked in Rome 500 years after Hippocrates and was even more respected. He wrote over 300 medical books that were still trusted by doctors in the Middle Ages.

What did Hippocrates and Galen say? The triangle below gives you a summary and the speech bubble and illustrations on the right explain their ideas about what caused illnesses (you will read more about these ideas on page 28).

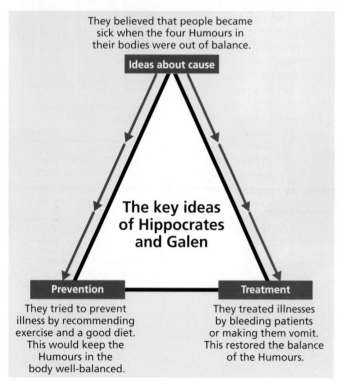

They believed that people became sick when the four Humours in their bodies were out of balance.

Ideas about cause

The key ideas of Hippocrates and Galen

Prevention
They tried to prevent illness by recommending exercise and a good diet. This would keep the Humours in the body well-balanced.

Treatment
They treated illnesses by bleeding patients or making them vomit. This restored the balance of the Humours.

▲ Hippocrates (c.460BC–c.370BC) was a Greek doctor and teacher of doctors.

The body contains four Humours or liquids: blood, phlegm, yellow bile and black bile. When we are healthy these Humours are perfectly balanced in our bodies but we fall sick when we have too much or too little of one Humour. You can see the evidence when you are sick and your body gets rid of excess Humours as shown in the illustrations below.

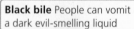

Black bile People can vomit a dark evil-smelling liquid

Blood People may cough blood or have nosebleeds

Phlegm The sick sometimes sneeze revolting phlegm

Yellow bile Sick people can vomit up their half-digested food

THE IDEAS OF HIPPOCRATES AND GALEN

1. Explain the Theory of the Four Humours in your own words.
2. What did people often see when they were ill that made the Theory of the Four Humours believable?
3. How does the Theory of the Four Humours explain Hippocrates' and Galen's methods of treating and preventing illness?
4. Which detail in the illustration on page 11 does this page help to explain?

Understanding the Middle Ages

The questions on page 11 introduced some key features of medieval life. Understanding these features is vital for understanding medieval medicine. It is also vital to respect the people of the Middle Ages in order to understand them properly, not laugh at them because they were different. The diagram below summarises the key features of medieval life.

The questions on page 11 introduced some key features

KEY FEATURES OF MEDIEVAL LIFE

1. Do any of the features in the diagram below help to explain the illustration on page 11?
2. Which of these features might have:
   a) helped improve medicine and people's health
   b) prevented improvements?
3. What connections can you see between any of the features in the diagram?

The Church
The Christian Church was an organisation which spread all over Europe and was headed by the Pope. In England the head of the Church was the Archbishop of Canterbury. Every region had a bishop and every village had a priest. This network of priests gave the Church great influence over everyone's ideas. The largest libraries were in monasteries where monks read and copied books by hand.

The king and his government
The king's main tasks were to defend his people in wartime and to keep the country peaceful by punishing lawbreakers. Taxes were only raised to pay for wars. Keeping streets clean and towns healthy was the work of local councils, but they had little money to pay for this.

Work and harvests
90 per cent of people worked as farmers to grow the food everyone needed. This was hard, back-breaking work. This constant hard work meant there was little time for education or reading. There were years when poor harvests meant that people went hungry.

Key features of medieval life c.1000–c.1500

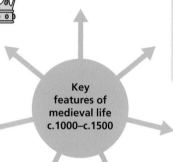

Communications
Printing came to England in the 1470s but until then books had to be written out by hand. This meant there were not many books and knowledge was slow to spread.

Food supplies and transport
Animals were taken to towns to be killed for food. The animals' dung and their butchery created a lot of dirt in the streets. Horses were the main form of transport and also pulled carts so they added considerably to the dirt in the streets that needed cleaning up.

Education
The Church controlled education, especially in the universities where physicians were trained. By the fifteenth century up to 50 per cent of people in large towns could read. The books most commonly read were prayer books and other religious books.

Attitudes
People were taught to respect what was written in the Bible and other ancient books. They were not encouraged by the Church to think for themselves or challenge traditional ideas.

ASKING QUESTIONS ABOUT MEDIEVAL MEDICINE

Learning to ask good questions is an important historical skill. On page 14 we introduce the main Enquiry Question on medieval medicine, so this is a good time to focus on asking questions.

On page 14 we intoduce the main Enquiry Question on medieval medicine

1. Some questions are 'bigger' – more important – than others. Which of these four questions are the bigger ones for understanding the history of medicine – and why?
   a) What diseases did people die from in the 1800s?
   b) Why was Pasteur's work so important in the history of medicine?
   c) Why was the pace of change in medicine so fast in the twentieth century?
   d) What was Vesalius's first name?

2. Make a list of questions you want to ask about medieval medicine. Divide your list into 'big' and 'little' questions. Use the question starters below to help you.

When ...?	What effects ...?
What ...?	How significant ...?
Why ...?	Did it really ...?
How ...?	Who ...?
What happened ...?	Did they ...?
Where ...?	

2.2 Your Enquiry Question

Like you, we thought of lots of questions about medieval medicine. Did you think of these?

What did they know about anatomy?

Did they care about keeping the streets clean?

What other treatments did they use to help the sick?

Why was there so little change in medicine during the Middle Ages?

These are all good questions, but we have chosen the question in the pink bubble as our Enquiry Question, the question to investigate in this chapter. We chose it for three reasons:

1   It's the 'biggest' question in the list because the answer helps you understand medicine throughout this period.
2   It's a puzzling question. Medieval people were just as intelligent as us and they did want to be healthier and stop diseases spreading – but medicine did not improve. Why not?
3   Change and continuity are important ideas in your exam course.

Beginning your enquiry

Before you begin to investigate why medicine changed so little, you need to find out what medicine was like in the Middle Ages. You are going to research this on pages 15–21 and record a summary of your findings on a memory map like the one below.

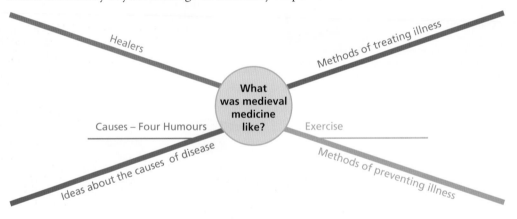

The memory map is the first Knowledge Organiser in this book. On page 4 we said we would help you to avoid common mistakes. One mistake is to make notes so full of detail that you cannot see the key points you need. Memory maps are excellent for recording key points. They help with revision too. This is how to build up your memory map.

Step 1: Use A3 paper. Space is important. The final version should not be cramped.

Step 2: Add information to the map as you read pages 15–21. Use pencil so you can make corrections later. Remember:

■   Use key words or phrases. Do not write full sentences.
■   Use pictures/images/diagrams to replace or emphasise words. Some of you will find it easier to remember visual images than words.
■   PRINT words to make them stand out.

Step 3: When you have finished, redraft your map to make sure everything is clear.

Use the information on pages 12 and 13 to begin filling in your memory map.

2.3 Case study: dealing with the Black Death 1348–49

The pestilence mentioned in the illustration on page 11 is also known as the Black Death, or the plague. Studying the ways people reacted to the Black Death provides a good introduction to medieval medicine, but first this page tells you about its terrifying impact.

The Black Death probably first broke out in China then spread to India and across Europe until it reached England. What happened next was described by a monk writing at a monastery in the south of England:

> In 1348 the cruel pestilence arrived at a port called Melcombe in Dorset. It killed numberless people in Dorset, Devon and Somerset and then it came to Bristol where very few were left alive. It then travelled northwards, leaving not a town, a village or even, except rarely, a house, without killing most or all of the people there. There was such a shortage of people that there were hardly enough living to bury the dead.

Historians estimate that at least 40 per cent of the population died, with an even higher death rate in towns and ports. To many people the world seemed to be ending. One survivor scratched these words on the wall of a church in Hertfordshire:

> 1349 the pestilence 1350 pitiless, wild, violent, the dregs of the people live to tell the tale.

Whoever scratched those words was desperately afraid, wondering what the future would bring. Normal life seemed to have ended. It was a feeling shared by an Irish monk, Brother John Clynn, who wrote:

> I, waiting among the dead for death to come, leave parchment for continuing the work, in case anyone should still be alive in the future and any son of Adam can escape this pestilence and continue my work.

Even now historians are not completely certain what the pestilence was. It may have been the bubonic plague, which spreads when fleas bite an infected rat and then pass the disease onto other rats and to humans. People bitten by infected fleas or rats developed painful swellings called buboes in their armpits and groins. Blisters appeared all over their bodies, followed by a high fever, severe headaches, unconsciousness for several days and then death.

The pestilence did not go away after the first outbreak in 1348–49. Every few years it broke out again and carried on killing large numbers of people, especially in towns, for 300 years.

▲ A **chronicler** in London in the 1300s described how 'they dug broad, deep pits and buried the bodies together, treating everyone alike, except the most eminent'. Archaeologists excavating towns have discovered the evidence to support the chronicler's statement. In the 1980s graves containing victims of the Black Death were found in London, stacked five deep. More burial pits have been found since then, such as the one shown here, in London and in other towns. Skeletons provide historians with a lot of useful evidence: about the height and strength of people, sometimes what injuries and diseases they suffered from, and what kinds of work they did.

THE BLACK DEATH

1. Information speed test! How quickly can you find the answers to these questions?
   a) When did the Black Death arrive in England?
   b) What percentage of people died?
   c) What were buboes?

2. How do skeletons provide valuable evidence for historians?

3. From what you have read so far, why do you think people were unable to stop the Black Death spreading and killing so many?

The Black Death: causes, treatments and prevention

The Black Death was terrifying. Fear and panic drove people to try desperate remedies. However, most ideas about what caused the Black Death were rational, fitting people's ideas about how the world worked. Monks scoured books in monastery libraries to find treatments and cures. People stopped strangers entering their villages in case they were carrying the plague. People did everything they could to prevent plague spreading, given the knowledge and skills they had. The headings on these pages identify people's ideas about what caused the Black Death. In those sections you will also find information about prevention and a little about treatments. There is more information about treatments in a separate box on page 17.

God's punishment

The most widely believed explanation was that God had sent the pestilence to punish people for their sins. In September 1348 the Prior of Christchurch Abbey, Canterbury wrote:

> Terrible is God towards the sons of men … He uses plagues, miserable famines, wars and other suffering to arise and to terrify and torment men and so drive out their sins. Thus England is struck by the pestilence because of the increasing pride and numberless sins of the people.

This was a logical explanation as people believed that God controlled all significant events. Plague was therefore part of God's plan to make people less sinful and save them

from Hell. The clinching evidence that God had sent the pestilence was that no human being could stop or cure it. Only God could do that.

Therefore the only way to stop the pestilence spreading was to show God that people were sorry for their sins and plead for forgiveness. The Archbishop of York wrote:

> The only hope is to urge God with prayers that he, the kind and merciful Almighty God, should turn away his anger and remove the pestilence and drive away the infection from the people.

Many attempts to prevent plague were therefore linked to religion:

- The king and bishops ordered services and processions in every church at least once a day, in which people prayed for forgiveness and asked God to stop the disease.
- People lit huge numbers of candles in churches as offerings to God or fasted (stopped eating) to show they were sorry for their sins.
- Many went on pilgrimages to pray for God's forgiveness at the tombs of saints.
- Activities that might be insulting God were ended. In Suffolk they stopped using churchyards for wrestling matches.
- Some people punished themselves in public and begged God for forgiveness, as you can see in the picture below.
- People prayed to God to let their family and friends who had plague recover.

◄ This picture shows the Flagellants who arrived in London from Holland, according to the chronicler Robert of Avebury. They walked barefoot through the city twice a day, wearing only a linen cloth.
They whipped themselves to show God they had repented their sins and asked God to be merciful.

Bad air

People also blamed miasma – bad, stinking air – for the Black Death. In April 1349, King Edward III wrote to the Mayor of London ordering him to have the 'filth lying in the streets removed' and the city cleansed:

> …from all odours so that no great mortality may arise from such smells …the filth from the houses is infecting the air, endangering people through the contagious sickness which is increasing daily.

People therefore believed that dirt poisoned the air and the poisoned air then made them ill. However, this was not a separate theory. They knew God allowed the air to be poisoned as part of his plan to cleanse people of sin.

London's records show how people tried to prevent dirt creating bad air. By the 1370s there were at least twelve teams of rakers clearing animal dung from the streets. Fines for throwing litter were increased. Butchers were punished for letting blood and the remains of slaughtered animals dirty the streets. Other towns used the same methods to clean streets and water supplies.

Cleaning was not the only way of purifying the air. People:

- carried sweet-smelling herbs or lit fires to overpower the bad air
- kept the air moving by ringing bells or keeping birds to fly around the house.

The impact of the planets

Another explanation was that movements of the planets had caused the disease. People believed that God controlled the planets so this explanation also linked to religion. One writer said:

For God has said, 'At my command, let the planets poison the air and corrupt the whole earth.'

Physicians believed the stars and planets affected people's bodies, so it was logical that planets could cause disease. The science of **astrology** was an important part of the training of doctors in the 1300s.

The Theory of the Four Humours

The wealthy could also consult a university-trained physician. A physician, John of Burgundy, wrote in 1365 that Galen (of course!) had explained the cause of plague:

> Many people have been killed by the plague, especially those stuffed with evil humours. As Galen says, the body does not become sick unless it contains evil humours.

TREATMENTS

We know far less about treatments than about prevention for two reasons. There was little time for treatment because victims died quickly. Frantic, fearful people (even those who could write) did not write down treatments. We do know that people put holy charms round the necks of sufferers and prayed to God to heal the sick. They cut open the buboes to let out the pus and even tried putting bread round the buboes and then burying the bread.

Physicians may have tried bleeding and purging if the sick survived long enough, or tried treatments based on Galen's 'treatment by opposites'. This involved using heat or hot food to treat patients who were cold or using cold and cold foods to treat fevers. Cold foods and baths were used to treat the Black Death and people were told to avoid hot food such as garlic and onions.

THE BLACK DEATH: A CASE STUDY

1. Complete this table showing the treatments and methods of prevention linked to each cause.

Cause	Treatments and methods of prevention
God's punishment	
Bad air	
The impact of the planets	
The Theory of the Four Humours	

2. Which of the causes in the table would you describe as:
   a) based on religion
   b) logical and rational because there was evidence to support it
   c) supernatural because there was no evidence to support it?
   Causes can go in more than one category: a), b) or c).

3. These causes were not completely separate but had links in people's minds. Draw a diagram to show the links and annotate it to explain them.

4. Which of the factors below had the greatest influence on treatments and prevention of the Black Death and ideas about its causes? Give evidence to support your choice.
   a) Government
   b) Individuals
   c) People's attitudes
   d) The Church

5. Use the information in your table to add to your memory map from page 14.

2.4 The main features of medieval medicine

Use pages 18–21 to complete your memory map from page 14. The questions on these pages help you pick out the key points.

Medieval healers

Who would you get help from if you were sick? It depended on how rich you were, whether you lived in a town or the countryside, and how desperate you were. Below is a summary of the main kinds of healers.

Women: wives, mothers and midwives

Women treated most illnesses and knew a wide range of remedies. Sometimes the local wise woman or lady of the manor was called to use her skills and knowledge. Women acted as midwives. In some towns midwives were apprenticed, had licences and were paid. Women could qualify as surgeons by working as apprentices, but were not allowed to become physicians.

Hospitals

The first wave of hospitals appeared in towns in the eleventh century. They mostly cared for older people who could no longer look after themselves. They were run by monks and nuns who provided food, warmth and prayers. Everyone could see the altar where priests said mass seven times each day. They rarely admitted the sick in case they spread infection. One of the most famous early hospitals was St Bartholomew's in London, founded in 1123. From the thirteenth century a second group of much smaller hospitals were founded, often by guilds, organisations of wealthier townspeople who worked in the same trade – shoemakers, silversmiths, etc. These hospitals cared for guild members and local citizens who could no longer look after themselves. By 1400 there were over 500 hospitals, many with only five or six beds. St. Leonard's in York was unusually large with over 200 beds. Occasionally, hospitals were set up to care for particular cases. In London, Richard Whittington, the Lord Mayor, paid for an eight-bed hospital for unmarried pregnant women. In Chester there was a hospital for the care of 'poor and silly persons'.

Physicians

Physicians trained at universities for seven years, reading books by Hippocrates, Galen and Arab medical writers such as Rhazes and Ibn Sina [Avicenna]. However there were fewer than 100 physicians in England in 1300 and only the rich could afford their fees.

Surgeons (also called barber surgeons)

Surgeons did not go to university but trained as apprentices through observing others. They improved their skills through practice and reading books on surgery. They did basic surgery such as bleeding, removing surface tumours, sewing up wounds and making splints for broken bones. There were no effective anaesthetics but occasionally they had to amputate a limb or remove painful bladder stones. Some surgeons used fine needles to remove cataracts from eyes to restore or improve sight.

Apothecaries

Apothecaries mixed ingredients to make ointments and medicines for physicians. They learned from other apothecaries. They also made their own medicines to sell to the sick.

1 Who treated:
  a) the rich
  b) pregnant women
  c) those unable to look after themselves?
2 Who provided most medical care?

3 Who would usually not be let into a hospital?
4 How did surgeons and apothecaries learn their skills?

Treatments

Herbal remedies

A

1 Take onions and garlic

2 Pound them together

3 Take wine and bull's gall

4 Stand for nine nights in a brass vessel

5 Strain mixture through a cloth

6 Apply to stye with a feather

The modern verdict: Onion and garlic kill bacteria

Bull's gall also attacks bacteria

Wine contains acetic acid which reacts with copper in the brass vessel to form copper salts which also kill bacteria

The result: a practical cure

The cure for a stye in the eye shown in diagram A above comes from Bald's Leechbook, a tenth-century collection of treatments. **It continued to be used throughout the Middle Ages**. Many remedies did help the sick. Honey and plantain were often used in treatments for cuts, wounds and dog bites and they do contain ingredients which fight infection.

The most common remedies were made from herbs, minerals and animal parts. Most women knew them by heart, but they were written down in books called 'herbals', with pictures of the ingredients and explanations of the exact quantities of each ingredient and how to mix the potion. They included prayers to say while collecting the herbs to increase the effectiveness of the remedy.

> **SCIENCE NEWS**
> In 2015 scientists tested the cure shown above and have proved that it can kill MRSA, the hospital 'superbug'. Don't underestimate medieval treatments!

Some cures combined prayer, magic and folklore, such as this cure for toothache recommended by John of Gaddesden, an English doctor in the 1300s.

> Write these words on the jaw of the patient. 'In the name of the Father, Son and Holy Ghost, Amen. + Res + Pax + Nax + In Christo Filio.' The pain will cease at once. I have often seen it.

Another cure unlikely to work was for treating quinsy (an abscess in the throat):

> Take a fat cat, flay it well and draw out the guts. Take the grease of a hedgehog, the fat of a bear, resins, fenugreek, sage, honeysuckle gum and virgin wax and crumble this and stuff the cat with it. Then roast the cat and gather the dripping and anoint the sufferer with it.

Bleeding to re-balance the humours

Bleeding, urine and zodiac charts were the three most common illustrations in medical books. This bleeding chart (B) showed the surgeon where to take blood from. Bleeding was usually done by a surgeon who warmed a bleeding cup, placed it over a cut and let the warmth draw out blood. Alternatively, leeches were used to sink their teeth into the patient and draw off blood, a method still used in the nineteenth century. Bleeding and purging the stomach were used to restore the balance of the humours. Purging meant swallowing herbs and animal fat to make the person sick or taking a laxative to empty their bowels.

Physicians used zodiac charts to decide the best time for treatment because they believed that parts of the body were linked to signs of the zodiac and the planets. The zodiac chart showed the doctor when to avoid treating each part of the body. When the moon was in Pisces, for example, the feet should not be treated.

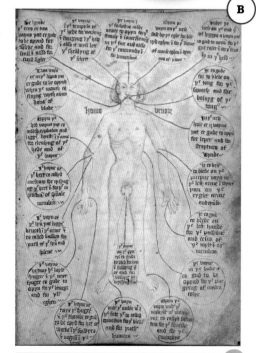

B

1 Were herbal remedies helpful?
2 What were zodiac and bleeding charts used for?

Surgery

Surgeons improved their techniques and instruments through practice. A skull discovered in Yorkshire shows their skills. It belonged to a man who'd been hit, leaving bone splinters in the brain; but a medieval surgeon cut a hole, removed the splinters and the man lived after the operation.

A surgeon saved King Henry V when, as a 16-year-old prince in 1403, he was wounded in battle. An arrow pierced his cheek and penetrated to the base of his skull. The royal surgeon, John Bradmore, knew that pieces of arrow in the wound would poison and kill the prince. So Bradmore designed metal forceps to pass through the wound, take hold of the arrowhead and pull it out. When the forceps were made, Bradmore removed the arrowhead and dressed the wound for three weeks with clean linen, barley and honey, which keep wounds free of infection. The wound healed.

A 'wound man' (C) was a common illustration, showing surgeons how to deal with different wounds. However, surgeons could not do complex surgery inside the body. They did not have enough knowledge of anatomy, nor effective anaesthetics. They used herbs such as opium or hemlock to make patients drowsy, but risked putting the patient to sleep permanently. Wine, vinegar or honey were used to clean wounds, but could not prevent infections spreading or stop heavy bleeding.

> 1 What could surgeons not do?
> 2 What kinds of surgery did surgeons do?

Ideas about the cause of illness

As you read in the case study on the Black Death (pages 15–17), people believed that God sent diseases. This belief was linked to other ideas, most of which were logical – but wrong. Physicians, such as the one shown here (D), believed in the Theory of the Four Humours. This was another logical theory – but it too was wrong! Nobody knew what really caused diseases and so no major progress could be made in treatments or prevention.

> 3 Why were ideas about causes so important for all aspects of medicine?
> 4 What did a physician use a urine jar for?

A picture of a physician from c.1400. He is shown carrying a urine ▶ jar because examining a patient's urine was a crucial part of diagnosing an illness. The physician matched the patient's urine against the colours, smell and thickness shown on a urine chart and might taste the urine to check it was normal. This method of diagnosis fitted the Theory of the Four Humours. For example, very white urine was a sign of too much phlegm in the body.

Preventing disease and illness

Physicians advised wealthy clients how to stay healthy, suggesting regular washing, cleaning teeth, combing hair, exercise in fresh air and bathing in hot water. The wealthy sent their urine to physicians to make sure that they were not falling ill. Simple, hand-copied guides to healthy living and how to avoid plague were sold in towns and around the country and so reached a wide audience. Many were written in rhyme so the details could be more easily remembered.

People also tried hard to keep their towns clean. Historians did not always believe this; 150 years ago Victorian historians described medieval towns as places of complete squalor, full of dirt. Nobody, they said, made any effort to keep towns clean. However, modern historians have done research which proves that Victorian writers were wrong. Many medieval towns, especially in the 1400s, were cleaner than industrial towns of the early 1800s. Town councils and individuals worked hard to keep streets clean, especially after outbreaks of plague. We should not be surprised – medieval people were just as interested in staying healthy as we are today.

The diagram below shows that great efforts were made to keep towns clean. London was the first town in Europe to have a piped water supply. People were proud of their towns, wanting to be cleaner than neighbouring towns and attract visitors as pilgrims or for trade. Many individuals left money in their wills to pay for improvements such as building latrines or improving piping systems to bring fresh water. They expected this charity would help them reach Heaven sooner after they died. However, it was impossible to get rid of all the dirt created by animals, industries and people themselves. Cleaning cost more money than towns had when war or plague stopped trade. Therefore, despite all the efforts, medieval towns would have seemed to us dirty, smelly and very unhealthy places.

1 Why were towns so hard to keep clean?
2 What did people do to stay clean and healthy?

Too many animals

Problem: Cattle, sheep and geese continually arrived to be butchered for food. Horses were the main form of transport. These animals left trails of dung in the streets.

Solution: A small number of rakers were employed to clean the streets. Newcastle was one town where streets were paved to make them drier and easier to clean.

Keeping towns clean: problems and solutions

Dirty water

Problem: Water supplies were dirty because of industrial and human waste.

Solution: Gloucester was one of many places where monasteries and townspeople collaborated to bring fresh water to public wells through lead pipes. In Exeter aqueducts were built to bring fresh water to the town.

Waste and litter

Problem: People dropped waste and litter of all kinds and sometimes used streets as latrines. Butchers threw bloody waste and animal parts in the street.

Solution: Laws were passed to punish throwing waste. Butchers had to get rid of waste outside city walls. Public latrines were built in Norwich and many other towns, including over a dozen in London.

Leaking latrines

Problem: Latrines and cesspits were sometimes built by house-owners near water supplies and their contents emptied into streams and rivers used for washing and drinking water.

Solution: Regulations were introduced about where to build private latrines. Cesspits were lined with brick or stone and so were less likely to leak into drinking water supplies. In Hull, Southampton and other towns, night carts went round collecting human waste from cesspits.

Medical moments in time: 1390 – London in the time of plague

MEDIEVAL MEDICINE: A SUMMARY

This page gives you the chance to summarise what you have learned about medieval medicine.

1. Each of the bubbles and boxes in the picture starts a conversation or provides information. Work with a partner to complete the conversations or information boxes. This will involve including information about all four parts of your memory map from page 14:
   – healers
   – ideas about the causes of disease
   – methods of treating illness
   – methods of preventing illness.

   If you look carefully you will also find some clues in the picture.

2. Which healers are not included in this picture?

3. One of the pictures on the cover of this book is a medieval illustration. What does its tell you about medieval medicine?

My father's sick. I took him to the monks at the hospital …

People tried to keep towns clean by …

The main problems keeping the towns clean were …

Some houses had toilets and wells but …

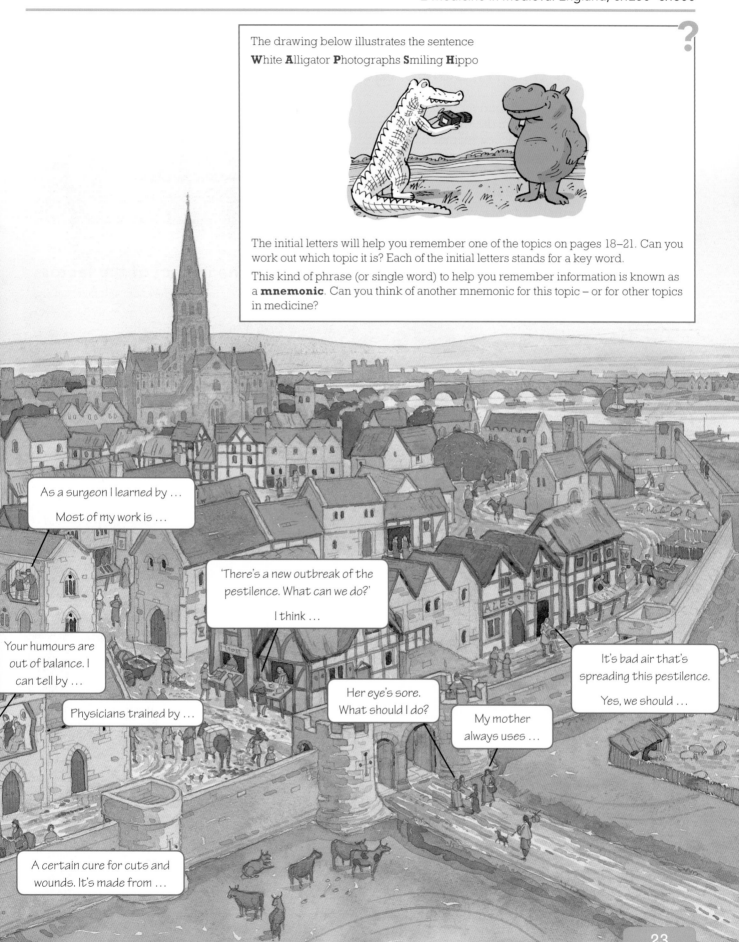

The drawing below illustrates the sentence
White **A**lligator **P**hotographs **S**miling **H**ippo

The initial letters will help you remember one of the topics on pages 18–21. Can you work out which topic it is? Each of the initial letters stands for a key word.

This kind of phrase (or single word) to help you remember information is known as a **mnemonic**. Can you think of another mnemonic for this topic – or for other topics in medicine?

As a surgeon I learned by …

Most of my work is …

'There's a new outbreak of the pestilence. What can we do?'

I think …

Your humours are out of balance. I can tell by …

Physicians trained by …

Her eye's sore. What should I do?

My mother always uses …

It's bad air that's spreading this pestilence.

Yes, we should …

A certain cure for cuts and wounds. It's made from …

2.5 Your enquiry: why was there so little change in medicine in the Middle Ages?

Your completed memory map will continue to be useful later when you compare medicine in the Middle Ages with medicine in later periods. However, now it's time to work out your answer to the Enquiry Question above.

Creating your hypothesis

To create a hypothesis – the first draft answer to our question – you can use the Factor Diamonds. We have picked out the factors that were most important in preventing medical change in the Middle Ages (therefore omitting Science and Technology). Here they are:

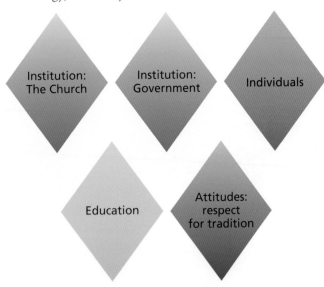

1. Now use the diamonds to create your hypothesis. Arrange them in a pattern like the examples below. You do not have to copy one of these patterns, but do not just guess. Use your knowledge to decide on the most likely pattern. The information on page 13 will act as a reminder.

Preventing change	Hypothesis A	Hypothesis B
THE MOST IMPORTANT FACTORS	◇ ◇	◇
VERY IMPORTANT FACTORS	◇ ◇	◇ ◇
QUITE IMPORTANT FACTORS	◇	◇ ◇

2. Now use your pattern to write a short paragraph answering the Enquiry Question. You can use these sentence starters and links as a guide:

One of the most important reasons why there was little change in medicine in the Middle Ages was …

Another vital reason was ….

Other factors ….. also played a part in hindering medical developments

Researching the impact of the factors

Use pages 26–28 to research the effects of each factor. Take one factor at a time:

a) Read the section about the factor quickly to get an overall sense of its content. The questions on each page will help you think about the factor's influence.
b) Use a table like the one below as a Knowledge Organiser. After your first reading fill in column 2 in pencil.
c) Now read the section again. Make separate notes explaining how the factor explains continuity. Then finalise your entry in column 2. Prove the link by using connectives (see page 25).
d) Fill in column 3. Revise your hypothesis if you can improve it. Use language such as 'most important', 'very important', 'quite important'.

1. Factors	2. How does the factor explain continuity in medicine?	3. How important is the factor in explaining continuity?
The Church		
Education		
Attitudes (respect for tradition)		
Individuals		
Government		

Revisiting the word wall

It is time to return to the word wall (introduced on page 10) because you need a strong command of the words on the wall to develop a good answer to the Enquiry Question.

These words are not only useful for writing your answer. They are just as important when you are thinking and talking about your answer. They help you use exactly the right words and so explain your ideas more precisely.

On the word wall at the bottom of the page are some more words and phrases to add to your own wall. We have used the same colour coding that we used on page 10 – one colour for each group of words as follows:

Red – words related to the history of medicine.

Green – the factors that explain change and continuity.

Black – words that make your arguments and ideas answers clear to a reader.

And what about the words on the **golden background**?

They are the **golden words** – the words that really help you think, talk and write effectively when you are answering questions. You use them to:

■ Link your answer strongly to the question
■ Make your argument clear, for example when writing about which factors were most important or explaining how factors were linked together
■ Show that there is evidence to prove your argument.

Visible learning

This meant that … using connectives to tie in what you know to the question

When talking or writing about a factor, you cannot just say that it affected medicine. You have to **prove** that the factor affected medicine. You can do this effectively by using some of the **golden words** and phrases below such as 'this meant that …', 'this led to' and 'this resulted in …'

We call these words and phrases **connectives** because they connect what you know to the question and prove they are strongly linked. Look out for examples on pages 26–28.

Visible learning

How does talking help?

Some people think that students are only working effectively if the classroom is quiet. This is wrong. Experience shows that students write better answers if they have first talked through their answer with other people. Talking helps us organise ideas in our minds, choose the right words and decide what evidence we need to prove a point.

Visible learning

What is an argument?

The black words on the word wall help you make your argument clear. An argument in History is not a punch up! Argument is another word for hypothesis. It's what you believe the answer is – supported by evidence to show why you think this.

physician	bad air	pilgrimages	rakers
miasma	pestilence	flagellants	sewers
The Church	respect for tradition		attitudes
influential	continuity	inhibit	also important
hindered	challenge	most significant	argument
progress	reason	change	explanation
this led to …		this meant that …	this resulted in …

Why was there so little change in medicine?

> What is the importance of the three phrases in bold on this page? Check page 25 if you are not sure.

THE CHURCH

Until the 1500s there was only one religious organisation in Europe – the Christian Church led by the Pope in Rome, Italy. The Church was extremely rich because it owned a great deal of land in every country. It was also very powerful because it had a priest in every village and a bishop in every region. Through its bishops and priests it controlled education. You can read more about education on page 27.

Here are three ways in which the Church made it difficult for new medical ideas to develop:

- The Church had a major influence on people's ideas about what caused disease. The Bible said that God controlled every aspect of life so it was logical that God also sent diseases. They also believed that God had sent the Black Death to punish them for their sins. So if God sent diseases **this meant that** there was no need to look for other causes. This was an important reason why ideas about what caused disease did not change.

- The Pope, bishops and priests told people that everything in the Bible was true and you could not challenge what the Bible said. If anyone did dare to challenge the Bible and the Church they were told they would go to Hell when they died. In the Middle Ages people believed that Hell was a real place where they would suffer eternal pain from punishments such as being roasted over fires. This was a very real fear – there were wall paintings of Hell in churches to show people what happened there. Fear of Hell **meant that** hardly anyone dared to challenge what the Church said, including what it said about medicine.

- The Church supported the ideas of Galen. Galen had not been a Christian but he had said that the body had been created by one god who made all the parts of the body fit together perfectly. The Christian Church said that God had created human beings and did not make mistakes so the two ideas fitted together perfectly. As a result the Church supported Galen's work and **this meant that** no Christian dared to question Galen's ideas. If you questioned Galen you would be accused of challenging the Church and God.

1. Complete the sentences to summarise the impact of the Church.

a) God sends diseases	This meant that …
b) You will go to Hell if you challenge the Church	This meant that …
c) Galen was correct about the human body	This meant that …

2. Complete activities a–d in 'Researching the impact of the factors' on page 24 for this factor.

EDUCATION

This factor is strongly linked to the influence of the Church because the Church controlled education, including how physicians were trained at universities. There were in fact very few physicians in England (fewer than 100 in the 1300s), partly because the training took seven years and very few people could afford the cost.

The main part of doctors' training was reading the books of Hippocrates and Galen, along with translations of books by Arab doctors such as Ibn Sina (known as Avicenna in Europe) and al-Razi (known as Rhazes). These Arab writers included many of the ideas of Hippocrates and Galen in their work. Doctors were taught to believe that Hippocrates and especially Galen were correct in every detail. This meant that doctors were not encouraged to experiment or to think for themselves about what caused disease or about how to treat diseases. Following the work of Galen was all that was needed.

A good example of this total belief in Galen comes from how doctors learned about anatomy – the structure of the body. Doctors attended dissections of human bodies (as Galen had recommended) but they were NOT trying to make new discoveries. Dissections were simply another way of demonstrating that Galen's descriptions of the human body were correct. The trainee doctors just watched a surgeon carry out the dissection while a section of one of Galen's books was read aloud. This meant that hardly anyone tried to find out more about the structure of the human body or how it worked.

1. Complete the sentences to summarise the impact of education.

a) Doctors learned in training that Galen and Hippocrates were correct about all aspects of medicine	This resulted in …
b) Dissections were carried out to show that Galen was correct about anatomy	This meant that …
c) The Church controlled education	This resulted in …

2. Complete activities a–d in 'Researching the impact of the factors' on page 24 for this factor.

ATTITUDES: RESPECT FOR TRADITION

The result of the influence of the Church and of the way doctors were educated was that most people had great respect for the past and for traditional ideas. They wanted to keep everything as it was (this attitude can also be called conservative) unless there was a very, very good reason for change! In any case it was hard for new ideas to spread because books were written out by hand until printing came to England in the 1470s. Only after that were books manufactured in large numbers.

Later in history doctors and scientists believed it was important to question and test older ideas and not just rely on books written in the past. This was a vital change in attitude which led to many important breakthroughs, but this attitude did not develop in the Middle Ages. This meant that doctors were not trained to challenge existing ideas. What happened to one man was a warning to everyone else. When the English scientist Roger Bacon (1214–92) suggested that doctors should do their own research and carry out experiments he was thrown into prison by Church leaders.

1. Complete the sentences to summarise the impact of respect for tradition.

a) Books were made by copying by hand.	This meant that …
b) Doctors did not believe in questioning existing ideas.	This resulted in …

2. Complete activities a–d in 'Researching the impact of the factors' on page 24 for this factor.

INDIVIDUALS

Later in history some of the most important breakthroughs were the work of determined and inspired individuals: Harvey, Jenner, Pasteur and others (see the Big Story on pages 6–7). However, no individual made a great breakthrough in the Middle Ages. One reason was that education was very limited and controlled by the Church which did not encourage new ideas. As a result the key individuals in medieval medicine were Hippocrates and Galen – who had died centuries earlier!

Galen's work was especially important in the Middle Ages. He built on the work of Hippocrates and wrote over 350 books on medicine. These were the main books studied by doctors throughout the Middle Ages. He made new discoveries, especially about the anatomy of the body. Galen, unlike Hippocrates, thought it was very important to dissect dead bodies to find out more about anatomy and about how the body works. For example, he proved that the brain controls speech and that arteries carry blood round the body.

However, doctors did not just believe Hippocrates and Galen because they were trained to follow old ideas. There were two parts of their work that persuaded doctors their ideas were right:

■ **There seemed to be evidence to prove their ideas were correct.**

People's symptoms when they were sick seemed to show that the Theory of the Four Humours was correct. When a medieval doctor saw a sick patient he often saw one of the Humours (see page 12). For example, a sick

person might vomit yellow bile or black bile or sneeze phlegm or have a nosebleed. This sickness seemed to prove that the body was unbalanced and trying to get rid of too much of one Humour. Just as importantly, nobody suggested an alternative theory about what caused disease that was more persuasive or had more evidence to support it.

The books by Hippocrates and Galen also made doctors believe they had all the answers. The books seemed to cover everything in an extremely detailed and organised way. For example, they contained the first detailed descriptions of symptoms and treatments. For example, in AD167 Galen made a precise and thorough record of plague symptoms. Galen's descriptions of dissecting human bodies and animals also made his work very believable and hard to challenge.

■ **Their ideas seemed logical and reassuring if you were sick.**

Hippocrates and Galen did give very good advice. They told doctors to observe and note down the symptoms and development of diseases, including the pulse rate. These notes could be used to diagnose and treat other patients. Galen also developed the idea of using 'opposites' to balance the humours. For example, he treated someone shivering with cold with hot food such as peppers. These treatments seemed very rational.

GOVERNMENT

Since the early twentieth century governments have spent a great deal of money on medical research and care. This has played a major part in improving medicine. In the Middle Ages the king's government never did this. The major tasks of the king were to defend the country in war and to keep the country peaceful. Kings did order towns to be cleaned (as Edward III did in 1349 during the Black Death) but they did not do this regularly and did not pay for cleaning. No taxes were collected by the king's government to improve people's health or medicine. This meant that no money was spent to find medical breakthroughs.

THE IMPACT OF INDIVIDUALS AND GOVERNMENT

1. Create your own table for each factor like the tables on pages 26–27. Use these ideas as a guide:

   Individuals
   a) Who were the key individuals in medieval medicine?
   b) Which two aspects of their work seemed logical?

   Government
   a) What were the king's main duties?
   b) Did the government spend money on improving health?

2. Complete activities a–d in 'Researching the impact of the factors' on page 24 for the factors Individuals and Government.

How did the factors work together to inhibit change?

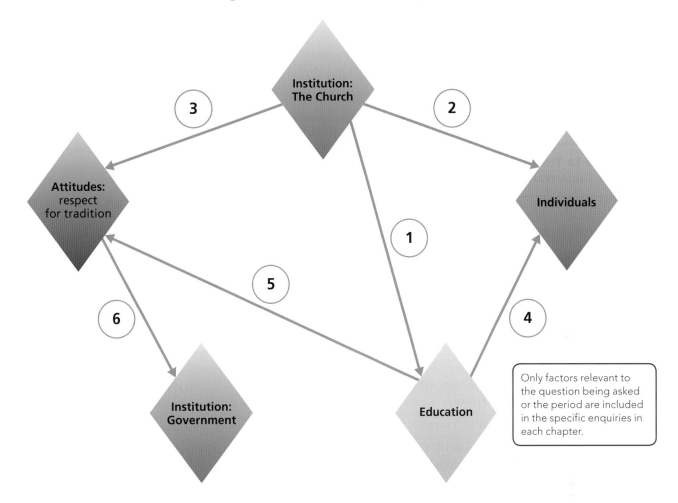

Only factors relevant to the question being asked or the period are included in the specific enquiries in each chapter.

LINKING THE FACTORS TOGETHER

On pages 26–28 you have explored how each factor helps to explain why there was little change in medicine. Now we are going to look at how the factors were linked and how these connections made change even more difficult.

The diagram above is called a Factor Map. The lines between the factors show you which factors were interlinked. Your task is to write at least one sentence explaining each of the six links. You can find most of the explanations on pages 26–28 but you will also have to think for yourself.

The best way to do this is to draw your own version of the Factor Map on a piece of large (A3) paper and write your explanations onto your map.

Visible learning

Why are Factors Diamonds, Factor Maps and card sorts useful?

These all help you think more clearly and at a higher level. This improves your explanations because you can write more clearly about the complexity of what happened in the past.

- **The card sort using the Factor Diamonds helps you develop a clear line of argument**. It is a lot easier to write a good answer that is focused on the question if you have a clear line of argument in your head **before** you begin your answer. The cards help you decide which factors were the most important before you begin your answer. Successful students spend time thinking about their approach to the question before they start to write.
- **The Factors Map helps you decide which factors were most important.** The most important usually have the most links to other factors.
- **The card sort and the Factors Map help you to select what to include in an exam answer.** The Diamond card sort makes sure you include the most relevant and important factors. The Factors Map helps you identify and explain the links between the most important factors.

2.6 Communicating your answer

It's time to THINK about the answer

Now it's time to write your answer and ...

STOP! We have forgotten something very important:

Revise your hypothesis and get your summary answer clear in your mind before you write.

This is a really vital stage because one of the biggest mistakes that students make is starting to write their answer without having the answer clear in their minds. These activities help you do that and they will work better if you do them with a partner.

1. Return to the illustration on page 11. Can you explain all the references in that illustration?
2. Use that illustration and your completed table from page 24 to organise the Factor Diamonds into the pattern you think best answers the question.
3. Now use the Diamond pattern to revise your hypothesis paragraph for the last time. This will make sure you have a clear answer to the question.

Now it's time to write your answer!

Now you are fully prepared to write your full answer to our question:

Why was there so little change in medicine in the Middle Ages?

Pages 24–29 have given you a good deal of help but you will find more guidance in the writing guide on pages 148–162. However, the person who will give you the best advice is your teacher because he or she knows exactly what help you need to improve your work in History.

And remember – mind your language!

Use words from your word wall to help you write accurately and with confidence and use connectives like those in the paragraph below. Which connectives can you find in the paragraph and why are they important?

> During the Middle Ages religion had a major impact on the development of medicine. The most common belief was that God sent illnesses such as the Black Death to punish people for their sins. People believed that the sick could be healed if they prayed for forgiveness. This meant that people did not look for scientific ways to explain the causes of disease and as a result medical treatments did not improve. Also, the Christian Church supported Galen's ideas, controlled universities and said that his work should not be questioned. This resulted in doctors being discouraged from researching and developing new ideas.

Practice questions

1. 'The role of the Church was the main reason why there was so little change in medicine in the Middle Ages.' How far do you agree? Explain your answer.
2. 'There was little progress in medicine in the Middle Ages.' How far do you agree? Explain your answer.

Some of your exam questions (such as question 4, 5 and 6 in the exam paper) will suggest two topics you could use in your answer. You can see examples on page 149. We have not included topics in the practice questions in this book to give teachers the opportunity to change these from year to year.

2.7 Visible learning: Revise and remember

Yes, there is something to do after you have answered the Enquiry Question. It's something that's easily put off – getting ready for revision! Successful students plan their revision while they are studying. They do not leave revision until close to the exam. This page starts that revision process. So how can you revise?

1 Building up summaries on Knowledge Organisers

You used three Knowledge Organisers:

a) The memory map to record the key features of medieval medicine.

b) The table to record how factors inhibited change in medicine.

c) The factors map to show how some of the factors were linked together.

What you have to do now is make sure those Knowledge Organisers are complete. When you come back to them for revision you do not want to start again from scratch!

2 Rewrite the Big Story

It's important for your exam to keep the whole picture of the history of medicine clear in your mind. On pages 6–7 you told the whole story in outline and wrote it down. Now revise the section on medieval medicine but this time you can write more and include these words:

continuity	pestilence
hindered	factors
progress	this meant that …
The Church	respect for tradition

3 Test yourself

You need to work at making your knowledge stick to your brain! The more you recap what you have learned and **identify what you're not sure about**, the more chance you have of success. Answer these questions, identify what you don't know and keep repeating this.

1 What is dissection?	2 What were the Four Humours?	3 Name four different kinds of medieval healers.	4 List three ideas people had about the cause of disease in the Middle Ages.
5 List three kinds of treatment used in the Middle Ages.	6 When did the Black Death arrive in England and what percentage of people did it kill?	7 Give two reasons why it was hard to keep medieval towns clean.	8 Give two ways people used to keep towns clean and healthy.
9 List three reasons why people continued to believe the ideas of Hippocrates and Galen.	10 Which three factors were most important in inhibiting change in medicine?	11 What did you find hardest to understand in this chapter? How are you going to help yourself understand it?	12 Name one thing that you learned in this chapter that surprised you or that you now think differently about. Explain why.

4 Set questions yourself

Work in a group of three. Each of you set four revision questions on medieval medicine. Use the style of questions on page 11. Then ask each other the questions – and make sure you know the answers!

2.8 Visible learning: Developing independence

The author and editor think that this is the most important page in the book. Why?

A few weeks ago you did not know very much about medieval medicine. Now you know a great deal. It's important to identify how you learned so much so quickly. This is an important example of making how you learn VISIBLE – the idea introduced on page 4.

Why is it important? In the future you will need the skills to study for yourself, with much less help from a teacher. This might be at A level, at university or at work. The process you have used in this chapter will help you work independently and more effectively. Here's the process – in six stages:

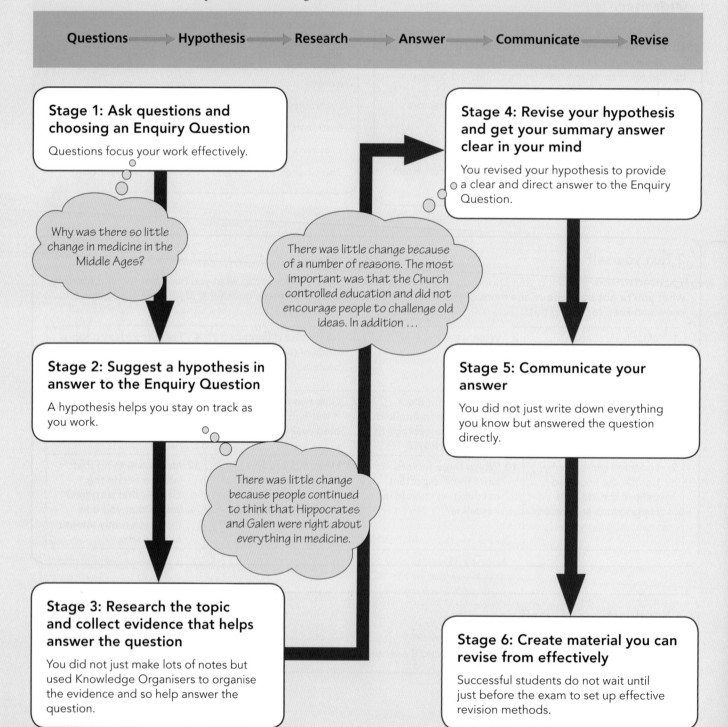

Questions ➡ Hypothesis ➡ Research ➡ Answer ➡ Communicate ➡ Revise

Stage 1: Ask questions and choosing an Enquiry Question

Questions focus your work effectively.

Why was there so little change in medicine in the Middle Ages?

Stage 2: Suggest a hypothesis in answer to the Enquiry Question

A hypothesis helps you stay on track as you work.

There was little change because people continued to think that Hippocrates and Galen were right about everything in medicine.

Stage 3: Research the topic and collect evidence that helps answer the question

You did not just make lots of notes but used Knowledge Organisers to organise the evidence and so help answer the question.

There was little change because of a number of reasons. The most important was that the Church controlled education and did not encourage people to challenge old ideas. In addition …

Stage 4: Revise your hypothesis and get your summary answer clear in your mind

You revised your hypothesis to provide a clear and direct answer to the Enquiry Question.

Stage 5: Communicate your answer

You did not just write down everything you know but answered the question directly.

Stage 6: Create material you can revise from effectively

Successful students do not wait until just before the exam to set up effective revision methods.

In 1700 people were no healthier and did not live longer than in the Middle Ages. This suggests that the story of medicine between 1500 and 1700 is again about continuity. Yet, as you read on page 7, Vesalius and Harvey made important discoveries in this period. So is the story really about continuity or is it about progress? We begin at the death-bed of King Charles II as his doctors battle to save his life.

3.1 Introducing Renaissance Medicine

FIGHTING TO SAVE KING CHARLES

On 2 February 1685 King Charles II was taken ill. He could not speak and became unconscious. The royal doctors clustered round, trying to save his life. The details of the treatment were later written down by the chief **physician**, Sir Charles Scarborough.

For each decision below, choose the option or options you think the royal doctors used.

Decision 1

Will you:
a) open a vein in the king's arm to **bleed** 16 ounces of blood?
b) call in Mistress Holder who successfully treated the king's poisoned hand five years ago. It is said she 'has a strange wisdom in the curing of wounds'?
c) do nothing and wait to see if the king recovers?

Decision 2

After an hour the king has not improved. Will you:
a) bleed the king again?
b) give more time for the first bleeding to work?
c) purge the king by giving him pills that will empty his bowels?

Decision 3

There is still no improvement. Will you:
a) give the king more pills to purge him some more?
b) place pigeons against the soles of the king's feet?
c) shave the king's head and put burning tongs on his scalp to blister the skin?

Decision 4

February 4: The king seemed better, but in the afternoon has another attack. Will you:
a) continue bleeding the king?
b) continue purging the king?
c) prescribe this medicine recommended by a colleague: spirit of human skull, 40 drops, taken in an ounce and a half of cordial julep?

Decision 5

February 6: The king's strength is fading rapidly. Should you use this **remedy**?

Every other hour take two scruples (two and a half grams) of bezoar stone, a green stone found in the stomach of Persian goats, known as a famous remedy.

TREATING CHARLES II – EVIDENCE OF MEDICAL CHANGE?

Charles II died, exhausted, later that day.

1. Now you have made your decisions above, look on page 164 at the decisions made by Charles II's doctors and add up your score. The more points you score, the more you understand about the work of doctors in the 1680s.

2. What does the treatment of Charles II suggest about how much medicine had progressed in the 200 years since the Middle Ages?

King Charles II was 54 years old ▶ when he died in 1685.

3.2 Case study: The Great Plague in London, 1665

Plague had not disappeared after the Black Death of 1348. Leicester, for example, suffered ten outbreaks between the 1550s and 1640s. A third of the population of York died from plague in 1604 and plague killed 20 per cent of the people in London in 1603, in 1625 and again in 1665 when 75,000 died. Many more thousands died all over Britain. Had medical knowledge and methods improved at all since the Middle Ages?

CONTINUITY OR CHANGE? ❓

Look at the illustration on these pages.

1. When plague was raging in London in 1665:
   a) what did people think was causing plague?
   b) how did they try to treat or prevent plague spreading?

2. What evidence can you see in the streets to explain why it was still hard to keep towns clean?

3. Draw your own version of the scales below. Add to your drawing as many examples of changes and continuities as you can find in the illustration. You can include information used in answering question 1.

4. How much progress had there been in medicine by the 1660s according to the information on these pages?

Visible learning

Many students find it helpful to use the scales diagram to record changes and continuities. The diagram makes the concepts of change and continuity more concrete – they aren't just ideas to hold in your mind. The diagram is particularly helpful for keeping track of the overall pattern of change and continuity and then making your final decision about how much medicine had changed by 1700.

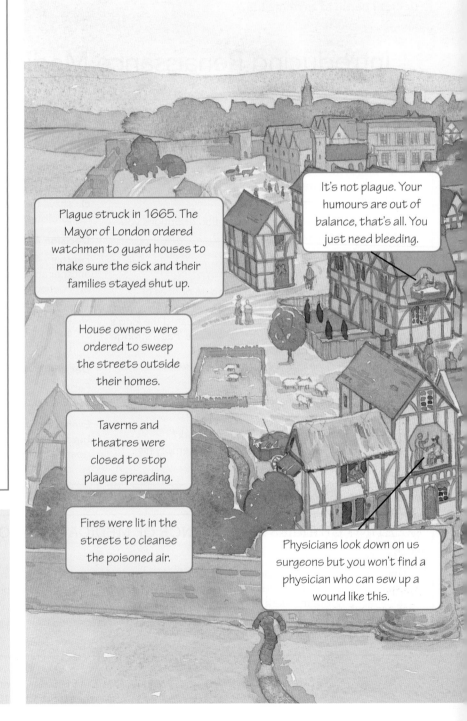

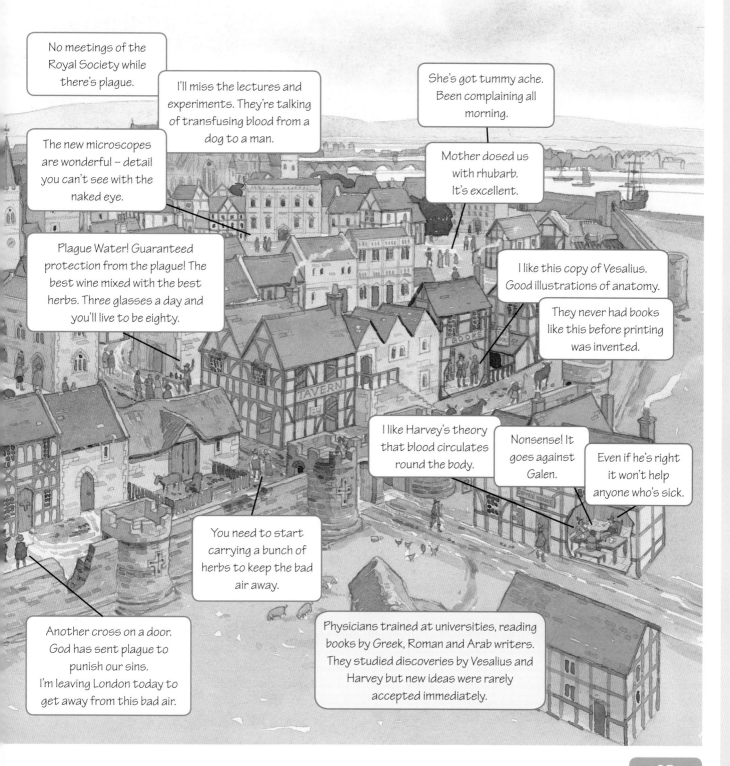

The plague in 1665 – explanations, treatments, prevention

Explanations for the plague had not changed since the Black Death of 1348, as you can see in the diagram below. These were still rational explanations, given people's beliefs and understandings, even if they seem very strange today.

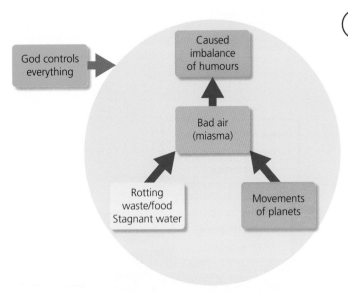

A

The Diseases and Casualties this Week.

Abortive	6	Kingsevil	10
Aged	54	Lethargy	1
Apoplexie	1	Murthered at Stepney	1
Bedridden	1	Palsie	2
Cancer	2	Plague	3880
Childbed	23	Plurisie	1
Chrisomes	15	Quinsie	6
Collick	1	Rickets	23
Consumption	174	Rising of the Lights	19
Convulsion	88	Rupture	2
Dropsie	40	Sciatica	1
Drowned 2, one at St. Kath. Tower, and one at Lambeth	2	Scowring	13
Feaver	353	Scurvy	1
Fistula	1	Sore legge	1
Flox and Small-pox	10	Spotted Feaver and Purples	190
Flux	2	Starved at Nurse	1
Found dead in the Street at St. Bartholomew the Less	1	Stilborn	8
Frighted	1	Stone	2
Gangrene	1	Stopping of the stomach	16
Gowt	1	Strangury	1
Grief	1	Suddenly	1
Griping in the Guts	74	Surfeit	87
Jaundies	3	Teeth	113
Imposthume	18	Thrush	3
Infants	21	Tissick	6
Kild by a fall down stairs at St. Thomas Apostle	1	Ulcer	2
		Vomiting	7
		Winde	8
		Wormes	18

Christned { Males — 83 Females — 83 In all — 166 } Buried { Males — 2656 Females — 2663 In all — 5319 } Plague — 3880

Increased in the Burials this Week — 1289.
Parishes clear of the Plague — 34. Parishes Infected — 96.

The Assize of Bread set forth by Order of the Lord Maior and Court of Aldermen; A penny Wheaten Loaf to contain Nine Ounces and a half, and three half-penny White Loaves the like weight.

▲ A mortality bill for 1665. These bills listed the numbers of dead in each parish and the causes of death. These bills show that the highest numbers of plague deaths were in the poorest, dirtiest, most overcrowded parishes and so provided evidence that plague was linked to dirt and bad air.

Treating the victims

Treatments for plague were very similar to those used against the Black Death. People prayed for the sick, gave them magical or religious charms to wear or cut open the buboes to let the **pus** out. Traders sold 'Great Medicines' which they claimed had saved 'vast numbers' of lives. One such medicine, Theriac, or London Treacle, contained wine, herbs, spices, honey and opium. Desperation also drove people to try remedies such as this:

> Wrap in woollen clothes, make the sick person sweat, which if he do, keep warm until the sores begin to rise. Then apply to the sores live pigeons cut in half or else a plaster made of yolk of an egg, honey, herb of grace and wheat flour.

Physicians may have tried bleeding and purging if the sick lived long enough but most physicians left London for the countryside. Dr George Thomson stayed and carried out an autopsy on a plague victim, hoping to learn more about the disease. Thomson caught plague but survived, despite his own remedy of putting a dried toad on his chest when he felt the first symptoms!

How to avoid catching plague

Methods of avoiding plague were strongly linked to ideas about its causes. People believed it was vital to keep the air sweet to ward off the bad air that brought plague. Bunches of strong-smelling herbs (such as lavender or sage) were hung in doorways and windows to stop bad air coming into the house. People also held bundles of herbs under their noses as they walked through the streets or drank 'plague water' made from herbs mixed with wine, which was thought to give protection against plague. Many people simply stayed at home to avoid contact with others. When they had to buy food, coins were soaked in vinegar to avoid passing on plague.

Some used even more powerful smells to fight off the plague-carrying **miasma**. Many people chewed tobacco, hoping the strength of its smell would give them immunity from plague. A schoolboy at Eton College said that he was flogged in 1665 for not smoking often enough. The same theory explained the recommendation from Dr Francis Glisson, a professor at Cambridge University, to keep in your room a piece of dried manure from someone who had died of plague.

Preventing the spread of plague

The methods used to try to stop plague spreading were very similar to those used in the 1300s. The King and his government ordered days of public prayer and fasting (not eating) so that people could publicly confess their sins and beg God to be merciful. The Mayor of London published detailed orders which show that a great deal of thought and effort went into trying to prevent plague spreading. However, the orders were not always easy to enforce.

Orders published by the Mayor of London	Why were the orders hard to enforce?
A. Examiners were appointed in every parish to identify those who caught plague. Families were expected to report plague symptoms inside two hours.	1. Parliament refused to turn the orders into laws because members of the House of Lords refused to be shut in their houses.
B. Victims and their families were shut up in their homes. Watchmen stood guard to stop anyone going in or out. Some victims were taken to specially built pest-houses away from the crowded parts of the city.	2. People ignored the rules. Plague symptoms were not reported. Over 20 watchmen were murdered by people escaping from houses that had been shut up.
C. Bodies were examined by 'women searchers' to check that plague was the cause. Their findings were confirmed by surgeons.	3. The King and his council left London. They discussed what to do about plague three times in seven months and two of those discussions were about the King's safety.
D. Bedding had to be hung in the smoke of fires before being used again. Barrels of tar and bonfires were lit in streets to cleanse the air of poisons. Rotten food was banned from sale to reduce bad air.	4. Nine men were put in charge of dealing with plague in London. Six of them left London as soon as they could.
E. Householders were ordered to sweep the street outside their doors every day and wash down the area twice a day to prevent dirt building up.	5. Not enough men could be found to work as watchmen. Some watchmen and women searchers took the chance to steal from the sick.
F. Pigs, dogs, cats and other animals were banned inside the city. Stray animals were killed by newly appointed dog-killers; 40,000 dogs and 200,000 cats were killed.	6. Beggars and other homeless people caught plague but still stayed in the streets, begging for help.
G. Plays, bear-baitings and games were banned to prevent the assembly of large crowds which might spread plague.	
H. Carts collected dead bodies at night and took them for burial in mass graves at least six feet deep.	

THE END OF PLAGUE

It took a combination of cold weather, the disease reaching the end of its natural course and the Great Fire of London to put an end to the Great Plague. In 1666 London was destroyed by fire and was completely rebuilt. Narrow streets and wooden buildings were replaced by stone and brick buildings, and wider, better-paved streets. For a time London was healthier, but as the city became more and more crowded again, the benefits of the rebuilding disappeared.

COMPARING REACTIONS TO PLAGUE, 1348 AND 1665

1. Identify two similarities between:
   a) ideas about the causes of plague in 1348 and 1665
   b) methods of preventing plague in 1348 and 1665
   c) methods of treating plague in 1348 and 1665.
2. Why were people's reactions to plague so similar in 1348 and 1665?

3.3 The Renaissance battle of ideas: tradition versus change

One of the main features of the Renaissance was a slow change from respect for tradition to the search for change. If you think of this as a boxing match, tradition had knocked out enquiry in the Middle Ages. This wasn't surprising, as tradition had the experienced and powerful Christian Church in its corner.

What helped change fight back? The Black Death began to encourage change back on its feet. Survivors were paid higher wages because employers had to attract workers. Some people spent their money on educating their children and in time education helped trigger the Renaissance.

Renaissance means 're-birth'. The Renaissance was a time of re-born interest in all things Greek and Roman – their books, ideas, buildings and sculptures. The development of printing helped people publish many new editions of Greek and Roman books, including nearly 600 editions of Galen's books.

This work changed attitudes. People now realised that the Greeks had loved enquiry – asking questions, challenging old ideas and suggesting new ones. If it was OK for the Greeks to ask questions and challenge old ideas, then so could the people of the Renaissance! One famous example is that Copernicus, a Polish scientist, proved that the Earth revolves around the sun. Until then it was believed that the sun circled the Earth.

So, what was also re-born was a love of enquiry and willingness to challenge existing ideas. Once they began to ask questions some people began to realise that Galen had not known everything – and had even made mistakes!

Of course not everyone agreed. Many people stuck to tradition, still saying it was wrong to challenge Galen. So, what developed between 1500 and 1700 was a battle between attitudes – between tradition, people defending the old ideas, and people seeking change and improvement.

THE RENAISSANCE BATTLE OF ATTITUDES

1. What was re-born in the Renaissance?
2. Look back at the information about Charles II and plague on pages 33–37.
   a) What evidence is there that tradition was still strong in 1700?
   b) What was happening that would give change a chance against tradition?
   c) Who do you think was winning by 1700? Use the Big Story on pages 6–7 to help you decide.

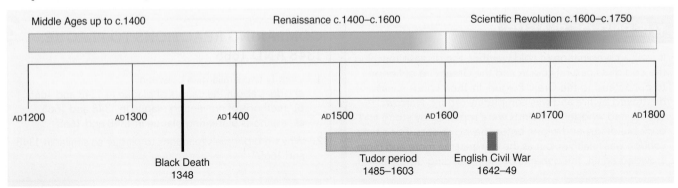

3.4 Your enquiry: Was there really so little progress in medicine c.1500–c.1700?

The methods used to treat Charles II and plague victims were very similar to methods in the Middle Ages. Ideas about the causes of disease did not change either. Therefore there seems to have been little progress in medicine, despite the Renaissance beginning to change attitudes. However, you have only seen two snapshots of medicine in this period – do they tell the whole story?

On pages 40–49 you can research Renaissance medicine and develop your answer to the question above. Here are the tasks which help you build your own hypothesis and conduct your research.

1. Creating and developing your hypothesis

The continuum line helps you create your hypothesis and keep track of your answer. It includes two criteria to help you decide whether there was progress in medicine:

- Did people become healthier by 1700?
- Did developments lead to long-term improvements?

   a) Draw the continuum line below. Then use what you learned from pages 33–38 and pages 6–7 to place the cards where you think they go on the line. Use pencil so you can move them later as you do more research.

   b) Write a short paragraph answering the enquiry question above, using the cards on the continuum line to guide you. This is now your hypothesis.

   c) As you work on each topic on pages 40–48 decide whether you want to move any cards. If you do, revise your hypothesis paragraph. This keeps your answer to the question in your mind.

   d) On page 47 we explain how to finalise your answer. When you write your answer it will be essential to use the criteria on the continuum line.

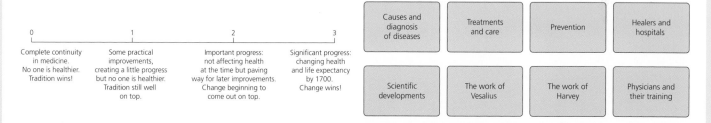

2. Collecting evidence for your judgements

This table helps you record evidence to justify where you place each card on the continuum line.

   a) Complete the row on Prevention straightaway because you have covered this on pages 34–37.

   b) Read about each topic on pages 40–48. Then fill in each section of your table. Use A3 paper so there's plenty of room for the evidence.

   c) Use the evidence to decide whether to change your first thoughts on where that topic goes on the continuum line.

Topics	Ideas and methods in the Middle Ages	Changes that improved health by 1700	Changes that paved the way for long-term improvements in health after 1700
Prevention			
Causes and diagnoses of diseases			

3.5 The main features of Renaissance Medicine

Causes and diagnoses of diseases

As you read on page 36, ideas about the causes of disease had not changed since the Middle Ages. However, this does not mean that some doctors were not trying to learn more about diseases. Thomas Sydenham was a pioneering doctor who did make progress, especially in how to diagnose diseases. He believed that each disease was different and that it was important to identify the exact disease so the correct remedy could be chosen to cure it. Taking a patient's pulse, for example, was an important part of diagnosis.

Sydenham became one of the most respected physicians in London, telling young doctors 'You must go to the bedside. It is there alone that you can learn about disease'. He stressed that doctors needed to take a full history of the patient's health and symptoms, observing and recording the illness with great care so that the correct diagnosis was made.

Sydenham became known as the 'English Hippocrates' because the legendary Greek doctor had placed great importance on this kind of careful observation. Sydenham contributed to the progress of medicine by making detailed descriptions of many illnesses, including the first description of **scarlet fever**. He also believed in allowing the body to fight the illness by itself. Patients who were used to physicians ordering bleeding or purging must have been delighted when Sydenham prescribed roast chicken and a bottle of wine to restore their strength!

▲ Thomas Sydenham (1624–89). Sydenham's practical approach to medicine may have developed because he spent several years fighting in the English Civil Wars and so spent less time at university.

Scientific developments

The first meetings in England of people interested in discussing new scientific ideas took place in London in 1645. The group met weekly to discuss new ideas in physics, botany, astronomy, medicine and other sciences. Members also demonstrated experiments (such as the one shown in Picture A) because the Society had its own laboratory and equipment such as microscopes. It also published books and articles to spread new ideas and discoveries. In 1662 the group became known as the Royal Society after King Charles II attended meetings to hear talks and watch experiments. He even had a laboratory and an observatory built in one of his palaces.

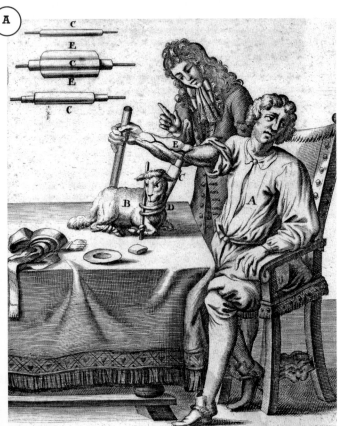

▲ In 1665 Richard Lower, a member of the Royal Society, made the first experimental blood transfusion. He transfused blood from a dog to another dog and later from a sheep to a man, a 'crackbrained' student called Arthur Coga. It was said that people hoped this would make Coga cleverer!

> **?**
> Complete the row of your table for these two topics, using the information on these pages. Then use the evidence in your table to decide where to place these topics on the continuum line.

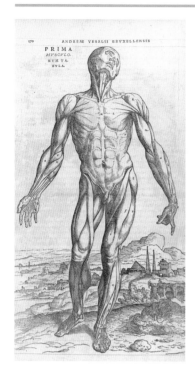

The importance of printing

Earlier in this chapter there have been references to the development of printing. Printing was a crucial development which helped change ideas in medicine and many other subjects because it spread new ideas far more rapidly. Books could be printed faster and more cheaply than when they were copied by hand. The printing press was invented by Johannes Gutenberg in the 1450s. By 1500 printing presses were being used throughout western Europe. Some books were highly illustrated such as this page from Andreas Vesalius's book on **anatomy** *The Fabric of the Human Body* (1543). You will read more about Vesalius on page 44.

A new kind of science

Don't worry, this isn't part of a GCSE science book – but it does show how much history and science have in common! During the 1600s changing attitudes created a 'scientific revolution'. Scientists challenged old ideas, experimenting to make new discoveries, using the methods outlined in the diagram below.

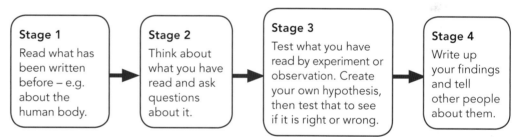

Stage 1
Read what has been written before – e.g. about the human body.

Stage 2
Think about what you have read and ask questions about it.

Stage 3
Test what you have read by experiment or observation. Create your own hypothesis, then test that to see if it is right or wrong.

Stage 4
Write up your findings and tell other people about them.

Stepping stones to the future

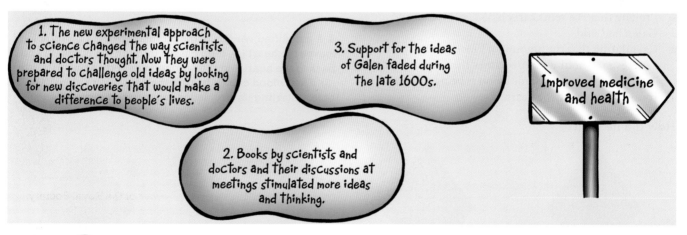

1. The new experimental approach to science changed the way scientists and doctors thought. Now they were prepared to challenge old ideas by looking for new discoveries that would make a difference to people's lives.

3. Support for the ideas of Galen faded during the late 1600s.

Improved medicine and health

2. Books by scientists and doctors and their discussions at meetings stimulated more ideas and thinking.

BUT ...

1. This change of attitude was only the beginning. Many more discoveries were needed before people's health would be much better. Medical treatments in the late 1600s still included ingredients such as frogspawn and 'cold deadman's skull'.
2. It took time to end opposition to experimental science from supporters of Galen.

Case study: William Harvey and the circulation of the blood

William Harvey made one of the most important breakthroughs in medical history when he discovered how the blood circulates around the body. These pages explain his discovery and its effects on medicine, at the time and later.

Blood – the story so far

Galen had said:

1. New blood was constantly manufactured in the liver to replace blood burned up in the body.
2. The veins carried blood and air round the body.
3. Blood passed from one side of the heart to the other through invisible holes in the septum.

Other doctors, including Vesalius (as you will discover on pages 44–5), had begun to question these ideas although nobody could explain how blood moved around the body.

Harvey's discovery

In 1628 Harvey published his book *An Anatomical Account of the Motion of the Heart and Blood* which described how the blood circulates round the body. Harvey proved that Galen's ideas listed above were wrong. He showed that the heart acts as a pump, pumping blood around the body. He did this by:

■ **Dissecting** live cold-blooded animals whose hearts beat slowly so he could see the movement of each muscle in the heart.
■ Dissecting human bodies to build up detailed knowledge of the heart.
■ Proving that the body has a one-way system for the blood. He tried to pump liquid past the valves in the veins but could not do so.
■ Proving that the veins carry blood, not blood and air as Galen had said.
■ Calculating that the amount of blood going into the arteries each hour was three times the weight of a man. This showed that the same blood is being pumped round the body by the heart.

Complete a row of your table for Harvey's discovery, then use the evidence to decide where to place Harvey on the continuum line from page 39.

William Harvey was born in 1578 and died in 1657. He studied medicine in Cambridge and in Padua in Italy and worked as a doctor in London. He became doctor to King Charles I.

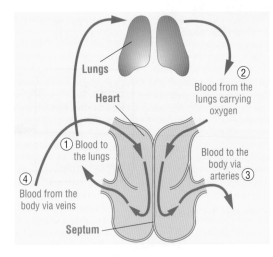

▲ A simplified version of the circulation of the blood. Blood leaves the heart (1), then passes through the lungs (2) and back to the heart and then around the body along arteries (3). Then blood comes back to the heart along veins (4) before starting its circulation around the body again.

How did he do it?

Individuals

Harvey was exceptionally thorough in his work, spending many hours repeating experiments and going over every detail.

Attitudes: seeking improvement

Harvey was not satisfied to believe that Galen was correct. He tested Galen's ideas through his own experiments. Harvey said 'I prefer to learn and teach anatomy not from books but from dissections.'

Science and Technology

Mechanical water pumps in London (see Picture A) *may* have given Harvey the idea that the heart pumps blood. He used modern scientific methods, reading about other scientists' work, carrying out experiments and carefully observing the results.

Communications

Harvey had read the work of earlier doctors and used their work to build up his theory. For example, Harvey's tutor at Padua, Fabricius (1533–1619), proved there are valves in the veins. Valves control the way liquids flow.

A

▲ A water pump being used to fight a fire in the 1600s. Pumps like this had valves to direct the flow of water.

Harvey could not explain everything about how blood ▲ circulates. He did not know how blood moves from the arteries to the veins. In 1661, four years after Harvey died, Professor Marcello Malphigi solved this puzzle. He used one of the first effective microscopes to discover the capillaries, which carry blood from arteries to veins. The development of microscopes was a vital technological development, helping to transform medical knowledge.

Stepping stones to the future

B

1. Harvey's discovery laid the groundwork for future investigation of the blood and physiology (the workings of the body).

3. Harvey provided more evidence for the importance of dissection and experiments. He wrote 'I prefer to learn and teach anatomy not from books but from dissections.'

2. Many aspects of medicine depend on understanding the blood system. Surgery, for example, could not develop until after Harvey's discovery.

Improved medicine and health

WARNING

BUT …

1. **There was still much more to discover about the blood**. Doctors could not make blood **transfusions** until they discovered blood groups in 1901.
2. **Harvey's discovery was only gradually accepted**. Some doctors ignored his theory. Others said that he was wrong because he was contradicting Galen. It was 50 years before teachers at the University of Paris taught Harvey's ideas rather than Galen's.
3. **Harvey's discovery did not make anyone better**. The writer John Aubrey noted 'All his profession agree Dr Harvey to be an excellent anatomist, but that I never heard any that admired his treatment of the sick.' Harvey himself said that after he published his discovery fewer patients came to see him because many thought his idea mad.

The work of Andreas Vesalius – breakthroughs in anatomy

Vesalius's achievements

Doctors believed Galen had given a complete and fully correct description of the anatomy of the body. Vesalius respected Galen's work but proved, through dissecting bodies, that Galen could be wrong. He proved that:

- The human jaw bone is made from one bone, not two as Galen said.
- The breastbone has three parts, not seven as Galen said.
- Blood does not flow into the heart through invisible holes in the septum, as Galen suggested. Such holes do not exist.

Vesalius published his work in *The Fabric of the Human Body* in 1543, the first highly illustrated book describing human anatomy. The illustrations showed the body in far more detail and far more accurately than had ever been done before. This book was used to train doctors in England who, therefore, gained more detailed and accurate knowledge of anatomy. Records show that his book was being used in Cambridge by 1560 and led to doctors writing corrections about anatomy in older medical books. In addition, doctors realised they could learn more about anatomy by dissecting bodies themselves. The first dissection by an anatomist in Cambridge was carried out in 1565.

▲ Vesalius (1514–64) was Professor of Surgery in Padua in Italy.

How did he do it?

Science and Technology

Printing. Vesalius supervised the engraving of the illustrations and the printing himself. Printing meant that everything came out the same with no mistakes – which had not happened in books copied by hand. Thousands of copies of his book were used all over Europe.

Individuals

Vesalius was inventive and determined. Once he stole the body of a criminal from the gallows to dissect, and he worked in Padua where dissection was encouraged.

Attitudes: seeking improvement

Vesalius believed that it was vital to ask questions and challenge traditional ideas by carrying out dissections.

Vesalius is shown in the centre, dissecting the body himself. In the Middle Ages professors had sat and read Galen aloud while demonstrators did the dissection.

Galen and other Greek doctors are shown at the same level as Vesalius, not higher up as if superior.

Students crowd round the body so they can see what Vesalius is doing rather than simply listening to Galen being read out.

◀ The title page of Vesalius's *The Fabric of the Human Body* tells us about his attitudes to dissection.

Physicians and their training

For most of this period from c.1500–c.1700 physicians still learned about medicine from the books of Galen and other ancient writers. Even in 1668 diarist Samuel Pepys noted that the leading expert on eye problems in London had only ever seen animals' eyes dissected, but not a human eye. However, very gradually, especially in the late 1600s, the training of doctors did begin to change as you can see in this chart:

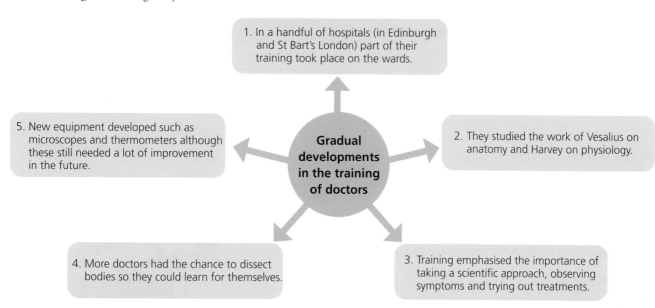

Gradual developments in the training of doctors

1. In a handful of hospitals (in Edinburgh and St Bart's London) part of their training took place on the wards.

2. They studied the work of Vesalius on anatomy and Harvey on physiology.

3. Training emphasised the importance of taking a scientific approach, observing symptoms and trying out treatments.

4. More doctors had the chance to dissect bodies so they could learn for themselves.

5. New equipment developed such as microscopes and thermometers although these still needed a lot of improvement in the future.

Healers and hospitals

Although physicians were trained in universities, most people preferred more familiar and cheaper remedies from surgeons, **apothecaries** and their families. Thomas Hobbes, one of the greatest philosophers in history, said he would 'rather have the advice or take medicine from an experienced old woman, who had been at many sick people's bedsides, than from the learnedest but unexperienced physician'.

Women still played a major part in everyday medicine. The first person to treat nearly all sicknesses was the wife or mother of the sick person. Wealthy ladies often provided care for local families. Lady Grace Mildmay (1552–1620) was set to read William Turner's book *A New Herbal* as a child and later read books by Galen and Ibn Sinna. She also kept records of her patients and the treatments she used. Margaret Colfe, a Londoner, was remembered after her death in 1643 as 'Having been above forty years a willing nurse, midwife, surgeon and, in part, physician to all both rich and poor, without expecting reward'.

The story of hospitals was also mostly of continuity. Many medieval hospitals were part of monasteries so they closed when Henry VIII closed the monasteries in the 1530s. However, some were taken over by town councils, especially the almshouses that looked after the elderly poor. In London the city council and charity helped to keep St Bartholomew's Hospital open. By the 1660s it had 12 wards and up to 300 patients, looked after by three physicians and three surgeons, fifteen nursing sisters and a larger number of nursing helpers. The nursing sisters treated patients with **herbal remedies** but the nursing helpers did the heavy, manual work – washing, cleaning and preparing food – and had no medical training.

St Bartholomew's was one of hospitals that were beginning to take in the sick and treat their illnesses. However, most still did not admit people with infectious diseases but just provided food, warmth and prayer for the poor. Anyone with any money paid for a doctor or nurse to look after them at home.

VESALIUS, TRAINING PHYSICIANS, HEALERS AND HOSPITALS ❓

1. On pages 41 and 43 we used the 'Stepping stones to the future' sign to summarise the struggle between conservative attitudes and enquiry. Create your own set of stepping stones and warning signs to summarise your conclusions about:
   - Vesalius
   - training physicians
   - healers and hospitals.
2. Complete the rows of your table on page 39 for these three topics. Then use that evidence to decide where to place each of them on the continuum line.

Treatments

? TREATMENTS

1. On page 43 we used the 'Stepping stones to the future' sign to summarise the struggle between traditional attitudes and enquiry. Create your own set of stepping stones and warning signs to summarise your conclusions about the topic Treatments.

2. Complete the Treatments row of your table on page 39, building on the information you compiled from pages 33–7. Then use that evidence to decide where to place this topic on the continuum line.

Bleeding and purging

Bleeding and purging were still very common medical treatments and also continued to be used to prevent illness. Physicians still believed in the Theory of the **Four Humours**, that people became ill when the Humours in the body were out of balance. Therefore they used bleeding and purging to correct the balance, even though they must have weakened the patients considerably, as you saw with the treatment of Charles II on page 33. European travels to America and Asia brought new ingredients for treatments to England. Rhubarb from Asia was widely used to purge the bowels. Ipecacuanha from Brazil was prescribed for **dysentery** and used to make people vomit.

Herbal remedies

Herbal remedies were handed down through generations from mother to daughter. Girls learned how to mix up remedies, using ingredients such as honey, which we now know kills some **bacteria**. More people were writing down home remedies because more people could now read and write. Mary Doggett, wife of a London actor, noted a remedy for scurvy which used horseradish roots, white wine, water and a quart of orange juice or 12 thinly cut oranges. We know that scurvy, which leads to internal bleeding and death, is the result of not eating enough fruit and vegetables. Mary did not know this but she did know, from experience, that this remedy worked. Less helpfully, tobacco from America was greeted as a cure-all, being recommended for toothache, poisoned wounds, joint pains, and as protection from plague.

▲ The printing revolution meant that more people had books in their homes containing advice on herbal remedies. One of the most popular was Nicholas Culpepper's *Complete Herbal* which recommended simple homegrown herbal remedies.

God and the King

Between 1660 and 1682 over 92,000 people visited the King's court, believing that if Charles II touched them they would be cured from **scrofula**, a skin disease known as the King's Evil. The King was God's representative on earth so being touched by the King was as close as you could get to being touched by God. There are records of people travelling from as far as Bamburgh in Northumberland in the hope that the King's touch would heal them.

Folk remedies

Many treatments seem rational and would have helped the sick person. However, the treatment below, published in a book called *The New London Dispensary* in 1682, shows that people still used cures based on magic. Such ideas must have been used because people were desperate for help.

> To cure malaria, take the hair and nails of the patient, cut them small and either give them to birds in a roasted egg or put them in a hole in an oak tree or a plane tree. Stop up the hole with a peg of the same tree.

In fact, a new cure for **malaria** had arrived when the bark of the cinchona tree was imported from South America because it treated fevers effectively. It became known as quinine and helped many who suffered from malaria.

3.6 Communicating your answer

Now you have completed your research it is time to write your answer to the enquiry question:

Was there really so little progress in medicine c.1500–c.1700?

First, however, as you did in Chapter 2 (page 30) you need to have your answer clear in your mind.

Great medical discoveries! No one healthier!

Great medical discoveries! They'll help make breakthroughs in two hundred years' time!

1. Return to your completed continuum line on page 39. Check that you are happy where you have placed each topic now you have completed your research.
2. In your answer you are making a judgement about how much progress took place. The newspaper sellers on the right show you two criteria for deciding whether there was progress. Explain in your own words what these two criteria are. You could begin by saying 'One way of judging progress is to assess whether ...'
3. Now use the continuum line and the criteria in the drawing to revise your hypothesis paragraph for the last time. This will make sure you have a clear answer to the question.

Now you are fully prepared to write your full answer to our question.

Practice questions

1. Explain one way in which people's reactions to plague were similar in the fourteenth and seventeenth centuries.
2. Explain one way in which ideas about the causes of disease were similar in the fourteenth and seventeenth centuries.
3. Explain one way in which treatments for illness were similar in the fourteenth and seventeenth centuries.
4. Explain why some changes took place in medical knowledge during the period c.1500–c.1700.
5. Explain why there was little change in methods of treating and preventing disease during the period c.1500–c.1700.
6. 'Vesalius's work on anatomy was a major breakthrough in medical knowledge during the period 1500–1700.' How far do you agree? Explain your answer.
7. 'Harvey's discovery of the circulation of the blood was a major breakthrough in medical knowledge during the period 1500–1700.' How far do you agree? Explain your answer.

Before answering any of these questions look at 'Writing better history' section on pages 148–62. For questions 4 and 5 also see pages 48–49.

We have given you a good deal of help but you will find more guidance in the writing guide on pages 148–162. In addition use the words from your word wall to help you write accurately and with confidence. The additions to the word wall below may be helpful for answering this question, especially the **golden words** – but you don't have to use them all!

On the one hand ...   on the other ...   In some ways ...   but in others ...   at the end ...

Overall, the evidence shows ...   At the beginning of this period ...   The pace of change

physiology   microscope   blood transfusion   mortality bill   pesthouse   pulse   scrofula   cure-all   veins   arteries   capillaries   valves

gradual   significant   turning point   breakthrough   impact   relevance

3.7 Explaining the pattern of change c.1500–c.1700

The history of medicine in this period looks like a signpost pointing in two different directions. Some events point back to the Middle Ages, to medical ideas and methods that are very familiar. Other developments point forward – although people at the time could not see that part of the signpost at all clearly. They did not know what lay ahead. King Charles II provides a good example of this two-way signpost – the details on the signpost show how Charles's involvement in science and medicine points both forward and back in time.

Who was winning – tradition or change?

On page 38 we introduced the idea of this period being a battle between tradition and the search for change. In 1700 tradition was still winning but changes were taking place. One example of change is that doctors were now learning about the discoveries of Vesalius and Harvey while they were being trained instead of just reading and believing every word written by Galen and other ancient writers. Doctors were being encouraged to think for themselves, ask questions and make new discoveries.

However, this change was very slow. Methods of treating and preventing illness were not changing. This was partly because some treatments, such as some herbal remedies, did work. The methods used to prevent the spread of plague in 1665 were very logical and did help a little. However, the biggest reason by far why methods of treating and preventing diseases had not changed was because understanding of the causes of disease had not changed. Remember the triangle on page 6 – treatments and prevention have always been directly linked to ideas about causes of disease.

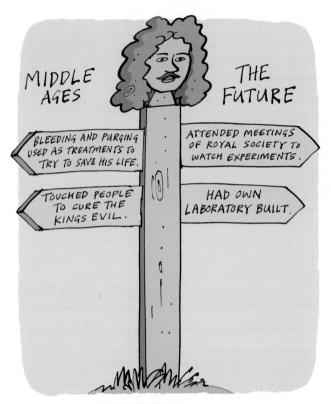

Visible learning: more ways to revise

Revision can be a chore, so it helps to have a variety of techniques to use. Here are two more to add to your collection.

1 Time travel

Imagine you were born in the late 1600s and travelled back in time to the 1350s. What would you find familiar and what would you find strange about fourteenth-century medicine?

2 Repeat your memory map

In Chapter 2 you drew a memory map recording the main features of medieval medicine. Draw a similar memory map for Renaissance medicine, using blue for continuities from the Middle Ages and red for changes.

HOW DID THE FACTORS LEAD TO CHANGE OR CONTINUITY BETWEEN 1500 AND 1700?

You did a lot of work in Chapter 2 on how we can use the factors to explain the continuities in medieval medicine. This activity helps you answer questions 4 and 5 on page 47.

Explain why some changes took place in medical knowledge during the period c.1500–c.1700.

Explain why there was little change in methods of treating and preventing disease during the period c.1500–c.1700.

Take each question in turn.

1. Which cards below provide evidence to help answer each question?

2. Which cards provide evidence for the impact of the factors? (A factor can lead to both continuity and change.)

3. Decide which factors were most important in leading to either change or continuity.

4. Write an answer to each question using the guidance on page 14 and in the 'Writing better history' section on pages 148–162.

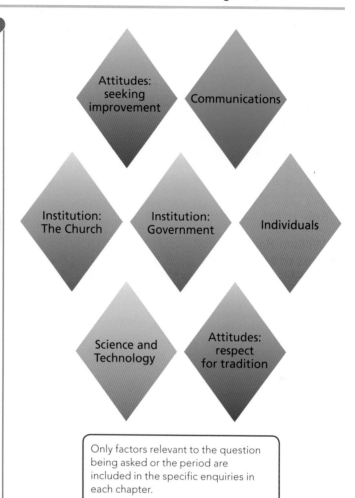

Only factors relevant to the question being asked or the period are included in the specific enquiries in each chapter.

1. New ideas about science encouraged people to challenge old ideas.	2. Some herbal remedies worked and encouraged people to keep to old ways of treating illnesses.	3. The Church was still very powerful and people were told that God controlled every aspect of life.
4. The development of printing spread details of new ideas and discoveries far faster than in the past.	5. The work of Galen and other ancient doctors was still a central part of medical training for doctors.	6. New discoveries by Vesalius and Harvey did not improve anyone's health.
7. There were still very few trained doctors and scientists so there were very few people to try to find new ideas.	8. Groups such as the Royal Society helped to spread news of new experiments and discoveries.	9. Technology was gradually improving so that new equipment such as microscopes made new discoveries possible.
10. Doctors such as Thomas Sydenham were more prepared to learn from their daily experience rather than from books.	11. Doctors had believed in the complete accuracy of Galen's work for so long that it was very hard to change that view.	12. Ideas about what caused disease had not changed despite changes in scientific thinking.
13. Discoveries in other areas of science such as astronomy encouraged doctors to seek new knowledge in medicine.	14. Governments did not spend money on trying to improve people's health or finding out more about medicine apart from when there was a major outbreak of plague.	15. Methods of preventing the spread of plague were already carefully thought out and organised.

3.8 Visible learning: Revise and remember

Recording and assessing the role of an individual

During your course you will need to record and assess the achievements of a number of key individuals – Pasteur, Lister and others. It will be much easier to revise their achievements and write about them in exams if you use the same kind of chart for each of them. This means the pattern of the chart will be clear in your mind when you need it. The questions included below will help you create charts for other individuals, but don't be afraid to think for yourself about what needs to be included.

1. Complete this 'Role of the Individual' chart for William Harvey in order to establish the pattern of the chart.
2. Complete a similar chart for Andreas Vesalius.

▼ 'Role of the Individual' chart

William Harvey (1578–1657)
Area of Medicine: Physiology   **Discovery: Circulation of the blood**
Career: studied medicine in Cambridge and Padua in Italy and worked as a doctor in London

BEFORE this breakthrough
What kinds of ideas or methods did doctors have before this breakthrough?

What was the breakthrough?
Explain the key aspects of this breakthrough.

Short-term impact
What was the immediate impact on medical ideas or treatments?

Did this discovery improve health in the short-term?

Did other discoveries need to be made to make full use of this breakthrough?

Long-term impact
Why did this breakthrough lead to others?

How did this change thinking about medicine?

What other aspects of medicine changed as a result?

Why did this breakthrough happen?
Explain the reasons for the breakthrough. Remember to refer to the factors on page 8.

Making your brain stickier

'I don't need to worry about revision. There'll be plenty of time for that before the exams.'

You might agree with the thought above – but before you turn over and ignore this revision page take a look at the graphs below. They should convince you that leaving revision until just before your exam is not the way to success!

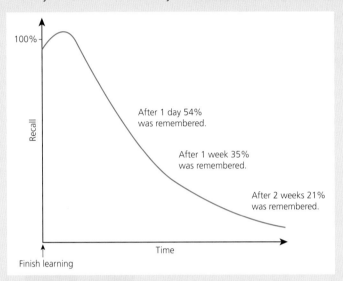

▲ Graph 1 The Ebbinghaus Curve of Forgetting. That sounds impressive but the graph is alarming. We forget the detail of what we study very quickly.

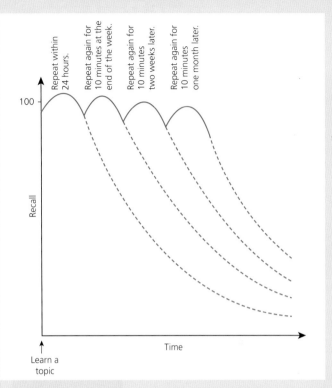

▲ Graph 2 How do you stop yourself forgetting?

1 Test yourself!

The more you think about what you have learned and **especially what you're not sure about**, the more chance you have of succeeding in your exam. So answer these questions and don't be surprised if we ask you these questions again.

1. What were the four Humours?	2. What discovery did Harvey make and in which century did he make it?	3. Name four different kinds of medieval healers.
4. List three ideas people had about the cause of disease in the Middle Ages and the Renaissance.	5. List three kinds of treatment used between 1500 and 1700.	6. Why was Vesalius important in the history of medicine and in which century did he do his work?
7. Give two reasons used to try to prevent plague spreading in 1665.	8. Why was Thomas Sydenham's work important?	9. List three reasons why some doctors still believed the ideas of Hippocrates and Galen in the 1600s.
10. Name three reasons why some changes were taking place in medicine by 1700.	11. What did you find hardest to understand in this chapter? How are you going to help yourself understand it?	12. Name one thing that you learned in this chapter that surprised you or that you now think differently about. Explain why.

2 Set questions yourself!

Work in a group of three. Each of you set four revision questions on Renaissance medicine. Use the style of questions on page 11. Then ask each other the questions – and make sure you know the answers!

3 Revise the Big Story

It's important to keep the whole picture of the history of medicine clear in your mind. Revise the story you told on pages 6–7, making sure that you bring it up to date with what you have learned about medicine c.1500–c.1700.

So far there has been far more continuity than change in the story of medicine but now it's time for some of the most important medical discoveries in history, ones we are all grateful for. By the end of this chapter you will understand which discoveries were the most significant, why so many breakthroughs happened in the 1800s and why, finally, people were starting to live a little longer.

4.1 The breakthroughs

The breakthroughs shown on these pages were the most significant in this period. These boxes help you understand which one of them was the most important of all.

1798: Edward Jenner – the development of vaccinations

In 1798 Edward Jenner proved that **vaccination** prevented people catching **smallpox**, one of the great killer diseases. Jenner's work was based on observation and scientific experiment. However, he did not understand what caused smallpox or exactly how vaccination worked.

At first there was also opposition to making vaccination compulsory by law. Over time Jenner's discovery saved many thousands of lives in Britain and millions worldwide as vaccination eventually wiped out smallpox.

INTRODUCING THE BREAKTHROUGHS ❓

1. Which breakthroughs changed:
   a) ideas about the cause of disease
   b) methods of treating the sick
   c) methods of preventing people becoming sick?
   Some breakthroughs can be included more than once.

2. There are lines connecting some breakthroughs but not others.
   a) What do you think these lines represent?
   b) Choose one pair of linked breakthroughs and suggest why they were linked.
   c) What does the overall pattern of links suggest about which breakthrough was most important?

3. We always start by asking you to ask questions so here we go again! How many good history questions can you ask about these breakthroughs?

1847: James Simpson – the first effective anaesthetic

James Simpson showed that **chloroform** could be used as an effective **anaesthetic** during surgery. He used it to help women in childbirth and patients undergoing operations and wrote articles which led to other surgeons using it. However, chloroform was not problem-free. Sometimes patients died because too much chloroform was used or because they developed **infections** which could not be cured. Deaths during surgery actually increased for a time after Simpson's discovery.

1854: John Snow – preventing cholera

In 1854 cholera killed over 500 people around Broad Street in London, near Dr Snow's surgery. Snow mapped out the deaths, showing that people had caught cholera from the water they used for washing and drinking. Snow proved that clean water prevented cholera but governments still did not make laws forcing towns to provide clean water and improve living conditions. Many scientists continued to believe that diseases were spread by 'bad air'.

1875: Public Health Act

The Public Health Act was a major change in the attitudes of governments to improving people's health. This law was the first to say that it was *compulsory* for local councils to improve sewers and drainage, provide fresh, clean water supplies and appoint **medical officers** and sanitary inspectors to inspect **public health** facilities.

1861: Louis Pasteur – germ theory

Louis Pasteur published his **germ theory** in 1861, suggesting that **bacteria** (also called **microbes** or **germs**) cause human diseases. He based his theory on experiments which proved that germs make milk go bad and cause diseases in animals. In 1864 more experiments convinced many doctors that this theory was correct, though it took time to convince everyone. Some still insisted that bad air caused disease. Later Pasteur developed the first vaccines to prevent disease since Jenner's vaccination for smallpox.

1867: Joseph Lister – effective antiseptics against infection

After reading Pasteur's germ theory, Joseph Lister, a Scottish surgeon, experimented with carbolic acid spray to produce the first **antiseptic**. This greatly reduced the chances of patients dying from infection developed during an operation and made longer, more complex operations possible. However, at first there was still opposition because some surgeons refused to accept Pasteur's theory and did not believe that bacteria existed.

1882: Robert Koch – identifying bacteria that cause diseases

Robert Koch and his research team used Pasteur's work to discover the bacteria that cause individual diseases, such as tuberculosis and typhoid, which killed many thousands of people. Koch's methods were copied by other scientists, who discovered the bacteria that cause other diseases. Once they identified the bacteria they could develop vaccines to prevent people getting diseases.

1850s onwards: Florence Nightingale – hospitals and nursing

Florence Nightingale was a great organiser, working to improve conditions in hospitals and the training of nurses. During the Crimean War (1854–56) she improved hygiene and cleanliness for wounded soldiers. Her nursing schools trained nurses to keep wards totally clean, provide fresh air and keep patients clean and well fed. Her work improved hospitals a great deal. Pasteur's discoveries later provided more evidence to show why hospitals and patients had to be as clean as possible.

4.2 Case study: Jenner and vaccination

▲ Edward Jenner, 1749–1823. In 1808 Jenner received a letter from Thomas Jefferson, President of the USA, which included the words 'Medicine has never before produced any single improvement of such utility … mankind can never forget that you have lived'.

The first great breakthrough was Edward Jenner's use of vaccination to save people from catching smallpox. It's a good place to begin, not just because it was the first great breakthrough, but also because it will help you understand why some breakthroughs were more important than others.

In the 1700s smallpox was as frightening as **plague** had been. It killed more children each year than any other disease as well as thousands of adults. Survivors were often severely disfigured by scars from scabs on their skin.

Jenner was an experienced country doctor in Gloucestershire. Like other country doctors he knew that milkmaids who caught cowpox, a mild disease, never got smallpox. However, no one had made this widely known nor tested the idea scientifically. In the 1790s Jenner decided to carry out experiments to test the theory, observing and recording the details carefully. His experiments were so successful that in 1798 he published a book describing how to prevent smallpox by infecting people with cowpox. He called this method *vaccination* because the Latin word for cow is *vacca*. His book also described his evidence, recording 23 different cases to prove the theory (see Extract A).

 A

Case 17 James Phipps. I selected a healthy boy about eight years old. The matter was taken from the cowpox sore on Sarah Nelmes' hand and inserted on 14 May 1796 into the boy by two cuts each half an inch long. On the seventh day he complained of uneasiness, on the ninth he became a little chilly, lost his appetite and had a slight headache and spent the night with some degree of restlessness but on the following day he was perfectly well.

In order to ascertain that the boy was secure from the **contagion** of smallpox he was **inoculated** with smallpox matter but no disease followed. Several months later he was again inoculated with smallpox matter but again no disease followed.

THE SIGNIFICANCE OF VACCINATION

There are arguments about just how important Jenner's breakthrough was. You are going to look at the evidence and decide whether you agree with this statement:

'Vaccination against smallpox was a major breakthrough in the prevention of disease.'

1. Read the evidence cards on page 55. Decide where each card goes on this set of scales.
2. Which evidence do you think is most effective in:
   a) supporting the statement
   b) challenging the statement?
   Explain your choices.
3. Write a short answer summing up whether you agree with the statement. Include at least two pieces of evidence to support your view and also evidence to show why the opposite view is less strong.
4. What have you learned from this activity about why some breakthroughs can be seen as more significant than others?

A. Stopping smallpox was not new

Inoculation was already being used to prevent smallpox. Inoculation involved spreading **pus** from a smallpox pustule into a cut in the skin of a healthy person. If the person was lucky they got a mild dose of smallpox and did not catch it again because their body had developed **antibodies** against smallpox (though they did not know this). Inoculation became big business. For example, the Suffolk surgeons Robert and Daniel Sutton carried out thousands of inoculations, cutting deaths from smallpox.

B. Opposition to vaccination

There was a lot of opposition to vaccination. Some came from inoculators and doctors who were no longer earning money by giving inoculations. Other people did not like the idea of a treatment linked to animals or heard of cases when it was done clumsily and did not work. Others did not believe Jenner because he was not a famous London doctor!

C. Jenner showed the value of scientific method

Jenner had found a way of saving thousands of people from smallpox. His work was an excellent example of using scientific methods of experiment and enquiry, encouraging other scientists to solve medical problems.

F. Vaccination saved many lives

Although vaccination was not compulsory it was widely used and led to a significant fall in deaths from smallpox. Deaths fell even more rapidly after 1871 when compulsory vaccination was enforced. A century later, in the 1970s, smallpox was wiped out worldwide.

D. Inoculation had limited impact on smallpox

Inoculation was risky because the person inoculated could get a strong dose of smallpox and die or pass smallpox onto someone else. Vaccination did not have these risks. In addition, most people could not afford inoculation but Jenner offered free vaccinations and the government gave money to pay for free vaccinations.

E. Vaccination was not enforced for many years

Governments were slow to make vaccination compulsory. As Graph B shows, having children vaccinated was voluntary until 1852 because governments did not want to force people to vaccinate their children. At that time no government had passed laws forcing changes to improve health. Even after 1852 the government did little to enforce the law until 1871 when people were fined for not having their children vaccinated. Many children had died who might have been saved by vaccination.

G. Vaccination did not lead to other breakthroughs

Vaccination only dealt with one disease and did not help doctors stop other infectious diseases. Vaccination was a 'one-off' discovery, made because of the chance connection between cowpox and smallpox. Jenner did not know exactly how vaccination worked (he did not know that bacteria cause disease) so he could not use his method to prevent other diseases. Vaccination was very important but did not lead to other discoveries.

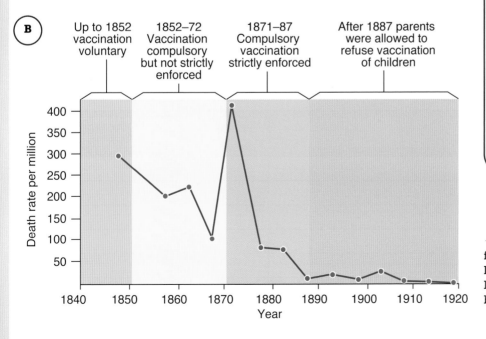

◀ This graph shows the death rate from smallpox between 1840 and 1920. It also shows when governments made laws to increase the number of people being vaccinated.

4.3 Your challenge: Proving that germ theory was the most significant breakthrough in the 1800s

Question: Which of these breakthroughs was the more significant?

a) Jenner's use of vaccination because it saved many lives immediately and has saved lives ever since.

b) Pasteur's germ theory which did not save a single life by itself.

Answer: Pasteur's germ theory! Vaccination did save many, many lives but it was a one-off discovery which did not lead to other breakthroughs. In contrast, germ theory completely changed the History of Medicine. For the first time doctors understood what really did cause diseases and this led to a torrent of medical improvements, eventually revolutionised medicine and saved far more lives than vaccination.

The answer in the box above contains several of the most dangerous things in history – generalisations. A generalisation is a very big statement such as 'completely changed the History of Medicine' or 'led to a torrent of medical improvements' or 'revolutionised medicine'. We call this kind of claim a generalisation because it's very general – there is no evidence provided to support it.

In the first part of this section we're setting you a challenge rather than an enquiry – the challenge is to collect the evidence to prove that germ theory was as significant as the generalisations above claim. You can collect the evidence on a memory map or in a table, depending on which Knowledge Organiser you prefer to use. Here they are for you to choose from.

THE IMPACT OF GERM THEORY

1. Read pages 57–66 and answer the questions on them. Use your answers to complete your table or memory map.

2. When you have completed your research choose:
    a) the three pieces of evidence that you think support the argument that germ theory was the most significant breakthrough in the 1800s.
    b) the evidence which most challenges the argument that germ theory was a significant breakthrough.

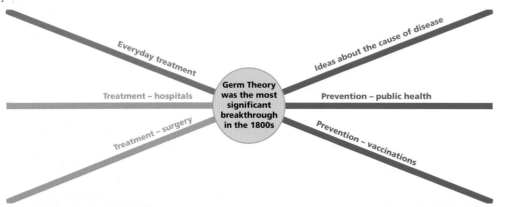

Practice question

'Germ theory was the most significant medical breakthrough in the 1800s.' How far do you agree? Explain your answer. Use the guidance in Part 3 from page 148 to help you.

Topics	What impact did germ theory have on this topic? (warning – not everything changed!)	What other reasons were there for changes in this topic?
ideas about the cause of disease		
prevention – public health		
prevention – vaccinations		
treatment – surgery		
treatment – hospitals		
everyday treatments		

4.4 Ideas about the cause of disease

Germ theory changed ideas about what causes diseases but it did not lead to instant revolution. This revolution took place in stages:

Stage 1: 1861–64 – theory and proof

Pasteur published his germ theory in 1861. In 1864 he carried out experiments that convinced other scientists that his germ theory was correct. However, his theory was very general – he said that bacteria cause diseases but could not identify the specific bacteria which cause individual diseases.

Stage 2: 1865–76 – struggling to prove the theory's value

In 1865 there was a cholera **epidemic** in France and Pasteur tried to find the exact bacterium that causes cholera. However, under his microscope he could only see a confused mass of bacteria. He could not discover which one was causing cholera.

Therefore, in the 1860s, Pasteur's germ theory seemed less useful than Jenner's vaccination. Jenner did not know that bacteria cause smallpox but he could prevent people catching it! The invisibility of bacteria was one reason why many people still believed that bad air (**miasma**) was the cause of disease. They could see rotting food and flesh and even **faeces** in the streets. They knew this dirt gave off terrible smells and assumed that these smells caused and spread disease. This miasma theory was still believed by educated people such as Florence Nightingale (see page 63) and Edwin Chadwick, the civil servant who had done a lot of research to improve public health in England.

Stage 3: 1876 – gotcha! Identifying the bacterium causing anthrax

In 1876 a German doctor called Robert Koch and his research team made a practical breakthrough. They found the bacterium that was causing **anthrax**. This was the first time anyone had identified the specific microbe that causes an individual disease.

Stage 4: 1876 and afterwards – vaccines to prevent diseases

Over the next 20 years Koch and other scientists identified more bacteria causing individual diseases and this led to the development of vaccines to prevent them (see page 58). This finally persuaded people that bad air was not the cause of disease.

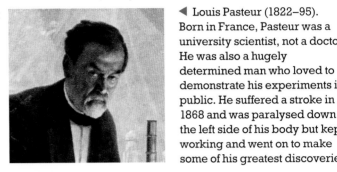

◀ Louis Pasteur (1822–95). Born in France, Pasteur was a university scientist, not a doctor. He was also a hugely determined man who loved to demonstrate his experiments in public. He suffered a stroke in 1868 and was paralysed down the left side of his body but kept working and went on to make some of his greatest discoveries.

Stage 2

It's OK. He knows we're here but he can't tell which of us is causing cholera.

Stage 3

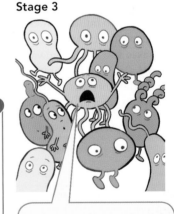

You've got me! I give in. I'm the one that causes anthrax.

GERM THEORY AND THE CAUSE OF DISEASE

1. What did Pasteur fail to do in 1865 that suggested his theory was not useful?
2. Why did the belief that bad air causes disease continue after Pasteur published his germ theory?
3. How did Koch prove the usefulness of germ theory?
4. Complete your table or memory map on page 56 for this topic.

What about the four Humours ... and God?

The idea that the **four Humours** caused disease had faded away in the 1600s and 1700s as doctors discovered more about the human body. In contrast some people continued to believe that God sent diseases to punish people for their sins. Not even the scientific proof of Pasteur's germ theory could stop that.

Bacteria, microbe, germ
These words all mean the same thing. The drawings on this page illustrate the development in knowledge about bacteria.

4.5 Germ theory and preventing diseases

Germ theory changed ideas about what causes disease – the top of our medical triangle. Now we will travel down its left-hand side to investigate how germ theory changed methods of preventing disease and how quickly this happened.

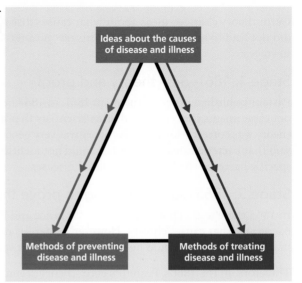

Prevention 1: Vaccinations

Stage 1: The 1860s – theory

Pasteur published his germ theory in 1861 and three years later carried out experiments that convinced other scientists that it was correct. However, this did not immediately lead to vaccinations to prevent diseases. Nevertheless, Pasteur's theory did play a part in persuading the government to enforce compulsory vaccination against smallpox (see page 55).

Stage 2: The 1870s and 1880s – identifying individual bacteria

In 1876 Robert Koch made the first identification of the bacterium causing an individual disease when he identified the bacterium causing anthrax. In 1882 his team of scientists found the bacterium that caused a second disease, tuberculosis (TB). After this, other scientists followed Koch's methods and quickly identified the bacteria causing these diseases:

| 1882 | Typhoid | 1886 | Pneumonia | 1894 | Plague |
| 1883 | Cholera | 1887 | Meningitis | 1898 | Dysentery |

Stage 2

There's nowhere to hide any more. You've got us. We surrender.

Stage 3: 1880s and after – developing vaccines

Koch's work identifying bacteria still didn't save people's lives by itself. What were needed were vaccines that worked like Jenner's vaccine against smallpox, giving people weak doses of disease to build up their immunity. The hero of this stage was once again Louis Pasteur. He knew all about Jenner's work and used it to find vaccines. He began with animal diseases and developed vaccines to prevent anthrax and chicken cholera. Then, in 1885, he tested a vaccine for rabies on a boy who'd been bitten by a rabid dog. The vaccine saved the boy's life. This was the first successful vaccine since Jenner's work on smallpox. Other scientists then developed vaccines to prevent other diseases.

Their successes included:

| 1896 | Typhoid | 1913 | Diphtheria |
| 1906 | Tuberculosis | 1927 | Tetanus |

However, scientific discoveries are one thing – the development of enough vaccine to use with the public took longer still.

> ### GERM THEORY AND PREVENTION: VACCINATIONS
>
> 1. Why had Jenner's use of vaccination not led to other vaccines?
> 2. Explain the links between:
>   - germ theory
>   - identifying the bacteria that cause individual diseases
>   - the development of vaccines that prevent those diseases.
> 3. Complete your table or memory map on page 56 for this topic.

Prevention 2: Public health

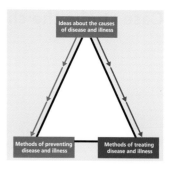

What is public health? A reminder

Governments organise public health systems to prevent diseases spreading and to help people become healthier. This includes providing fresh water, sewers and hospitals, for example, and making laws to force towns and people to try to prevent diseases spreading.

On pages 60–61 we will look at a case study on public health and the work of John Snow but, first, what had been happening to public health since the plague of 1665 (page 36)? For many people their living and working conditions had grown worse because of the growth of towns during the Industrial Revolution. The whole country's population had been growing rapidly but the growth of towns was phenomenal. People flocked to the towns to find work but many found themselves living and working in worse conditions than their ancestors had in the Middle Ages. One major reason was that workers had to live close to factories (there were no railways or other transport in the early 1800s) so houses were built rapidly and crammed together. Water came from stand-pipes in the streets and families shared **privies** (outside toilets). The results were described by one visitor to Leeds in *The Morning Chronicle in* 1848:

> The east and north-east districts of Leeds are, perhaps, the worst, a perfect wilderness of foulness. Conceive acre on acre of little streets, run up without attention to plan or health, acre on acre of closely-built and thickly-peopled ground, without a paving stone on the surface, or an inch of sewer beneath, deep trodden-churned sloughs of mud forming the only thoroughfares, privies often ruinous, all most horribly foul. Conceive such a surface drenched with the liquid slops which each family flings out daily and nightly.

One result of the overcrowding and poor conditions was the frequent outbreak of epidemics of disease such as cholera. These epidemics were just as frightening as plague had been in previous centuries because there was still no way of stopping them and they killed many thousands of people, as Table C shows. The shocking conditions led to a civil servant, Edwin Chadwick, compiling his 'Report on the Sanitary Conditions of the Labouring Population' in 1842. Chadwick detailed the effects of these conditions on people's lives, including statistics about the differences in average age at death. In country areas the average age of death for workers was 38. In Liverpool, chosen as an example of a rapidly growing town, the average age of death for labourers was 15.

Six years later, in 1848, the government took action – of a sort. It introduced a law called The Public Health Act.

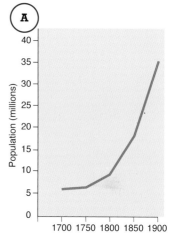

A

▲ The growth of the population of England and Wales 1700–1900.

The Public Health Act 1848

1. A national Board of Health was set up.
2. In towns where the death rate was very high the government could force the local council to make public health improvements to water supply and sewerage and appoint a medical officer of health.
3. Local councils were **encouraged** to make collect taxes to pay for public health improvements **if they had the support** of local tax-payers.
4. Councils were **allowed** to appoint medical officers of health to oversee public health.

Remember the Public Health Act came before Pasteur published his germ theory. There was no scientific evidence in 1848 to help persuade politicians to enforce public health changes.

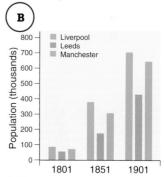

B

▲ The rapid growth of three major towns.

PUBLIC HEALTH IN THE EARLY NINETEENTH CENTURY

1. How had the growth of towns made public health worse?

2. What were the benefits and limitations of the 1848 Public Health Act? Look at the words in bold for the limitations.

3. How did ideas about the cause of disease in the 1840s hold back progress?

(You will find more questions on public health to help you complete your table or memory map on page 60.)

C

Year	Deaths
1831–32	26,101
1848–49	53,293
1853–54	20,079

▲ Death rates in cholera epidemics in Britain.

Case study: the cholera outbreak of 1854 and the story of public health

I will begin with the questions – though it's never the most exciting way to start a page! The questions show you what you can learn from these pages – three things that are important in the overall history of medicine.

CHOLERA AND THE STORY OF PUBLIC HEALTH

1. How different were methods of preventing the spread of cholera in 1854 from methods of preventing plague in 1665?
2. Why were governments reluctant to enforce public health reforms in the 1850s?
3. Why did the government finally enforce public health reform in 1875 and how important was the influence of the germ theory?
4. Complete your table or memory map on page 56 for this topic.

Cholera strikes!

The 1848 Public Health Act made little difference to people's health. Most towns did not set up Boards of Health and the National Board was abolished after six years. Then came cholera! Cholera seems to have broken out for the first time in Britain in 1831. It killed its victims in less than a day and when another epidemic broke out in 1854 over 20,000 people died. Table A shows you how people tried to prevent its spread – you may have seen these methods before!

A

Burning barrels of tar or vinegar to get rid of bad air
Smoking cigars as protection against bad air
Praying or wearing lucky charms
Taking medicines and pills that 'guaranteed' protection
Cleaning houses and scattering chloride of lime (great for making places look clean)
Burning the clothes and bedding of victims

▲ Trying to stop cholera in 1854

▲ Snow was born in Yorkshire in 1813, the son of a farm labourer. He was apprenticed to a surgeon at 14. He became a pioneer in surgery and public health, improving medical methods and using detailed evidence to challenge old ideas.

John Snow and the Broad Street pump

In 1849 John Snow published a book saying that people caught cholera from water they used for washing and drinking, not from 'bad air'. His suggestion was mocked by many doctors. The rest of this page will read like a western! While everyone else ran around frightened of cholera in 1854 a lone hero strode into Broad Street and 'did what a man's gotta do'. John Snow took on cholera and beat it – with a pump handle!

Snow's surgery was near Broad Street in London. Within ten days 500 people around Broad Street had died of cholera. Snow got to work – with a map! He mapped out the deaths in detail (see Map B) and proved that most of the local deaths were of people living close to the water pump in Broad Street. They got their drinking, cooking and washing water from that pump. Snow had the handle of the Broad Street pump taken away so no one could get water from it. There were no more deaths. It was discovered later that a **cesspit**, only a metre from the pump, was leaking into the drinking water.

Snow had proved that clean water was essential for preventing the spread of cholera but even this did not lead to a new Public Health Act enforcing change. Many scientists still clung to the 'bad air' theory.

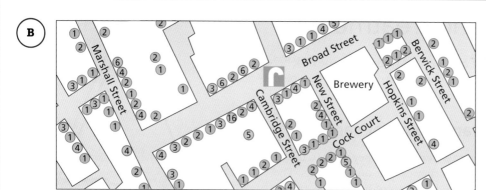

◀ A copy of part of Snow's map detailing deaths in the Broad Street area.

Why were major public health changes made in 1875?

Snow saved Londoners from cholera in 1854. People knew that dirty water was dangerous as Cartoon C shows but it was not until after Pasteur published his germ theory that anyone could begin to understand exactly why the water was causing cholera. Even another cholera outbreak in 1865, which killed 14,000 people, did not force the government to act. There were two main reasons why a new law was not passed.

1. Wealthy people did not want to pay taxes to pay the cost for water supplies, sewers, etc. that would benefit people in the poor parts of towns.
2. People did not want the government interfering in what happened in their own towns.

However, some changes did take place. In London, an effective, modern sewer system was built after the very hot summer of 1858. With no rain, river levels fell, especially in the Thames. The smell from the river grew worse and worse and The 'Great Stink' (as it was called) was worst at the Houses of Parliament which are right on the river bank. However, there was still no new Public Health Act to enforce improvements throughout the country.

Finally, in 1875, a Public Health Act was passed. It was now compulsory for local councils to improve sewers and drainage, provide fresh water supplies and to appoint medical officers and sanitary inspectors to inspect public health facilities. In addition, other laws improved the standards of housing and stopped the pollution of rivers (from which people got water).

There were two main reasons for this breakthrough.

1. Pasteur's germ theory

Pasteur had proved that there was a scientific link between dirt and disease. Snow had been correct in his arguments even if he did not know that it was bacteria in the water that spread cholera. The theory that illness was caused by 'bad air' finally faded away. Faced with scientific proof, people were more willing to pay taxes to cover the costs of public health reforms and more local towns began to make these reforms.

2. Governments needed votes

In 1867 working men in towns were given the right to vote for the first time. The numbers of voters had doubled. The numbers increased again in 1884 when many working men in country areas got the vote. If politicians wanted to win elections, they now had to promise laws to win the votes of working men, not just the wealthy and middle classes. The 1870s and 1880s saw many new laws passed designed to improve the lives of ordinary people.

▲ This cartoon published in 1860 was called Death's Dispensary.

4.6 Germ theory and treatments

Now it's time to look at the other side of our medical triangle, at the link between changing ideas about the cause of diseases and the treatments and care people received.

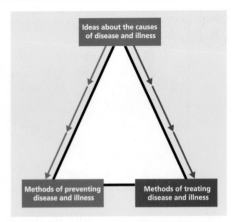

Treatment 1: Nightingale and hospital care

For many people in the early 1800s, hospitals were places they went to die – if not from the disease they had, then from another they caught on the wards. The illustration below shows you the problems and dangers of hospital wards.

Cramped, stuffy wards helped infections to spread quickly.

Death rates from infection were high, because wards were not cleaned often enough or effectively enough.

There were few toilets and the sewerage system was poor, so infections spread easily.

Nursing staff were not trained.

Nurses were often criticised for being dirty or drunk.

The lessons of the Crimea

The heroine of hospital reform was Florence Nightingale. She had horrified her wealthy family by wanting to be a nurse but she trained in Germany, then worked as a nurse and became Superintendent of Nurses in a London hospital. When the Crimean War broke out between Britain, France and Russia in 1854 she took 38 nurses to the Crimea, which lies between Russia and Turkey.

Arriving at the army hospital at Scutari, Florence was appalled by the dirty conditions. She concentrated on cleaning the hospital and patients and was so effective that the death rate in the hospital fell from 40 per cent of wounded to 2 per cent. She wrote back to the British government:

▲ Florence Nightingale at the age of 25 in 1845.

(i) 25 November 1854 'It appears that in these hospitals the washing of linen and of the men are considered a minor detail. No washing has been performed for the men or the beds – except by ourselves. When we came here, there was no soap or basins or towels in the wards. The consequences of all this are fever, cholera, gangrene, lice …'

(ii) 10 December 1854 'What we have achieved:

- A great deal more cleaning of wards – mops, scrubbing brushes given out by ourselves
- The supervision and stirring up of the whole organisation generally
- Repair of the wards for 800 wounded'.

Nightingale's impact on hospitals and care

Florence's work in the Crimea made her a national heroine, which helped her raise money to set up her first Nightingale School for Nurses in 1860. In 1859 she had written *Notes on Nursing* and in 1863 *Notes on Hospitals*. Both books were very influential all over the world, providing the basis for training nurses and hospital design.

She was not a hands-on nurse but a great organiser, convinced that her life's work was to improve conditions in hospitals and the training of nurses to improve the care of patients. She focused on improving:

- sanitation in hospitals – clean water supplies, good drains and sewers, toilet facilities, total cleanliness
- ventilation to make sure patients got fresh, clean air to breathe
- food supplies, clothing and washing facilities for patients.

One surprising thing was that she paid little attention to Pasteur's germ theory when it appeared in the decade *after* the Crimean War. She had been brought up to believe that miasma (bad air) was the main cause of disease and, in many ways correctly, she continued to associate disease with dirt. This is why she concentrated on improving hygiene and cleanliness in hospitals all her life. As a result, her nursing schools concentrated on training nurses in very practical skills. She did not let doctors teach nurses about germ theory because she felt that such ideas would simply get in the way of nurses' more important task – keeping patients and wards clean.

The impact of other factors on hospitals and care

The improvements in hospital buildings and sanitation could not have come about without improved engineering techniques and new government laws passed to enforce public health improvements. Changes in surgery increased the numbers of complex operations and so surgeons required better-trained nurses to assist them. And, despite Nightingale's relegation of germ theory, it had a very significant impact on all aspects of medicine, including surgery, and so in turn it affected the ways that nurses carried out their work.

Developments in hospitals

So far this page has talked about 'hospitals' as if they were all the same but there were important differences between the kinds of hospitals which developed from the 1850s onwards. It's also worth noting that the wealthy and middle classes never went to hospital. They paid fees to their doctors who treated them and even carried out operations at home because home seemed healthier than hospital wards.

Local hospitals were called 'cottage hospitals' because they were small, just like medieval hospitals run by abbeys and guilds. The first cottage hospital opened in 1859 and there were 300 by 1900, together with 18 **voluntary hospitals** in London. Local doctors gave their time for free. Wealthy local people gave donations to support these hospitals even if they did not use them themselves. Working people could use these hospitals if they subscribed to sick clubs, paying each week into a fund to cover the costs of treatment whenever it was needed. The out-patients department or the **dispensary** of a hospital also helped local people.

However, this still left the poor and disabled at home, people who could no longer support themselves. They were sent to live in **workhouses**, built since the 1830s, and run by local **Poor Law Unions**. Conditions in workhouses for the sick and elderly (perhaps blind, deaf or disabled) were often very poor. The sick or disabled were often the majority but little was done to separate them from the healthy inmates. Therefore, in 1867, the government ordered that the Poor Law Unions build infirmaries to care for the sick poor, using taxes raised from local people. These infirmaries were to be separate from the workhouses themselves and were to have a paid doctor to treat the sick. There were also to be new asylums for the mentally ill and fever hospitals for people with infectious diseases.

As ever, this system took time to develop and improve but it was an important improvement and by 1900 these new infirmaries had far more patients than the older voluntary and cottage hospitals. In the twentieth century they developed into the large general hospitals in many towns.

HOSPITAL CARE

1. What kinds of improvements did Nightingale make to hospitals and nursing?
2. Why did Nightingale pay little attention to germ theory?
3. How did hospital care for the sick poor improve in the later 1800s?
4. Did germ theory have any role in these improvements?
5. Complete your table or memory map on page 56 for this topic.

Treatment 2: Surgery

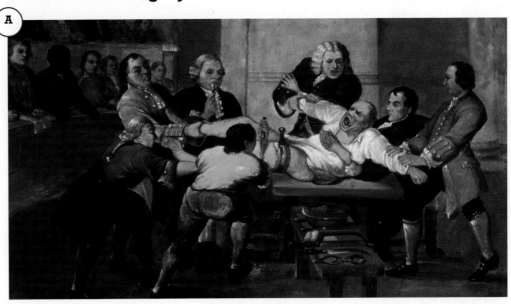

A

What else apart from the absence of an anaesthetic might endanger the patient's life?

This painting from the early 1800s captures the full horror of having an operation without an anaesthetic. The patient is having his leg **amputated** and the only way the surgeon can reduce his pain is to be as fast as possible. Surgeons prided themselves on their speed. Robert Liston once amputated a leg in two-and-a-half minutes but accidentally cut off his patient's testicles too. During another operation Liston amputated his assistant's fingers and slashed the coat of a spectator who dropped dead with fright.

Surgeons had tried to find effective anaesthetics. In the Middle Ages they used mandrake and hemlock, herbs which could kill if too much was used. In the early 1800s new ideas were tried as scientists learned about the effects of chemicals on the body. Laughing gas (nitrous oxide) reduced pain but not completely. Ether irritated eyes and lungs, causing coughing and sickness.

Simpson's use of chloroform as an anaesthetic

The answer came from James Simpson, Professor of Midwifery at Edinburgh University. He had used ether but wanted a better anaesthetic. One evening in 1847 he and his colleagues experimented with chemicals to see what anaesthetic effects they had. Simpson wrote:

> I poured some of the Chloroform fluid into tumblers. Before sitting down to supper we all inhaled the fluid, and were all 'under the table' in a minute or two, to my wife's consternation and alarm.

Simpson realised that chloroform was a very effective anaesthetic. Within days he used it to help women in childbirth and other operations. He wrote articles about his discovery and other surgeons started to use it in their operations. In 1848 John Snow (who you met on page 60) devised an inhaler to regulate the dose of chloroform and reduce the danger of using so much the patient died.

Surgery's 'Black Period', 1850–1870s

B

▲ James Simpson's discovery that chloroform was an effective anaesthetic was so important that over 30,000 people lined the streets of Edinburgh for his funeral in 1870 and flags flew at half-mast throughout Britain.

Using too much chloroform was only one reason why there was opposition to it. Some people, including some doctors, thought pain-free operations were unnatural! More importantly, anaesthetics had not necessarily made surgery safer. With patients asleep, doctors attempted more complex operations, thus carrying infections deeper into the body and also causing more loss of blood. The number of people dying from surgery may even have increased from the 1850s to early 1870s, which is known as surgery's 'Black Period'. In the 1870s some surgeons stopped using chloroform as they were concerned about the high death rate and returned to using ether mixed with nitrous oxide.

Joseph Lister and antiseptics

Chloroform changed surgery but surgeons were still wearing old pus-stained clothes, did not wash their hands before operations, nor did they **sterilise** equipment. Why? Because they did not know that bacteria caused infections in open wounds. The man who developed antiseptics to tackle infections was Joseph Lister. Lister was an outstanding surgeon but he also knew all about Pasteur's germ theory, which helped spark his own discovery as this imaginary conversation shows:

> There are bacteria in the air which cause rotting and infections such as gangrene.

> Then these bacteria must be causing infections in open wounds. I can save patients if I find a way of stopping these bacteria getting into operations' wounds.

Pasteur · Lister

The other part of Lister's answer came from sewage! He wrote:

> In 1864 I was struck by an account of the remarkable effects of using carbolic acid upon the sewage of Carlisle. It prevented all smell from the lands covered by the sewage and destroyed the parasites that usually infest cattle feeding on such land. The idea of using carbolic acid for the treatment of open fractures naturally occurred to me.

Lister experimented by treating fractures where the bone breaks through the skin. Infection often developed in these open wounds. Lister applied carbolic acid to the wound and used bandages soaked in carbolic. The wounds healed and did not develop **gangrene**, saving many lives. In 1867 Lister published his results, showing the value of carbolic acid. He also:

1. Insisted that doctors and nurses wash their hands with carbolic acid before operations to avoid infection from their hands getting into wounds.
2. Developed a carbolic spray to kill germs in the air around the operating table.
3. Invented an antiseptic **ligature** to tie up blood vessels and prevent blood loss.

The impact of these changes was spectacular. Between 1864 and 1866 there had been 16 deaths after 35 amputations – a death rate of 46 per cent. Between 1867 and 1870, after the introduction of antiseptic surgery, there were six deaths after 40 operations – a death rate of 15 per cent.

Lister's methods were a turning point. By the late 1890s Lister's antiseptic methods (killing germs on the wound) had developed into aseptic surgery (removing germs completely from the operating theatre). To ensure absolute cleanliness:

- Operating theatres and hospitals were rigorously cleaned.
- From 1887 all instruments were steam-sterilised.
- Surgeons stopped operating in ordinary clothes and wore surgical gowns and face masks and rubber gloves.

With the problems of pain and infection solved, surgeons began more ambitious operations. The first successful operation to remove an infected appendix was in the 1880s, the first heart operation in 1896 when surgeons repaired a heart damaged by a stab wound. The one major problem still facing surgeons was heavy blood-loss. The answer lay ahead in the twentieth century!

C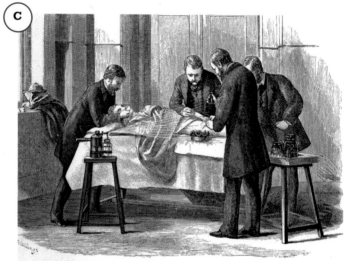

▲ An operation using a carbolic spray to disinfect the area while chloroform is used as an anaesthetic.

DEVELOPMENTS IN SURGERY

1. a) Draw up a chart listing the advantages and disadvantages of using chloroform as an anaesthetic.
   b) Why did surgery's 'Black Period' take place?
2. What part did germ theory play in Lister's development of antiseptics?
3. Sir Clifford Allbutt, a Professor of Medicine, wrote 'The obvious benefit of freedom from pain was the benefit of time. With anaesthesia ended slapdash surgery; anaesthesia gave the necessary time for the theories of Pasteur and Lister to be adopted in practice.'
   Explain what Allbutt meant.
4. Complete your table or memory map on page 56 for this topic.

4.7 Germ theory and everyday treatments

There had been major changes in medicine. At the heart of improvements was Pasteur's discovery that bacteria cause diseases. Until scientists had identified the cause of diseases it was impossible to develop effective methods of treatment and prevention. One-off discoveries such as Jenner's vaccination were very important but the idea could not be transferred to prevent other diseases.

However, it's important to remember that the impact on people's health was slow to develop. Life expectancy began to rise but by 1900 had only reached 46 for men and 50 for women. Towns were becoming cleaner. Public health facilities were beginning to improve. But the key words are 'becoming' and 'beginning to'. A great deal had not changed at all. Many still suffered major health problems because of dirt and poverty. The government gave no help to the sick, unemployed and elderly, no matter how poor they were. Those without help from friends, relatives or charities had to give up their homes and go into a workhouse run by the local council. Graph A shows the death rate of children under one year old between 1840 and 1980. This infant mortality was still shockingly high in 1900.

How did poor and working people treat everyday illnesses or even major sickness? In many ways treatments such as these home **remedies** still had a lot in common with medieval remedies:

a) For influenza either mix ginger into a drink of tea or mix half a pound of treacle with half a pint of vinegar and three teaspoonfuls of laudanum. Take three times a day.

b) To cure tuberculosis breathe into a freshly-dug hole in the turf or try the breath of stallions and cows.

c) To cure smallpox apply cool boiled turnips to the feet or make a drink out of ground ivy.

If home remedies did not work people bought 'patent' medicines, often known as 'cure-alls'. **Patent medicines** were big business, largely thanks to massive advertising campaigns by the manufacturers. James Morison (1770–1840) claimed that his pills cured everything from fever, scarlatina, tuberculosis, smallpox and measles to the effects of old age. They were actually made of lard, wax, turpentine, soap and ginger and had no ingredient that would cure illnesses but by 1834 Morison was selling over one million boxes of pills a year.

▲ Thomas Holloway became a multi-millionaire selling pills containing ginger, soap and aloes, a very powerful purgative, until a court case against him in the 1860s. There was no control over the manufacturing standards or the ingredients in patent medicines until the 1880s, so false claims about their effectiveness were made without fear of prosecution. Deaths and illnesses resulting from overdoses and addiction were common. In the 1880s governments introduced laws controlling the use of harmful ingredients but they still contained lard, wax and turpentine – and still claimed to cure all illnesses!

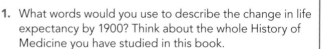

A

(Graph A: y-axis: Deaths of children under one, per 1000 live births, from 0 to 160; x-axis: years 1840, 1860, 1880, 1900, 1920, 1940, 1960, 1980)

▲ The rate of infant mortality – the death rate of children under one year old, 1840–1980.

EVERYDAY MEDICINE

1. What words would you use to describe the change in life expectancy by 1900? Think about the whole History of Medicine you have studied in this book.

2. Why do you think infant mortality was still so high in 1900?

3. What impact did germ theory have on the use of home remedies and 'cure-alls'?

4. Complete your table or memory map on page 56 for this topic.

4.8 Visible learning: Revise and remember: Part 1

This chapter has two sections, therefore we have divided your review work into two halves. This is the first half – four activities to consolidate your understanding of medical changes in the 1800s.

1 Why was germ theory so important?

Working in pairs, draw your own large version of the chart below. Summarise on it:
- **a)** the major changes in this topic in the 1800s
- **b)** to what extent these changes were linked to Pasteur's germ theory.

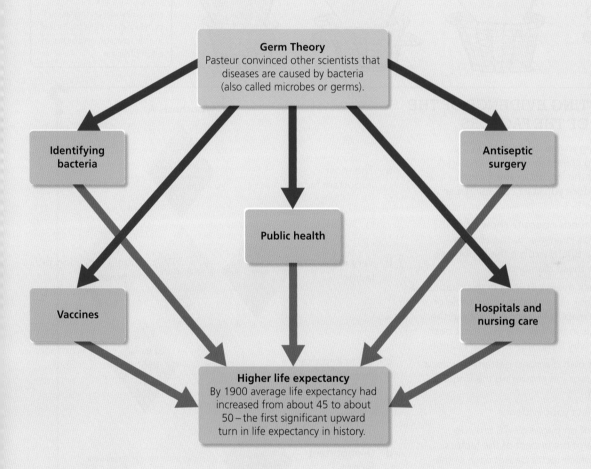

2 'Role of the Individual' chart

Look back at pages 52–53 and complete a chart for each of (deep breath!)

Jenner   Snow
Simpson   Nightingale
Pasteur   Koch   Lister

3 If you had been born in 1900 …

Some students remember things better if their imagination comes into play and they can think themselves back into the past. This doesn't suit some people but it does suit others. Try this activity:

Imagine you were born in 1900. Why would you be more confident about your medical future than if you were born in 1800? The page opposite will help you too.

4 Create a mnemonic

On page 22 we introduced the idea of using a mnemonic to help remember events or details. Can you think of a mnemonic to help remember the people behind the great breakthroughs in chronological order?

4.9 Your enquiry: Why were there so many medical breakthroughs in the nineteenth century?

While you have been finding out about the breakthroughs in the 1800s you will also have read about the reasons why they took place. This enquiry focuses on those reasons – why were there so many medical breakthroughs in the 1800s when there had been so few before?

Remember your chronology – the nineteenth century has dates beginning with 18, not 19.

Only factors relevant to the question being asked or the period are included in the specific enquiries in each chapter.

COLLECTING EVIDENCE OF THE IMPACT OF THE FACTORS

You are going to use the baskets in the illustration to collect evidence from pages 69–71 about the impact of the factors. However, before you start collecting, carry out activities 1–3.

1. The diamonds opposite show one hypothesis in answer to the enquiry question. Briefly explain the hypothesis shown in these diamonds.

2. Think back over your work in this chapter so far and look at your completed table or memory map from page 56. Set out the diamonds in the way that you think best explains why there was so much change.

3. Use your own diamond pattern to write a short paragraph answering the Enquiry question.

   Now collect your evidence.

4. Items A–K on pages 69–70 provide evidence of the impact of the factors. Decide which factor basket each of the items A–K goes in.

5. Read page 71. What other evidence can you find to go in the factor baskets?

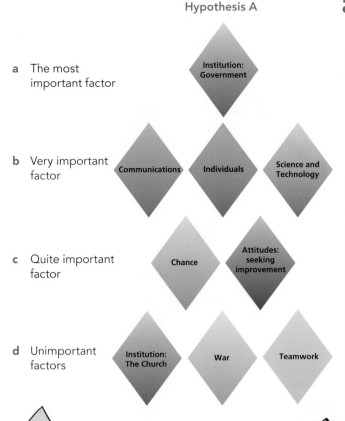

Hypothesis A

a The most important factor

b Very important factor

c Quite important factor

d Unimportant factors

What was behind the nineteenth-century breakthroughs?

A   Jenner was trained in London by John Hunter, a leading surgeon, who taught his students to observe carefully and carry out their own experiments instead of relying on knowledge in books. Jenner followed Hunter's methods, testing the connection between cowpox and smallpox in experiments and collecting evidence carefully as proof that catching cowpox really did protect people against smallpox.

B   The flushing toilet was an important late nineteenth-century invention. Instead of privies being emptied by hand and spade (and left rotting for days or weeks), the flushing system sent the waste instantly down into sewers. At first such toilets were only available to the rich but it was the beginning of a very important change. In addition in 1853 the government stopped taxing sales of soap so many more people could afford it, helping to kill germs (although no one knew this at the time!).

C

This drawing made in 1857 shows the impact of chloroform on James Simpson and his friends when they made their first experiment in 1847. It would be easy to say that this discovery was a chance factor but that would be unfair to Simpson who deliberately set out to test chemicals to see how effective they were as anaesthetics (see page 64).

D   In 1802 and 1807 Parliament gave Jenner £30,000 to develop his work on vaccination. Governments later made vaccination compulsory and enforced fines for failing to vaccinate children, which led to a steep fall in the number of smallpox cases.

E   In 1798 Jenner published his own account of his discovery, spreading the details of his method worldwide. Details of new discoveries were communicated in scientific journals so that scientists could learn from each other. Lister, for example, used the work of Pasteur, Koch and others in developing his ideas about using antiseptics in surgery.

Attitudes

Attitudes were clearly linked to individuals' work and to how scientific work was carried out. Individuals were willing to ask questions, challenge old ideas, experiment and collect evidence. Their attitude was that there was a great deal to discover. Each new discovery spurred on doctors to find out more. This all built on Renaissance ideas (see page 38).

F

This photograph shows sewers being built, one of the huge engineering projects to build sewers and water pipes under city streets. These projects used engineering knowledge that had not been available a hundred years earlier before the great improvements made in technology during the Industrial Revolution and the building of the railways (e.g. machinery powered by steam engines, methods of building pipelines and embankments). This knowledge was essential to make the laws effective. In London, engineer Joseph Bazalgette (1819–91) designed and built London's sewer system after the 'Great Stink' of 1858 (see page 61). This included 83 miles of main sewers, 1100 miles of sewers for each street (connecting to the main sewers) and pumping stations to drive the flow of sewage along the pipes.

Individuals

Breakthroughs were often initiated by the work of one person but there's more to this factor than identifying the name of an individual. It's important to identify the qualities that he or she had that led to the breakthrough – determination, observation, insight, attention to detail for example. Think about the individuals you have studied and identify the specific qualities they showed.

G Part of John Snow's description of his work identifying water as the cause of cholera in 1854.

On proceeding to the spot, I found that nearly all of the deaths had taken place within a short distance of the Broad Street water pump. There were only ten deaths in houses situated decidedly nearer to another street pump. In five of these cases, the families of the deceased persons informed me that they always used the pump in Broad Street as they preferred the water to that of the pump that was nearer.

There is a brewery in Broad Street. Perceiving that no brewer's men were registered as having died of cholera, I called on Mr. Huggins, the owner. He informed me that there were about 70 workmen employed in the brewery and that only two of them had been indisposed by cholera and then not seriously. The men are allowed to drink beer, and Mr. Huggins believed that they do not drink water at all and never obtained water from the Broad Street pump.

H

Developments in medicine were greatly helped by improvements in technology that resulted from the Industrial Revolution. Many pieces of scientific and medical equipment improved because industries developed the ability to create more precise equipment. The most significant development was probably the improvement in microscopes which allowed scientists to see and identify bacteria for the first time. Lister developed a microscope that magnified things 1000 times.

I Joseph Lister described part of the reason why he developed the use of antiseptics in surgery. He wrote:

In 1864 I was struck by an account of the remarkable effects of using carbolic acid upon the sewage of Carlisle. It prevented all smell from the lands covered by the sewage and destroyed the parasites that usually infest cattle feeding on such land. The idea of using carbolic acid for the treatment of open fractures naturally occurred to me.

J 1848 and 1875 were landmarks years when governments made new laws about public health. The 1848 Act made changes possible but was not as effective as many people hoped. The 1875 Public Health Act was far more important, forcing local councils to improve public health facilities (see page 53).

K Simpson's discovery of chloroform did not happen 'out of the blue'. Doctors had been trying other chemicals such as ether, because scientists had been learning more about the impact of chemicals on the human body.

How had society changed to make medical breakthroughs possible?

The changes described in this chapter were the result of rapid changes in society but they did also build on changes in ideas from earlier centuries. The illustration below shows how those earlier changes got closer to achieving the aim of longer, healthier lives.

Beginning of challenges to old ideas. Vesalius showed that Galen could be wrong about anatomy.

Development of scientific method – asking questions and testing hypotheses by observation and experiment. Harvey used this method to discover the circulation of the blood.

Doctors increasingly trained to use scientific method. Beginning of more professional training of doctors in hospital wards.

1500s Renaissance   **1600s Scientific Revolution**   **1700s**

The final leap was made in the 1800s. The diagram below shows the changes in society that contributed to medical change.

Urbanisation

For the first time more people lived in towns than in the countryside. Conditions were often crowded and filthy, leading to devastating epidemics of disease. This increased demands for solutions.

Communications

Communications were revolutionised. Trains allowed scientists and doctors to travel more quickly to attend conferences and learn from each other's ideas. News was reported more quickly, especially after the telegraph was developed in the 1850s, so details of scientific experiments could be reported in other countries on the next day. Scientific journals spread detailed accounts of new medical methods so they could be used worldwide.

Consequences of the Industrial Revolution

Political attitudes

In 1800 governments believed they should interfere in people's lives as little as possible. If people were unhealthy that was their business. By 1900 Parliament was making laws to improve people's health, forcing changes on people. This would have been unthinkable a century earlier.

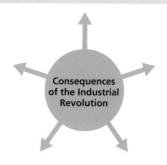

Have you noticed? Two famous medical names have not been mentioned in this chapter although they played a huge part in chapters 2 and 3. Who are they and why have they not been mentioned?

Technology

Industrialisation was not just about coal-mining and mills producing cloth and clothes from wool and cotton. Developments in steel-making helped produce a thin syringe needle that did not break; improvements in glass-making led to better microscope lenses and better thermometers.

Changes in voting

In 1867 working men were able to vote for the first time. It was still only a minority of working men but a major change had taken place and, in 1884, the numbers were increased. Now politicians had to make changes to win the votes of working men and this led to major reforms aimed at improving health.

4.10 Communicating your answer

Revise your hypothesis and get your summary answer clear in your mind.

Now you have completed your research it is time to write your answer to the enquiry question below. First, however, you need to have your answer clear in your mind.

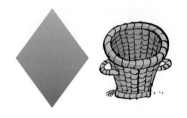

1. Return to your pattern of factor diamonds and collection of evidence baskets from page 68. Use these to reorganise the factor diamonds into the pattern you think best answers the question.
2. Use your reorganised diamond pattern to revise your hypothesis paragraph from page 68. This will make sure you have a clear answer to the question.

Now you are prepared to write your full answer to our question:

Explain why there were so many medical breakthroughs in the nineteenth century.

We have given you a good deal of help but you will find more guidance in the Guide to effective historical writing on pages 148–62. In addition remember to use **connectives** to tie in the factors to the question.

WHAT YOU KNOW   WHAT THE QUESTION ASKS

Remember connective phrases such as 'this meant that ...', 'this led to ...' and 'this resulted in ...'. And keep your **word wall** up to date.

Here are some of the words or phrases from this chapter that you will find useful.

microbes   anaesthetics   cottage hospital   chloroform   cholera   antiseptics

carbolic acid   infant mortality   vaccination   inoculation   sanitation   ether

patent medicines   antibodies   immunity   stand-pipes   Black Period

minimal   compulsory   voluntary   permissive   beginning to   essential

rapid   crucial   fundamental   highly/most significant   pre-requisite

critical   vital   of some value

Practice questions

1. Explain one way in which people's reactions to epidemics of disease were similar in the seventeenth and nineteenth centuries.
2. Explain one way in which people's reactions to the epidemics of disease were different in the seventeenth and nineteenth centuries.
3. Explain one way in which ideas about the causes of disease were similar in the seventeenth and nineteenth centuries.
4. Explain one way in which ideas about the causes of disease were different in the seventeenth and nineteenth centuries.
5. Explain why there were changes in understanding of the cause of disease during the period 1700–1900.
6. Explain why there was both continuity and change in treatments for sickness during the period 1700–1900.
7. 'There was rapid progress in methods of preventing disease between 1700 and 1900.' How far do you agree? Explain your answer.
8. 'Jenner's vaccination against smallpox was a major breakthrough in the prevention of disease during the period 1700–1900.' How far do you agree? Explain your answer.
9. 'Simpson's use of chloroform as an anaesthetic was a major breakthrough in surgery during the period 1700–1900.' How far do you agree? Explain your answer.

4.11 Visible learning: Revise and remember: Part 2

1 Revise the Big Story – with the help of a germ

After each chapter we have asked you to retell the Big Story. Here is a different way to do that – from the perspective of a germ! The task is to tell the story of medicine from the 1200s to 1900 from the perspective of a germ. First complete a living graph like the one opposite – when would you as a germ be happy, anxious, frightened, delighted by medical conditions and understanding? Then once you've completed the graph tell the story – and remember to explain why your feelings are changing.

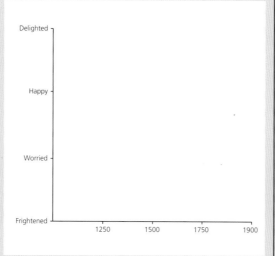

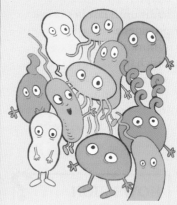

2 Test yourself!

The more you think about what you have learned and **especially what you're not sure about**, the more chance you have of succeeding in your exam. So answer these questions and don't be surprised if you have seen some of them before.

1. When did Pasteur announce his germ theory? (If not the year, which decade?)	2. What discovery did Harvey make and in which century did he discover it?	3. Which method of preventing smallpox was used before vaccination?
4. List three ideas people had about the cause of disease in the Middle Ages.	5. List three kinds of treatment used between 1500 and 1700.	6. What was so important about the 1875 Public Health Act? (Mention two details to support your answer.)
7. Give two methods used to try to prevent cholera spreading in 1854 before John Snow's work.	8. What did James Simpson use as an effective anaesthetic and what was surgery's 'Black Period'?	9. What did John Snow do to stop cholera spreading in 1854?
10. Name three reasons why changes were taking place in medicine by 1700.	11. Where did Florence Nightingale go to help British soldiers?	12. When did the Black Death arrive in England and what percentage of people did it kill?
13. What was Joseph Lister's big breakthrough?	14. What did you find hardest to understand in this chapter? How are you going to help yourself understand it?	15. Name one thing that you learned in this chapter that surprised you or that you now think differently about. Explain why.

3 Set questions yourself!

Work in a group of three. Each of you set four revision questions on nineteenth-century medicine. Use the style of questions on page 11. Then ask each other the questions – and make sure you know the answers!

Medical Moments in Time – London, 1854

Until now these Medical Moments illustrations have appeared earlier in the chapter. This time we have left it until last because it provides an excellent way of summing up the ways in which medicine changed – and did not change – by 1900. This illustration is set in 1854 so it's not at the end of the period you have just studied.

HOW MUCH CHANGE? **?**

1. What evidence is shown of:
   a) continuities in medical ideas and methods from before 1700?
   b) changes in medical ideas and methods since 1700?

2. What other changes and continuities could you add to build a fuller picture of medicine in 1854? Write a set of speech bubbles to illustrate them.

3. What would you put in a picture like this to show the development of medicine by 1900?

4. How would you describe the pace of change in medicine between 1800 and 1854 and then between 1854 and 1900?

5. What was the big difference between the 1848 and 1875 Public Health Acts and why was this so important?

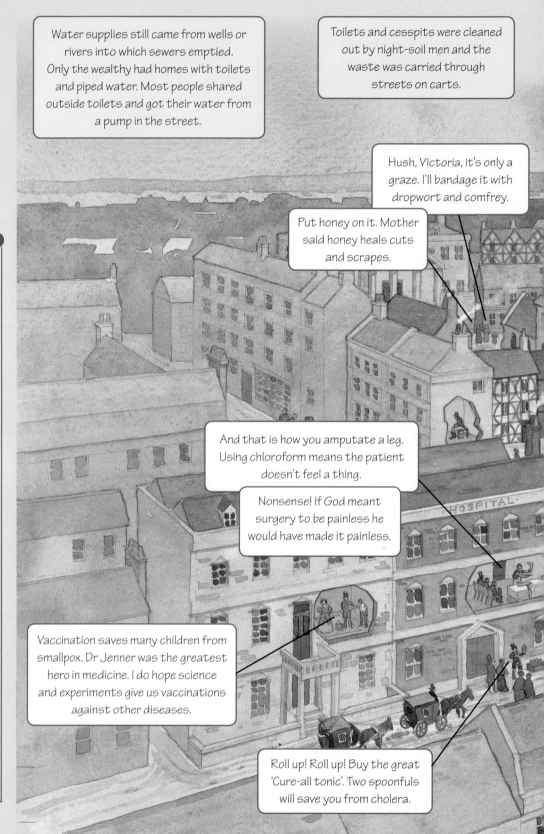

Water supplies still came from wells or rivers into which sewers emptied. Only the wealthy had homes with toilets and piped water. Most people shared outside toilets and got their water from a pump in the street.

Toilets and cesspits were cleaned out by night-soil men and the waste was carried through streets on carts.

Hush, Victoria, it's only a graze. I'll bandage it with dropwort and comfrey.

Put honey on it. Mother said honey heals cuts and scrapes.

And that is how you amputate a leg. Using chloroform means the patient doesn't feel a thing.

Nonsense! If God meant surgery to be painless he would have made it painless.

Vaccination saves many children from smallpox. Dr Jenner was the greatest hero in medicine. I do hope science and experiments give us vaccinations against other diseases.

Roll up! Roll up! Buy the great 'Cure-all tonic'. Two spoonfuls will save you from cholera.

In 1848 the government passed a Public Health Act setting up a national Board of Health. It said:

- local taxes could be charged to improve water supply and sewers

- the Board of Health could force towns to improve water supply and sewerage if the local death-rate was very high

- local Boards of Health with Medical Officers could be set up.

Cholera has broken out around Broad Street. There's so much bad air in that part of London. Those houses are so filthy they make the air bad.

Hold your arm out. Bleeding does you good. And I've a good laxative that'll clear out your body.

It's consumption. He's been coughing all week.

Back home people with coughs ride a donkey in a circle seven times. Worth trying.

There's talk of taxes to pay for cleaning streets and buildiing sewers and water pipes.

I'll pay for where I live but not for keeping anyone else clean.

That Dr Snow says people catch cholera from the drinking water. He's closed off the water pump in Broad Street.

There's not many agree with him though.

5 Medicine in modern Britain, c.1900–present

Improvements in medicine and health since 1900 have been amazing, astonishing, phenomenal! If you and your class had been born 150 years ago you would have lived in constant danger of death from infectious diseases or from cutting your finger and getting blood poisoning. So why have these medical miracles happened? Read on to find out!

5.1 The pace of change since 1900

The great breakthroughs before 1900 had been vital stepping stones to better health and longer lives but medicine had not been revolutionised overnight. Here are some key points about medicine in 1900 which show that change had been slow despite those breakthroughs:

- By 1900 life expectancy was beginning to increase but was still below 50 years of age.
- In 1899 163 out of every 1000 babies died before their first birthday – that's 3 out of every 20 births.
- The majority of families did not see a doctor because they could not afford to pay the fee.
- Vaccines had been developed against some infectious diseases. However, there was nothing to stop the spread of other diseases and many people did not have the vaccines that did exist.
- Many illnesses were not cured because there were no **antibiotics** or other medicines. Surgery was still very limited because of blood-loss during operations.

After 1900 change remained steady rather than rapid at first, as shown in this description by Kathleen Davys. She was one of a Birmingham family of 13 children growing up in the 1920s and 1930s.

> Headaches, we had vinegar and brown paper; for whooping cough we had camphorated oil rubbed on our chests or goose fat. For mumps we had stockings round our throats and measles we had tea stewed in the teapot by the fire – all different kinds of home cures. They thought they were better than going to the doctor's. Well they couldn't afford the doctor.

However, steady progress did give way to rapid change. The most obvious measure of change is that life expectancy has nearly doubled since 1900 as Graph A shows. Illustration B gives a summary of some of the changes that made this change in life expectancy possible:

Look at the developments in B.

Which two developments do you think have been most important in improving health and life expectancy? Explain your choices.

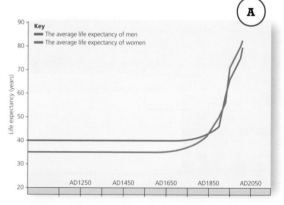

▲ This graph shows how average life expectancy has been transformed since 1900. The red line is for women, the blue for men.

B

	1800s	1900s and after
Ideas about causes of disease and illness	Bad air Germ Theory →	Discovery of DNA →
Treatments	Effective anaesthetics Effective antiseptics	Chemical drugs – sulphonamide drugs Antibiotics including penicillin Genetic medicine Blood transfusions Transplants, keyhole and micro-surgery
Prevention	Vaccinations against smallpox Vaccinations against increasing numbers of diseases 1848 Public Health Act 1875 Public Health Act	1911 National Insurance Act 1942 Beveridge Report 1948 NHS begins
	Governments increasingly involved in safeguarding health	

76

5.2 Your enquiry: Why has there been such rapid change in medicine since 1900?

Your core task in this chapter is to answer the question above. To do this you need to hunt down the factors which made each major development possible. Here is how to do it:

1. Create a set of index cards or sheets of A4 paper, each headed with the name of one of the factors below and divided in half as the example shows.

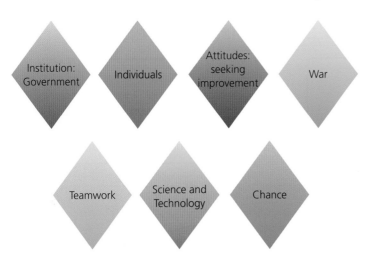

2. As you work on each section of this chapter add examples to your cards or sheets of A4, collecting evidence of the impact of each factor. In column 1 note down whether a development was linked to the causes of illness, treatment or prevention.
   You will have completed this task by the end of page 93. On page 94 we will help you to assess the importance of the factors and to answer the question.

Only factors relevant to the question being asked or the period are included in the specific enquiries in each chapter.

Effective reading

The most effective way to tackle each section is to read it at least twice. The first time read it quickly to identify the main points. Don't worry too much about the detail. Then read it again, this time focusing on the detail that supports the main points.

And before you begin ... create your hypothesis

By now you are used to beginning with a hypothesis. It makes completing an enquiry much more straightforward than if you just charge in without thinking what the answer might be. So ...

3. Use the factor diamonds above to create your hypothesis, arranging them in a pattern as you have before (see page 68). Use what you have learned about the impact of the factors in the nineteenth century plus your own ideas and knowledge of recent medical developments.
4. Use your pattern to write a short paragraph answering the enquiry question at the top of the page. You can use these sentence starters and links as a guide:

The major reasons why there was so much change in medicine in the twentieth century were ...

Another vital reason was ...

Other factors which played a part in creating medical developments were ...

5.3 Medical moments in time: London, 1935

This illustration provides a reminder that the pace of change was steady rather than rapid in the first half of the 1900s. You can see some of the changes that had taken place by the 1930s but also continuities, some of which went back a very long way. In the 1930s one home **remedy** for chilblains (painful swellings on the feet caused by cold and damp) was coating them in hot turnip mash, a cure that had been used by the Romans 2000 years earlier. The reason why this had lasted so long was that it did help and is still used today!

?

1. What changes can you identify that were the results of breakthroughs in the 1800s?

2. What new changes have taken place since 1900?

3. What continuities are there from earlier periods?

4. Which factors are having an effect on the development of medicine?

5. What major developments had not taken place by 1935? Do this **without** looking back to the chart on page 76, then look back and see how well you did.

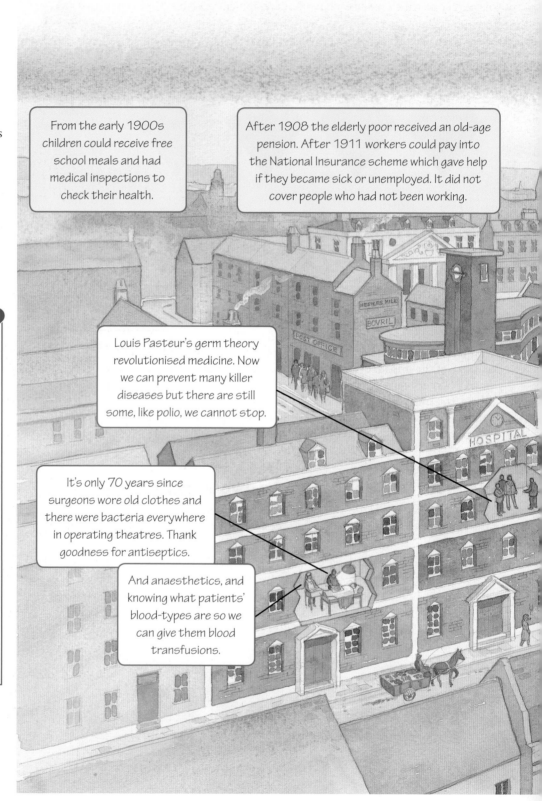

From the early 1900s children could receive free school meals and had medical inspections to check their health.

After 1908 the elderly poor received an old-age pension. After 1911 workers could pay into the National Insurance scheme which gave help if they became sick or unemployed. It did not cover people who had not been working.

Louis Pasteur's germ theory revolutionised medicine. Now we can prevent many killer diseases but there are still some, like polio, we cannot stop.

It's only 70 years since surgeons wore old clothes and there were bacteria everywhere in operating theatres. Thank goodness for antiseptics.

And anaesthetics, and knowing what patients' blood-types are so we can give them blood transfusions.

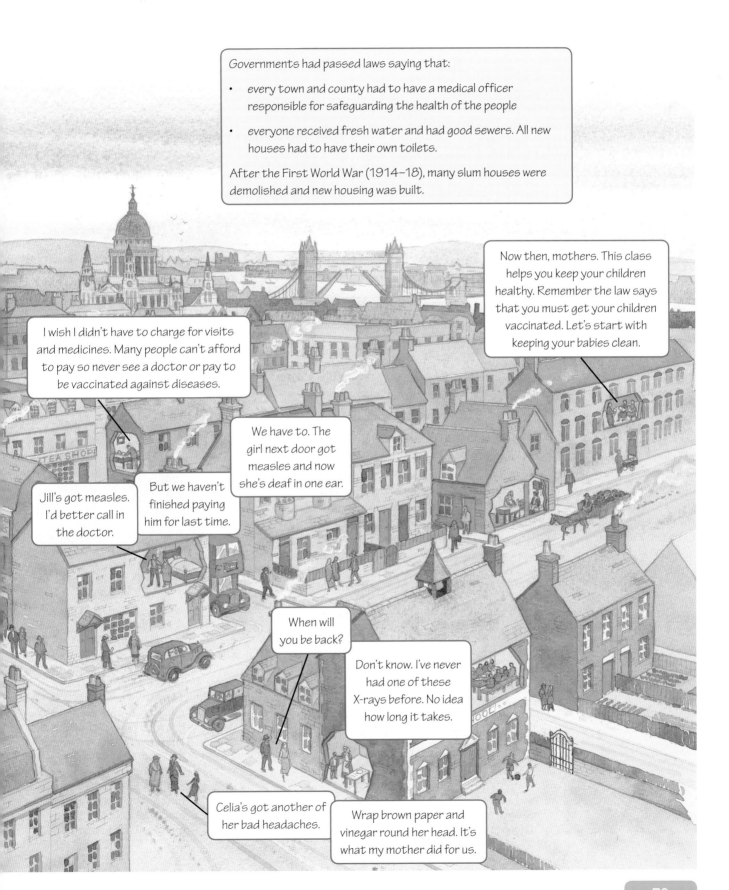

Governments had passed laws saying that:

- every town and county had to have a medical officer responsible for safeguarding the health of the people

- everyone received fresh water and had good sewers. All new houses had to have their own toilets.

After the First World War (1914–18), many slum houses were demolished and new housing was built.

Now then, mothers. This class helps you keep your children healthy. Remember the law says that you must get your children vaccinated. Let's start with keeping your babies clean.

I wish I didn't have to charge for visits and medicines. Many people can't afford to pay so never see a doctor or pay to be vaccinated against diseases.

We have to. The girl next door got measles and now she's deaf in one ear.

But we haven't finished paying him for last time.

Jill's got measles. I'd better call in the doctor.

When will you be back?

Don't know. I've never had one of these X-rays before. No idea how long it takes.

Celia's got another of her bad headaches.

Wrap brown paper and vinegar round her head. It's what my mother did for us.

5.4 Case study: Penicillin – Fleming, Florey and Chain

One crucial change has been the development of antibiotics. To us they are everyday treatments but when they first appeared they were described as 'magic drugs', 'almost miraculous' and 'wonder-working'. This was because throughout history people have died when simple cuts and scratches became infected. Antibiotics stopped life being on such a knife-edge! A miracle is exactly what antibiotics seemed to be when first used, as this account from 1943 during the Second World War shows. It was written by an army doctor, Lt Colonel Pulvertaft:

> We had an enormous number of wounded with infections, terrible burn cases among the crews of armoured cars. The usual medicines had absolutely no effect. The last thing I tried was penicillin. The first man was a young man called Newton. He had been in bed for six months with fractures of both legs. His sheets were soaked with pus. Normally he would have died in a short time. I gave three injections of penicillin a day and studied the effects under a microscope. The thing seemed like a miracle. In ten days' time the leg was cured and in a month's time the young fellow was back on his feet. I had enough penicillin for ten cases. Nine were complete cures.

Antibiotic
A drug made from **bacteria** that kill other bacteria and so cure an **infection** or illness.

DISCOVERING PENICILLIN ?

1. Create a timeline recording the key moments in the discovery and development of penicillin.
2. Explain the difference between the roles of a) Fleming and b) Florey and Chain in the development of penicillin.
3. a) List the factors that played a part in the discovery and development of penicillin.
   b) Which factor or factors do you think played the most important part? Explain your choice.
4. Use your findings to complete activity 2 on page 77.
5. Create a 'Role of the Individual' chart for a) Fleming and b) Florey and Chain.

Penicillin was the first antibiotic medicine and since the 1940s antibiotics have saved over 200 million lives. These pages tell the story of how the value of penicillin was discovered.

Stage 1: 1928 – Fleming's discovery of penicillin

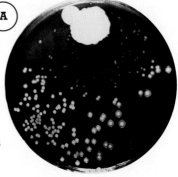

(A)

Many soldiers in First World War (1914–18) developed infected wounds. Chemical **antiseptics** were used successfully to kill many infections but they did not heal infections caused by **streptococci** and **staphylococci bacteria**. Soldiers with those infections died. A scientist called Alexander Fleming was sent to France to study these wounds and then, back in England, he worked on finding a way to deal with these bacteria. The hunt took ten years but in 1928 he found the answer. While away on holiday he left a pile of dishes containing bacteria on his laboratory bench. On his return he sorted out the dishes and noticed mould on one of them. Around the mould, as you can see in Picture A, the staphylococci bacteria had disappeared.

◀ Alexander Fleming (1881–1955) was working at St Mary's Hospital, London, when he discovered the potential of penicillin

Fleming then experimented with the penicillin mould on living **cells**. He discovered that if it was diluted it killed bacteria without harming the cells. He made a list of the **germs** it killed and used it to treat a colleague's eye infection. However, it did not seem to work on deeper infections and it took a very long time to create enough penicillin to use. In 1929 Fleming wrote about penicillin in a medical journal but nobody thought his article was important. He had not even used penicillin on animals to heal infections so had no evidence of it being useful.

▲ Fleming's original Petri dish. The mould is at the top. The bacteria originally around it have been killed but the bacteria further away have survived. The mould had probably been grown by another scientist in the room above Fleming's and spores had floated out of the window, then in through Fleming's window, before landing on the one place they could have an effect and be noticed.

Stage 2: 1938 – Florey and Chain's research and trials

In 1938 Howard Florey and Ernst Chain were researching how germs could be killed and read Fleming's article on penicillin. They realised that it could be very effective and tried to get funding from the government. They got £25. With war near at hand and no proof that penicillin could cure people the government had other things to spend its money on. Instead Florey asked for money from America and got enough to pay for five years' research.

They discovered that penicillin helped mice recover from infections but to treat one person they needed 3000 times as much penicillin! Even large drug companies could not afford to fund this quantity of work. So Florey and Chain began to grow penicillin themselves in whatever they could, using hundreds of hospital bedpans.

By 1941 there was enough penicillin to test on one person. The volunteer was Albert Alexander, a policeman who had developed **septicaemia** – a bacterial infection – from a tiny cut. Chemical drugs had not killed the infection and it was clear that Albert was dying. Florey and Chain requested permission to try penicillin and injections began. The penicillin worked and Albert began to recover. However, they ran out of penicillin after five days even though Florey and Chain were extracting unused penicillin from Albert's urine and reusing it in a desperate attempt to keep treating him. Without penicillin Albert died. Penicillin had shown that it worked and wasn't harmful to the patient – but how could they make enough of it?

B

▲ Howard Florey (1898–1968), Australian doctor and Head of Pathology at Oxford University

Stage 3: 1941 – Wartime need for penicillin

English factories were working flat-out on the war effort during the Second World War (1939–45) and couldn't be used to mass-produce penicillin. So Florey went to America – at just the right time. In 1941 America was attacked by the Japanese at Pearl Harbor and entered the war. The American government realised the potential of penicillin for treating wounded soldiers and made interest-free loans to US companies to buy the expensive equipment needed for making it. Soon British firms were also mass-producing penicillin, enough to treat the allied wounded on D-Day in 1944 – over 2.3 million doses.

▲ Ernst Chain (1906–79), a Jewish German who escaped persecution in Nazi Germany to become a scientist at Oxford

Stage 4: After the war

After the war ended in 1945 penicillin began to be manufactured and used by everyone, not just the armed forces. This still took time but antibiotics became more and more common in the 1950s and 1960s, gradually turning from a 'wonder-drug' into just an ordinary, everyday life-saver!

Tanks used to produce penicillin. ▶ The quantity needed is difficult to comprehend; 2000 litres were needed to treat one case of infection. In June 1943, 425 million units of penicillin were being produced – enough for 170 cases.

5.5 Understanding the causes of illness

Pasteur made a huge breakthrough in medicine with his **germ theory**, which led to many changes in methods of preventing and treating diseases. However, identifying bacteria did not find the cause of all illnesses. As the diagram below shows, two other major reasons for illness have played a big part in medical changes – the impact of genetic problems and of people's lifestyles.

▼ **Medieval and Renaissance medicine**

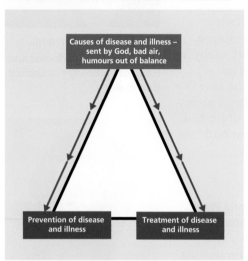

▼ **Modern medicine**

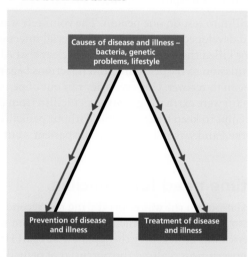

MORE CAUSES OF ILLNESS

1. Read pages 82–85 looking for reasons why genetic problems and lifestyles were identified as causes of illness. Use your findings to complete activity 2 on page 77.

2. When you have completed activity 1 draw a memory map which summarises the effects of the factors on understanding the causes of illness. Use the partly developed memory map below as a model.
    a) Add the other relevant factors on new blue lines.
    b) Add examples of each factor's impact on the red lines.

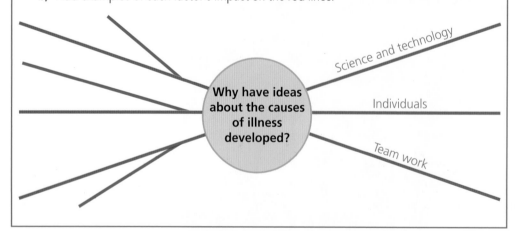

WHAT IS DNA?

- Inside every cell of your body are several identical strings of DNA.

- A tiny part of your DNA looks like this:

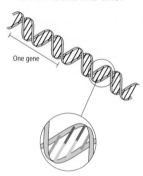

One gene

The structure of DNA is a double helix, a pair of interlocking spirals. They are joined by 'bases', set in pairs, which are like the rungs of a ladder.

- Think of DNA as a long list of instructions, like a computer program, that operate every cell of your body. There are more than 3000 million letters of code in your body's program.

- These instructions are grouped together into sets of instructions called **genes**.

- Each gene has a different function. Some decide your eye colour, some how much hair you have, some whether you will develop a disease or disability.

- Everybody's DNA carries slightly different instructions – which is why human beings are all different.

Genetic causes of illness – the discovery of DNA

DNA stands for deoxyribonucleic acid but you do **not** need to remember that – just talk and write about DNA. And you don't need to understand how DNA works or learn a list of scientific terms – this isn't preparation for a chemistry exam. We are interested in how the structure of DNA was discovered.

Turning point 1: Discovering DNA's structure

DNA wasn't 'discovered' in one brilliant experiment. It took a series of discoveries over a long period. In the 1800s scientists knew DNA existed and that it somehow controlled what we are like. However, they did not know how it did this. During the twentieth century two improvements in technology allowed scientists to take the first photographs of human cells. These improvements were electron microscopes (which allow people to see much smaller objects in much finer detail) and better X-rays, using a technique called crystallography which uses radiation to take a high-power X-ray photograph.

The first step came in 1953 when two scientists in Cambridge, Francis Crick and James Watson, discovered the structure of DNA illustrated. They proved that this DNA structure was present in every human cell and showed how it passed on information from parents to children. This was the launch pad for further discoveries.

There were several reasons why Crick and Watson made this discovery. They were great scientists, very adventurous in their ideas. They tried out ideas and methods other scientists did not try. However, they did not work alone. They had help from a team of scientists with a wide range of skills and knowledge. Maurice Wilkins was an expert in X-ray photography. Rosalind Franklin developed a technique to photograph a single strand of DNA and was the first person to take X-ray photographs of DNA.

Crick and Watson had the latest and best equipment, using the new technologies mentioned above, X-ray photography and improved microscopes. They also built on new knowledge in other types of science, such as **biochemistry**. All this meant that their research was very expensive because of the cost of complex equipment and the number of highly skilled people involved. Most of the money came from the government but industries also made a contribution.

Turning point 2: Mapping the human genome

The complete set of genes in a living creature is called a genome. In 1986 the Human Genome Project began to identify the exact purpose of each gene in the human body, compiling a complete map of human DNA. The task was completed in 2001, 15 years later.

This research was so complex it needed teams of scientists in 18 countries to take part, including the USA, Britain, Japan, France and Canada. Each team worked on a different part of human DNA. This work could not have been done before computers. The information carried in human DNA would fill 80,000 books the size of this one but the electronic equivalent can be passed around the world instantly via the internet.

Why is DNA so important?

To understand the importance of DNA in medicine it's helpful to compare this discovery with Pasteur's germ theory. Germ theory affected medicine in all kinds of ways but only helped doctors and scientists prevent diseases caused by bacteria. Many other illnesses have genetic causes, i.e. they are inherited in the sufferer's genes. Since DNA was first described scientists have identified the specific genes which pass on particular conditions and illnesses. These include:

Some forms of cancer	Diabetes
Down's syndrome	Cystic fibrosis
Parkinson's disease	Alzheimer's disease

This work holds out the hope that scientists can find ways of helping sufferers from these and many more genetic illnesses and, for example, help people paralysed in accidents. That is why the discovery of DNA may be an even more important breakthrough than germ theory.

Genetic medicine – the future?

When Pasteur developed his germ theory scientists did not know exactly what it would lead to. It took many years for its full impact to be clear. We cannot say for sure what DNA discoveries will lead to – even in five years' time, let alone a hundred. However, on pages 90 and 92 you will find details of some of the effects of this breakthrough – new ways of preventing and treating illness. Look out for the DNA/genes logo!

The impact of DNA discoveries

1. What did the Human Genome Project identify?
2. Why are the discoveries about DNA so important for the development of medicine?
3. Create a mnemonic (see page 23) to help you remember four factors which helped Crick and Watson make their breakthrough.

Lifestyle factors

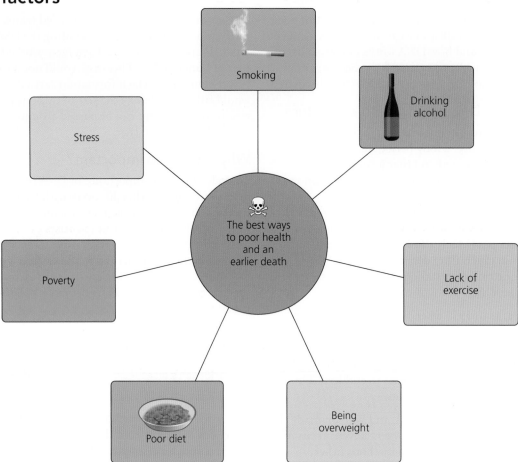

Another cause of illness is 'lifestyle'. 'Lifestyle' sounds like a new word but there is nothing new about the idea that how we live affects our health. Doctors in Ancient Greece, Rome and the Middle Ages gave advice about diet and exercise. In the nineteenth century there were also the first detailed reports about the impact of living conditions on people's health. The three most famous are:

1. **Edwin Chadwick's** *Report on the Sanitary Conditions of the Labouring Population,* **1842**. Chadwick was a civil servant who collected evidence of the impact of poverty on health. He used statistics to support his argument, showing how people in towns had, on average, much shorter lives than people in country regions.

2. **Charles Booth's** *Life and Labour of the People in London,* **1891–1903**. Booth was a businessman who financed research into poverty in the East End of London. His report contained detailed statistics, maps and descriptions, showing that 35 per cent of people lived in poverty and that this seriously affected their health.

3. **Seebohm Rowntree's** *Poverty: A Study of Town Life,* **1901**. Rowntree was a wealthy York businessman who collected detailed evidence showing that 25 per cent of the people of York lived in poverty, which had a serious impact on their health.

These reports were the forerunners of many modern investigations into the effects of lifestyle on health. 'Lifestyle' includes a number of specific issues and research shows how each issue leads to specific health problems. Some research is paid for by governments, some by universities and medical organisations or by charities such as the Joseph Rowntree Foundation. All must provide detailed evidence and statistics for their work to have an impact on government policy and on individuals with health problems.

The chart above shows the major 'lifestyle' problems that lead to health problems. They contribute to the development of a variety of forms of cancer, heart disease, type 2 diabetes, asthma, **ulcers**, mental health problems and a range of other major problems. One recent estimate suggests that smoking reduced life expectancy by at least seven years on average (see the case study on page 93).

LIFESTYLE AS A CAUSE OF ILLNESS

1. How has the impact of lifestyle on health been identified?
2. Identify three health problems caused by the problems in the chart.

Causes – improvements in diagnosis

Here is a news item from the *Guardian* website, the day this page was written, 4 June 2015:

New test uses a single drop of blood to reveal entire history of viral infections

Cheap and rapid test allows doctors to access list of every **virus** that has infected or continues to infect a patient, and could transform disease detection

Researchers have developed a cheap and rapid test that reveals a person's full history of viral infections from a single drop of blood.

The test allows doctors to read out a list of the viruses that have infected, or continue to infect, patients even when they have not caused any obvious symptoms.

The technology means that GPs could screen patients for all of the viruses capable of infecting people. It could transform the detection of serious infections such as hepatitis C and HIV, which people can carry for years without knowing.

The test could bring about major benefits for organ transplant patients. One problem that can follow transplant surgery is the unexpected reawakening of viruses that have lurked inactive in the patient or donor for years. These viruses can return in force when the patient's **immune system** is suppressed with drugs to prevent them rejecting the organ. Standard tests often fail to pick up latent viruses before surgery, but [this procedure] could reveal their presence and alert doctors and patients to the danger.

This is one example of major changes in diagnosis that have taken place in recent decades. Knowing the causes of diseases and illnesses has been the greatest step forward but some health problems are difficult to diagnose early in their development. Improvements in technology have led to the creation of complex machinery and instruments which can diagnose precisely what illness a person has. Such developments have cost huge amounts of money, paid for by governments, medical companies and universities. Some pieces of equipment are even available, often purchased from pharmacies, for use in the home. These include machines for monitoring blood pressure, blood sugar levels (for diabetics), heart monitors and cholesterol monitors.

The chart below shows some of the technology which enables illnesses to be diagnosed earlier and more accurately. These developments become widely known very quickly because detailed knowledge of techniques and methods spreads rapidly around the world in medical journals, the internet and at conferences attended by doctors and scientists.

Microscopes
The electron microscope, invented in 1931, allows doctors to see much smaller objects such as human cells in much finer detail.

Nuclear medicine
Radioactive elements are injected into the bloodstream where they track and diagnose changes in the body through disease.

Endoscopes
A camera inside a flexible tube is passed into the body so doctors can see inside the body without using surgery.

Scans and monitors
These machines scan the body to identify cancers and other illnesses. They are widely used in screening for breast cancer, for example, to catch the disease as early as possible.

Remember to complete activity 2 on page 77 for these pages.

5.6 Improvements in treatments

In 1892, one-year-old Maggie Wade was badly scalded by boiling soup. Her family lived in a village where people believed in the healing powers of a local woman, Mrs Brundish. Maggie's parents called in Mrs Brundish to charm the fire out of the little girl, repeating healing words and passing her hands over the injuries. Maggie's parents believed some good was done but she died next day.

This is a reminder that old treatments continued after the medical breakthroughs of the 1800s. Home carers used **herbal remedies**, treatments passed down from older generations, and some new ideas in medical books written for home use. Since then, helped by changes in the understanding of the causes of illnesses, treatments have improved. Pages 86–90 explore the changes shown in the diagram below and why they took place.

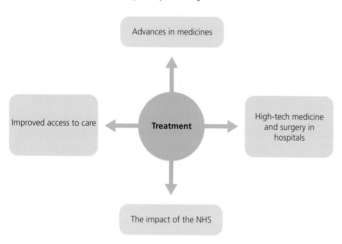

CHANGES IN TREATMENTS

1. Read pages 86–90 looking for the reasons why treatments have been developed. Use your findings to complete activity 2 on page 77.

2. When you have completed activity 1 draw a memory map summarising the effects of the factors on treatments. Use the partly developed memory map below as a model.
   a) Add the other relevant factors on new blue lines.
   b) Add examples of each factor's impact on the red lines.

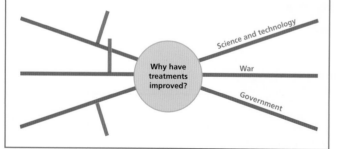

1. Advances in medicines

By the early 1900s 'cure-all' pills were being replaced by effective medicines for use in the home and by doctors. One of these medicines was aspirin which is used as a painkiller and remedy for fevers. It comes from willow bark which had actually been used as a medicine for centuries but no one knew why it worked. Developments in science enabled scientists to identify the exact chemical in willow bark that was beneficial. It was then manufactured in huge quantities and marketed as aspirin.

Pharmaceutical companies including Boots and Beechams became worldwide businesses. These companies were successful through:

- Investing in research and development (including employing scientists) to look for better remedies.
- Using improved scientific techniques and equipment to identify the precise chemicals that work as medicines.
- Using industrial technology to make huge quantities of each remedy and using commercial skills to market them worldwide.
- Using experiments and experience to find the exact dosages needed by patients.

'Magic bullets' – the development of sulphonamide drugs

In 1909 Paul Ehrlich (one of Koch's research team in Germany) developed the first chemical drug that killed bacteria inside the body. This was Salvarsan 606 which he called a 'magic bullet' because it homed in on and destroyed the bacteria that cause **syphilis**. Unfortunately Salvarsan 606 killed the patient too. It took until the 1930s to find a magic bullet that did not kill the patients. Gerhard Domagk tried out a chemical mix called Prontosil on mice and discovered it killed the bacteria causing blood poisoning. He didn't try it on people until his daughter developed blood poisoning. Normally she would have died but Domagk gave her Prontosil. She was the first human cured by a chemical cure. Scientists discovered the important chemical in both Salvarsan 606 and Prontosil was **sulphonamide** and drug companies then developed sulphonamide cures for diseases such as **pneumonia** and **scarlet fever** and mass-produced huge quantities for general use.

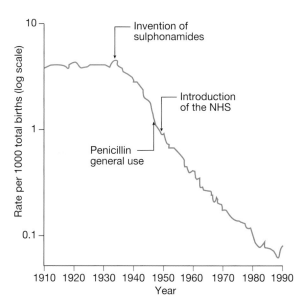

▲ This graph shows the pattern of deaths of mothers during and after childbirth in Britain between 1910 and 1990. What was the critical turning point in the pattern?

The development of antibiotics

War played a crucial part in the development of penicillin, the first antibiotic, as you read on pages 80–81. However, when the war ended in 1945, there was still a great deal to do to make antibiotics available for the whole population. This took place because of the following:

- There was investment in the discovery and development of other antibiotics by pharmaceutical companies.
- Scientific techniques and equipment were improved to develop antibiotics.
- After 1948 the government-funded NHS provided antibiotics free.
- Scientists and doctors communicated their research so they could learn from each other.

MAGIC BULLETS ❓

1. What does the phrase 'magic bullets' mean?
2. What was the importance of each of these medicines – Salvarsan 606, Prontosil, penicillin?

---

2. Improved access to care 1900–48

One major problem in 1900 was the cost of medical treatment. Many working people simply could not afford to pay a doctor or buy medicine. As a result, there were far fewer doctors in areas where the poor lived. During the early 1900s changes began which helped the very poorest get medical help. The Liberal government of 1906–14 carried out many of these changes. One reason the government acted was because during the Boer War

(1899–1902) a third of volunteers for the army were rejected because of ill health. This showed how common poor health was and worried the government. Could it recruit enough fit men if there was another war? Attitudes to government intervention in people's lives were also gradually changing. Knowledge of how bacteria cause diseases made people more accepting of laws to improve healthcare.

Here are some of the reforms. They may seem very ordinary today but a century ago they were revolutionary.

1902 Training for midwives was made compulsory.

1907 All births had to be notified to the local medical **officer of health**. A health visitor visited each mother to make sure she knew how to protect her baby's health.

1907 Nurses or doctors had to carry out medical checks on children in schools.

1911 The National Insurance Act provided help for workers who fell ill. Before this they had to carry on working or get no pay. The National Insurance Act required the worker, his employer and the government to pay into a sickness fund. When a worker fell ill he received ten shillings a week for up to 26 weeks and free medical care. It was a major step forward but only included workers, not their families or the unemployed, the elderly or anyone with a long-lasting illness.

1912 Clinics in schools gave children free medical treatment.

1919 The Ministry of Health was set up, the first government department to have an overview of health throughout the country. This was a major step in government involvement in health.

1919 The Nursing Act set up the General Nursing Council to enforce nursing standards.

The changes above meant that more people were able to get medical care and treatment and that care was improving. However, there were still many people who could not afford to see a doctor or pay for medicines. This situation grew worse in the 1930s when the rate of unemployment was extremely high. The most worrying evidence came from towns where unemployment was high. There the number of deaths among children under the age of one was rising again.

GOVERNMENT REFORMS TO 1920

1. How did the National Insurance Act of 1911 help some sick people?
2. Which groups of the sick were not helped by the 1911 Act?
3. Why were the reforms in this period important if they did not help everyone?

---

3. The impact of the NHS from 1948

The greatest change in care came with the introduction of the National Health Service (NHS) in 1948 which provided free care at the point of delivery for all. Two events played a part in this huge change.

Firstly, in 1918 all men and all women over 30 had the vote for the first time. In 1928 all adults over the age of 21 were able to vote. The development of real democracy increased demands from working people for the government to make changes to improve health care.

Secondly, the crucial change in attitudes came in the Second World War (1939–45), the first war in which people felt they were 'all in it together', with many people at home dying during bombing raids. The feeling of togetherness built the belief that everyone should have good health care, not just the wealthy. In addition:

- Many children were evacuated from towns to better-off homes in the countryside. Middle-class families were shocked at meeting some unhealthy and under-nourished children.
- After the sacrifices of the war, people wanted a better future. Better health care was an important part of this.
- During the war many people did get free health care to keep them fit for the war effort.

The Beveridge Report

In 1942 the wartime coalition government asked a leading civil servant, Sir William Beveridge, to write a report on what should be done to improve people's lives. He recommended:

- Setting up a National Health Service, free to everyone and paid for from taxes. Doctors, nurses and other medical workers would become government employees instead of charging the sick to create their wages.

- Everyone in work would pay National Insurance out of their wages. This would pay benefits (sick pay, old-age pensions, unemployment pay, etc.) to everyone who needed it whether they were working or not.

People queued outside shops to buy copies of the Beveridge Report; 600,000 copies were sold. Despite the enthusiasm for the report and the idea of creating a National Health Service there was opposition, chiefly from some doctors. However, this opposition ended when Aneurin Bevan, the Minister of Health, agreed that doctors could continue to treat patients privately and charge them fees as well as working for the NHS. Bevan summed up the importance of the new NHS in these words in Parliament in 1946.

> Medical treatment should be made available to rich and poor alike in accordance with medical need and no other criteria. Worry about money in a time of sickness is a serious hindrance to recovery, apart from its unnecessary cruelty.

The beginning of the NHS

In July 1948 the NHS was introduced. Now everyone could get free treatment at the point of delivery. About 8 million people had never seen a doctor before. Diagram A shows the range of services provided by the NHS. Many hospitals were rebuilt. Doctors and nurses got new improved equipment. The NHS played an important part in increasing people's life expectancy, particularly helping to reduce the numbers of women dying in or shortly after childbirth.

One major area of government spending since 1948 has been on hospitals. Some of this has been spent on much better qualified staff who can provide more specialist care. Many nurses develop specialist skills such as care of patients who have had breast surgery or cancer patients undergoing **radiotherapy** or **chemotherapy**. Some of these specialist nurses have the ability to prescribe a limited range of medicines – something which in the past could only be done by doctors.

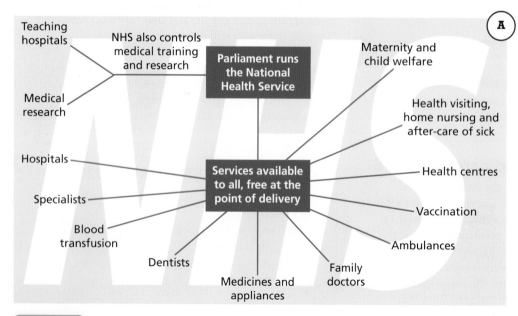

(A)

Teaching hospitals

NHS also controls medical training and research

Parliament runs the National Health Service

Medical research

Hospitals

Specialists

Blood transfusion

Dentists

Medicines and appliances

Services available to all, free at the point of delivery

Maternity and child welfare

Health visiting, home nursing and after-care of sick

Health centres

Vaccination

Ambulances

Family doctors

◀ Diagram showing the services provided by the NHS in 1948. Since then charges have been introduced for some items such as dentistry and prescription charges.

Protecting patients from acquiring new illnesses in hospital has also become a major aspect of hospitals' work. This was always a problem but became worse in the late 1900s as bacteria developed immunity to some antibiotics and outbreaks of '**Superbugs**' (such as MRSA) occasionally killed patients. Since then hospitals and governments have taken action to protect patients from such infections. The Care Quality Commission checks care in hospitals and forces hospitals to make improvements if necessary. Since 1999 NICE (the National Institute for Health and Clinical Excellence) has provided guidelines and recommendations for effective health care.

THE IMPACT OF THE NHS

1. How did the Second World War pave the way for the introduction of the NHS?
2. What was so revolutionary about the NHS?

4. High-tech medical and surgical treatments in hospitals

Hospitals have become the major centres of high-tech treatments, some of which are summarised here and on page 90. In some cases better treatments and care have meant the need for more care and treatments because, for example, patients with illnesses such as cystic fibrosis are now living longer because of better treatments.

Remember your core task and keep an eye out for those factors that produced change.

BLOOD TRANSFUSIONS

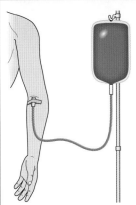

Blood **transfusions** were attempted in the 1800s but rarely worked. Nobody knew why until in 1901 Karl Landsteiner discovered blood groups. After this blood transfusions became possible, provided the patient and donor had the same type of blood and were in the same place. When doctors tried to store blood it clotted and could not be used for transfusions. The problem of storing blood was solved during the First World War. Firstly, sodium citrate was added to prevent blood clotting. Then scientists discovered how to separate and store the crucial blood cells and keep them in bottles for future use. This made possible the huge blood banks that supply blood today.

X-RAYS

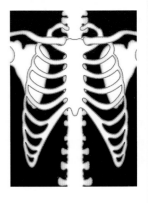

In 1895 a German scientist, Wilhelm Röntgen, discovered rays of light that could pass through black paper, wood and flesh and still light up a wall. He did not know what they were so called them X-rays. Within months, X-ray machines were in use in hospitals. The First World War led to a great increase in the use of X-rays to locate bullets and shrapnel lodged deep within wounded men. After this X-rays became routine and used in many different ways. For example, they changed the care of pregnant women and their babies as it became easier to monitor the development of babies in the womb.

RADIOTHERAPY AND CHEMOTHERAPY

Marie Curie and her husband, Pierre, continued research on X-rays. They discovered **radium** which has been used ever since to diagnose cancers, and in radiotherapy to treat cancers. Their research was the beginning of modern treatment of cancers. As the research continued it became so complex that they built up a team of research scientists to share ideas.

TRANSPLANT SURGERY

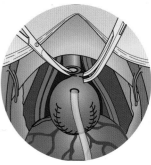

The first heart transplant was carried out in South Africa in 1967 by Dr Christiaan Barnard and a team of highly skilled and experienced doctors, nurses and scientists. Other organs had been transplanted before then – kidneys in 1954 and liver in 1963. Since then more ambitious transplants have been carried out including the first bone marrow transplant in 1980 and the first heart and lung transplant in 1982. All depend on high levels of technical and scientific expertise.

CUSTOMISED DRUGS

Drug treatments of the future could be designed to deal with one person's particular health problem which has arisen because of a particular gene in that person. These 'custom drugs' would be less haphazard than at present where the same drug is given to millions of different people regardless of their genetic make-up.

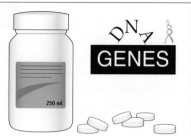
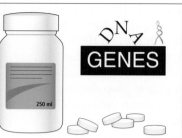

250 ml

DIALYSIS MACHINES

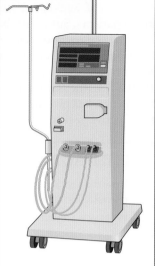

These machines keep kidney patients alive and give them the chance of living until a transplant becomes available.

GENE THERAPY

Research shows that some diseases and disabilities, such as cystic fibrosis, Huntington's chorea, sickle-cell anaemia and muscular dystrophy are caused by a single abnormal gene, passed on from parents to child. **Gene therapy** takes normal genes from a donor and puts them into the **DNA** of someone suffering from one of these illnesses. One approach uses 'stem cells' from embryos, for example using cells from an embryo to reverse a common form of blindness or to re-grow damaged nerves and restore movement to people paralysed in accidents. However, there is a major ethical debate about this stem-cell research because the process of taking the cells from the embryos usually kills the embryos.

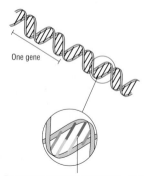

One gene

The structure of DNA is a double helix – a pair of interlocking spirals. They are joined by 'bases', set in pairs, which are like the rungs of a ladder.

PLASTIC SURGERY

The injuries of both World Wars led to a rapid improvement in techniques, especially the use of skin grafts. In the First World War injuries were mostly from bullet and shell damage. Surgeons carried out over 11,000 plastic surgery operations, increasing their experience and learning from each other. In the Second World War there were many more burns cases in tanks and aeroplanes. Archibald McIndoe alone carried out 4000 operations on burns cases.

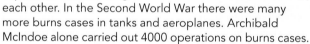

KEYHOLE AND MICRO-SURGERY

Nowadays surgeons cut into the body through as small a hole as possible – keyhole surgery. The tools needed are inside an instrument called an endoscope, which is controlled by the surgeon using miniature cameras, fibre-optic cables and computers. Micro-surgery has also developed because of improvements in technology. Surgeons can now rejoin blood vessels and nerves, restoring the use of damaged and even severed limbs.

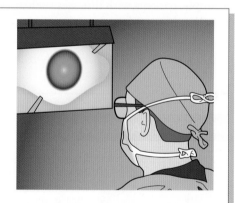

IMPROVED ANAESTHETICS

Anaesthetics in the later 1800s had to be inhaled through the nose and mouth. This made it difficult to control the dosage. In the 1930s Helmuth Wesse developed anaesthetics that could be injected into the blood stream, enabling precise doses, greater safety and longer operations. Nowadays local anaesthetics are so effective that they are used for major operations such as hip-replacements.

HEART PACEMAKERS

This technology has become an everyday item, being implanted to keep individuals' hearts working effectively.

5.7 Improvements in prevention

The bar graphs below show a remarkable change in the causes of death in the last century. As you can see, in 1911 infectious diseases such as TB (tuberculosis) and diphtheria were still responsible for a quarter of deaths. Today those same diseases, if they exist, account for less than 1 per cent of deaths. This is one major reason why people, on average, live much longer and so die from other health problems that usually strike later in life, such as cancers and heart disease. Pages 91–92 explore the methods that have developed to prevent illnesses and premature deaths.

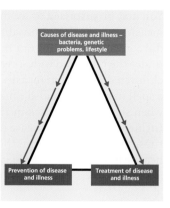

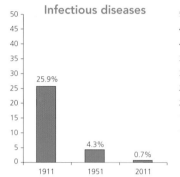

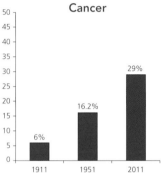

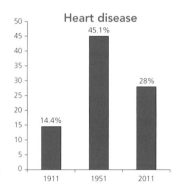

◀ Changes in major causes of death, 1911–2011

CHANGES IN PREVENTION

1. Read pages 91–92 looking for the reasons why methods of preventing illnesses have been developed. Use your findings to complete activity 2 on page 77.

2. When you have completed activity 1 draw a memory map summarising the effects of the factors on methods of prevention. Use the partly developed memory map opposite as a model.
   a) Add the other relevant factors on new blue lines.
   b) Add examples of each factor's impact on the red lines.

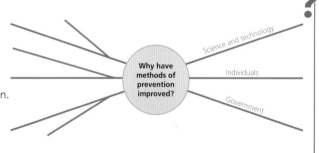

Preventing infectious diseases

Vaccines and **public health** reforms put an end to the devastating **epidemics** of **smallpox** and cholera but scientists needed more time to find vaccines for other infectious diseases that killed thousands of people. The table shows how long it took for these other diseases to be tamed. As a child in the 1950s I remember the fear created by **polio** epidemics, especially when it was announced in 1959 that even such a fit young man as Jeff Hall, a Birmingham City and England footballer, had died of polio. The **microbe** causing poliomyelitis wasn't identified until 1946. In 1954 American scientist Jonas Salk developed a vaccine that protected people from polio. Pharmaceutical companies invested in new technology to mass-produce the vaccine, which was then made available to use throughout Britain and the world. However, in Britain, people were slow to use the vaccine until Jeff Hall's death. This frightened people into being **vaccinated**, and so may have saved many lives. The demand for the vaccine was so great that emergency supplies had to be flown in from the USA.

◀ Iron lungs were used to keep polio victims breathing when they could no longer breathe for themselves. The thought of having to live in one of these machines was another deeply frightening aspect of the polio epidemics of the 1950s.

1896	Typhoid
1906	Tuberculosis (TB)
1913	Diptheria
1927	**Tetanus**
1952	Whooping cough
1954	Polio
1964	Measles
1988	MMR (Measles, Mumps, Rubella)
2008	Human papillomavirus (HPV)
2015	Meningitis B

▲ The development of vaccines for infectious diseases

You may be surprised to see measles in the table because people can think that measles is not a dangerous disease. This is because the vaccine developed in 1964 did a great deal to wipe out measles, aided by the availability of free vaccines under the NHS and widespread advertising campaigns. However, before this, children did die from measles. At best it led to many weeks off school and maybe a spell in hospital. It also caused other health problems. My mother had measles when she was three, back in 1928, and lost the hearing in one ear as a result. Influenza is another disease that can cause death, especially in the elderly and those already sick with another problem. That is why governments have invested heavily in providing free flu jabs for many groups of people including the elderly and key workers, for example those in hospitals.

Preventing illnesses caused by genetic problems

The breakthroughs linked to the discovery of DNA have led to important new ways of preventing illnesses developing. If doctors know the exact gene responsible for medical conditions they can test or screen patients as part of preventive medicine. This genetic screening or testing identifies potential illnesses, enabling doctors to take action even before an illness has developed. For example, they can identify whether a person's genes carry the risk of suffering from breast cancer and take action to prevent cancer developing. This kind of screening is done to check unborn babies for possible conditions such as Down's syndrome.

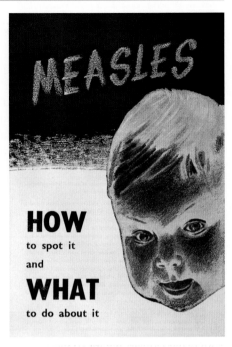

▲ Governments have used posters and television advertising to persuade people to take up vaccines and protect themselves from illnesses.

Preventing illnesses caused by lifestyle and other problems

When the NHS began in 1948 its main focus was on treatments because so many sick people had not been able to afford to see doctors before. Over the decades since then prevention has become a major part of the work of the NHS. This is not an entirely new approach as there were campaigns in the 1930s and earlier to warn people of the dangers of not getting enough exercise and the importance of diet. However, the evidence shown in the bar graphs on page 91 of the deadly impact of illness such as cancers and heart disease has led to much greater efforts to persuade people to improve their lifestyles.

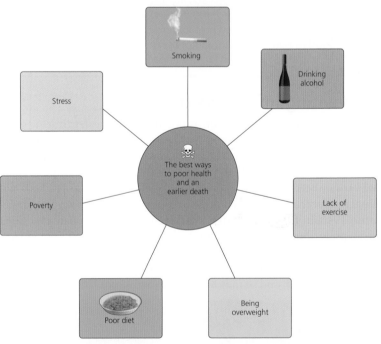

Therefore, there have been regular campaigns and initiatives to try to prevent illnesses linked to lifestyle. Single-issue campaigns have focused on warning of the dangers of smoking or of lack of exercise or have promoted healthier diets. In 1992 the government's 'Health of the Nation' initiative went further in setting the NHS targets to prevent and reduce deaths and illnesses in five major areas: heart disease, cancer, mental illness, HIV/AIDS and accidents. Everyone over the age of 40 is given the opportunity to have a health check every five years, focusing on blood pressure, weight and cholesterol levels alongside lifestyle advice.

More widely, governments have passed laws that attempt to ensure health by reducing air and water pollution and improving food safety to reduce outbreaks of salmonella and E.Coli poisoning.

5.8 Case study: fighting lung cancer in the twenty-first century

Lung cancer was extremely rare 150 years go. Its frequency increased greatly in the early 1900s and today it is the second most common form of cancer. Over 40,000 people are diagnosed with it each year. Medical evidence has proved conclusively that cigarette smoking (which first became common in the early 1900s and especially during the First World War) is the major reason for contracting lung cancer. Nearly 90 per cent of cases are the result of smoking, in some cases of **passive smoking**.

Lung cancer is particularly deadly because it is extremely difficult to diagnose in its early stages. It is usually diagnosed once symptoms have developed which means the cancer may have spread. Only one in three people live for as long as a year after diagnosis. Only 10 per cent live for more than five years. This compares very badly with survival rates from other cancers where 50 per cent live for at least ten years after diagnosis.

The devastation caused by lung cancer now means that huge efforts are made in prevention, diagnosis and treatment. Governments have launched major campaigns to prevent people developing lung cancer. Campaigns warn people of the extreme dangers of smoking, through advertising the dangers, banning advertisements for cigarettes and making them as invisible as possible in shops. New laws have made public places such as cafes, cinemas, sports grounds, workplaces and pubs smoke free, aiming both to reduce the effects of passive smoking and to help people give up smoking. Other campaigns, such as the one shown in the poster, aim to improve rates of early diagnosis.

Governments have also, through the NHS, invested large sums of money in improved treatments which in turn are dependent on developments in science and technology and on research undertaken by scientists. However, there is at this stage (2015) no national screening programme because the technology does not exist to pick up the earliest signs of lung cancer. As a step towards this, the screening of high-risk individuals is being developed.

Treatments

Treatments have taken four forms:

1. Surgery has been used since the 1930s but the majority of lung cancer sufferers have had other smoking-related health problems that have meant that surgery was too dangerous to use. New surgery techniques using remote-controlled micro-instruments and cameras have far less impact on the body and speed recovery.
2. Radiotherapy aims to kill the cancer cells using beams of radiation. Techniques have improved to target cancers more precisely.
3. Chemotherapy has been used since the 1970s if the cancer has developed so far that surgery and radiotherapy are not successful. Chemotherapy involves using particularly powerful chemical medicines to attack the cancer cells, although it can have significant side effects. New combinations of chemotherapy medicines are constantly being used and the results recorded.
4. **Immunotherapy**. Cancers are able to resist the body's immune system's attempts to block their growth. Trials have been taking place to boost the immune system and so stop the cancer cells from resisting it.

The fight against lung cancer therefore shows how inter-dependent the various factors are that help to improve medicine and health. Today the roles of government and science and technology overlap considerably and behind them are the many individuals who make significant contributions to preventing and treating such a dangerous illness.

◀ This poster was part of a national advertising campaign which began in 2012, funded by the NHS and so by the government. It aimed to diagnose lung cancer earlier and so give patients a much better chance of survival.

5.9 Communicating your answer

Now you have completed your research it is time to write your answer to the enquiry question:

Why has there been such rapid progress in medicine since 1900?

Before you write your answer to the enquiry question you need to have your answer clear in your mind.

1. Keeping your word wall up to date. Here are some words to add to your wall – how many of them can you explain now, before you begin? Keep a look-out for more words to add to your wall.

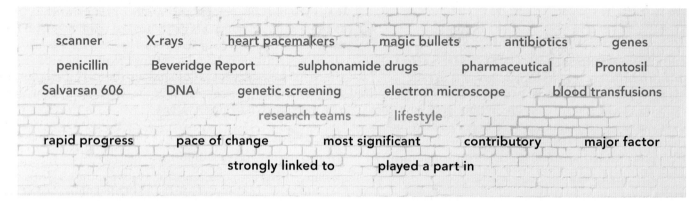

scanner   X-rays   heart pacemakers   magic bullets   antibiotics   genes

penicillin   Beveridge Report   sulphonamide drugs   pharmaceutical   Prontosil

Salvarsan 606   DNA   genetic screening   electron microscope   blood transfusions

research teams   lifestyle

rapid progress   pace of change   most significant   contributory   major factor

strongly linked to   played a part in

2. Use your completed index cards from page 77 to organise the factor diamonds into the pattern you think best answers the enquiry question.

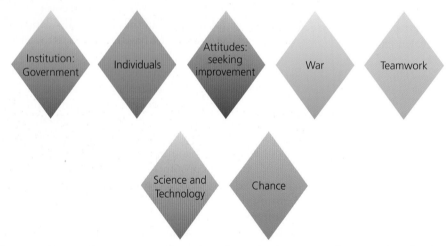

3. Use your diamond pattern to write a short hypothesis paragraph answering the enquiry question.
4. Now it's time to write your full answer.

Practice questions

1. Explain one way in which understanding of the causes of illness was similar in the late nineteenth and twentieth centuries.
2. Explain one way in which understanding of the causes of illness was different in the late nineteenth and twentieth centuries.
3. Explain why there have been changes in understanding the causes of illness during the twentieth century.
4. Explain why there have been changes in methods of preventing illness during the twentieth century.
5. Explain why there have been changes in methods of treating illness during the twentieth century.
6. 'The development of penicillin was a major breakthrough in the treatment of illnesses during the twentieth century.' How far do you agree? Explain your answer.
7. 'The discovery of DNA was a major breakthrough in medicine during the twentieth century.' How far do you agree? Explain your answer.

5.10 Visible learning: Revise and remember

1 Revise the Big Story

It's still just as important to keep the whole picture of the History of Medicine clear in your mind. Revise the story you told on pages 6–7, making sure that you bring it up to date with what you have learned about medicine since 1900.

2 Test yourself!

The more you think about what you have learned and **especially what you're not sure about**, the more chance you have of succeeding in your exam. So answer these questions and don't be surprised if you have seen some of them before.

1. When did Pasteur announce his germ theory? (If not the year, which decade?)	2. Who discovered that penicillin kills bacteria – and when?	3. What was average life expectancy in 1900 and what was it by 1911?
4. List three ways in which governments have tried to improve health since 1900.	5. List three kinds of treatment used between 1500 and 1700.	6. Which war began the much greater use of X-rays and blood transfusions?
7. What was the major difference between the Public Health Acts of 1848 and 1874?	8. Which two scientists were most responsible for the discovery of DNA?	9. What did John Snow do to stop cholera spreading in 1854?
10. What did Jonas Salk discover?	11. What was so significant about a) Salvarsan 606 and b) Prontosil?	12. List three methods used to prevent the Black Death spreading in the fourteenth century.
13. Identify two methods used to reduce deaths from lung cancer.	14. What did you find hardest to understand in this chapter? How are you going to help yourself understand it?	15. Name one thing that you learned in this chapter that surprised you or that you now think differently about. Explain why.

3 Set questions yourself!

Work in a group of three, each of you concentrating on a different theme – ideas about the causes of illness, treatments and methods of prevention. Each of you set three revision questions on developments in your theme since 1900. Use the style of questions on page 11. Then ask each other the questions – and make sure you know the answers to your own questions!

6 Medicine in Britain: revisiting the Big Stories

Finally let's go back to the very first question we asked on page 2 – why do we live, on average, so much longer than our ancestors? Pages 96–97 help you sum up the roles played by the factors. The rest of this chapter brings together the key points about developments in understanding the causes of illness, in treatments and in methods of preventing illnesses.

'History is not the story of strangers, aliens from another realm; it is the story of us had we been born a little earlier.'

This is a wonderful quotation. It reminds us that we aren't any different from people who lived many years ago – after all, they were our ancestors. Way back in time, in the 1800s, 1600s, the Middle Ages there were people with our **DNA**, people who looked like us, had the same colour hair or eye-colour, the same way of walking, the same energy or laziness!

But what if you'd been born in their time?

You now know that there is one very important way in which we are different from our ancestors. On average we live much longer, healthier lives. Let's take the example of one real family – John and Margaret Pepys and their children from the 1600s. John was an ordinary working man, a tailor who worked in London. They had 11 children, born between 1627 and 1641, shown below at their time of death. Only Samuel lived to anywhere near what is now the average age of death.

Mary
Died aged 13

Paulina
Died aged 3

John
Died aged 8

Robert
Died aged about 15

Sarah
Died aged 6

Ester
Died aged 1

Samuel
Died aged 70

Thomas
Died aged 30

Jacob
Died aged 6 months

Paulina
Died aged 49

John
Died aged 36

6.1 Assessing the impact of factors

The activity below helps you to sum up and revise the roles of the factors in improving medicine and health. This will also develop that very important skill – working as a team. It's amazing how a group of people working together can spark a whole host of good ideas that a person working by him or herself would have missed.

1. As a class agree on the criteria you will use to decide which of the factors below have been most important. (Think about these phrases to develop criteria – 'how long?', 'how many periods?', 'depth of impact'.)
2. Divide into groups and take one factor for each group. Make a list of the beneficial effects of your factor. There are starter clues below but you should be able to think of more. Then use the class criteria to decide how important your factor has been.
3. Feed back your results to the rest of the class. Which factor or factors have been most important in improving medicine and health?

6.2 Ideas about the causes of disease and illness

It is particularly important to repeat this familiar triangle on this page. It reminds you that people's ideas about what causes disease and illness determines how they treat and try to prevent disease and illness. That's why 'ideas about causes' is at the top of the triangle – the most important of all important aspects of medicine.

Pages 98–99 summarise those ideas, as you can see in the timechart across the bottom of page 99, which helps you see and understand the patterns of ideas across time.

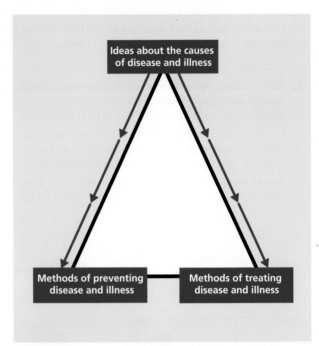

Medieval ideas c.1250–c.1500

Medieval ideas were so different from ours that it is easy to think they were just based on **superstition** or magic, that people were ignorant and even stupid. That is not the case. Most medieval ideas about what caused disease were rational and logical, fitting people's ideas about how the world worked. They believed that God controlled everything so God must send disease and illness. Ideas that blamed bad air and the movement of planets were also linked to God because it was God who made the planets move or sent the bad air to spread disease.

Physicians continued to believe in the Theory of the **four Humours** which had been developed by Hippocrates in Ancient Greece and continued by Galen. This too was a rational theory because the Humours, such as blood and phlegm, were often seen when someone was sick.

Renaissance ideas c.1500–c.1700

Ideas about the causes of disease and illness did not change in the Renaissance period. People's lives were still dominated by religion so they continued to believe that God sent sickness. Bad air was still a common explanation because the increasingly crowded towns were dirty and full of human and animal waste which created awful smells which made the air seem 'bad'. Physicians were still trained by reading the work of Hippocrates and Galen, so they continued to accept the Theory of the four Humours. Therefore, the **Plague** of 1665 was explained in the same ways as the Black Death of 1348–49.

Changing ideas c.1700–c.1900

The first major breakthrough came with Louis Pasteur's **germ theory** which he published in 1861. His later experiments proved that **bacteria** (also known as microbes or **germs**) cause diseases. However, this did not put an end to all earlier ideas. Belief that bad air was to blame continued, which is not surprising given the conditions in many industrial towns. In addition, Pasteur's theory was a very general one until scientists began to identify the individual bacteria which cause particular diseases. So while this was one of the two most important breakthroughs in ideas about what causes disease and illness it did not revolutionise medicine immediately. Scientists and doctors were the first to be convinced of this theory, but it took time for most people to understand it. This is shown in the example on page 86 of the little girl who was treated by a local **wise woman** who tried to charm her back to health – in 1892, thirty years after Pasteur's theory was published.

It is also important to remember that bacteria do not cause all illnesses. Many have other causes which you can read about in the next paragraph.

Modern ideas c.1900–present

One idea which has become much more central since 1900 actually goes back a long way – that is the idea that lifestyle affects health. However, in the twentieth century considerable research was undertaken to identify exactly how things such as lack of exercise and smoking lead to particular diseases. More dramatic was the discovery of DNA, which may turn out to be an even more important discovery than germ theory. From the initial discovery the Human Genome Project developed. This has identified the exact purpose of each **gene** in the human body, compiling a complete map of human DNA.

DNA is so important because many illnesses have genetic causes, i.e. they are inherited in the sufferer's genes. Since DNA was first described, scientists have identified the specific genes which pass on many particular conditions and illnesses such as Down's syndrome, cystic fibrosis and some forms of cancer. This work has already led to the development of treatments and to ways of preventing genetic illnesses (see pages 100–103) and more will follow. That is why the discovery of DNA may be an even more important breakthrough than germ theory.

THE CAUSES OF DISEASE AND ILLNESS ?

1. Take each of the four periods in turn and identify their key features (for an example see page 13).
2. Which of the key features explain continuities or changes in the ideas about the causes of disease and illness in each period?
3. Explain one way in which ideas about the causes of disease and illness were:
   a) similar in 1400 and 1700
   b) similar in 1700 and 1900
   c) different in 1700 and 1900
   d) different in 1900 and 2000.

Practice questions

1. 'There was no progress in understanding the cause of disease between 1250 and 1800.' How far do you agree? Explain your answer.
2. 'Pasteur's germ theory was the most important turning point in understanding the causes of disease and illness.' How far do you agree? Explain your answer.

▼ Ideas about the causes of disease and illness

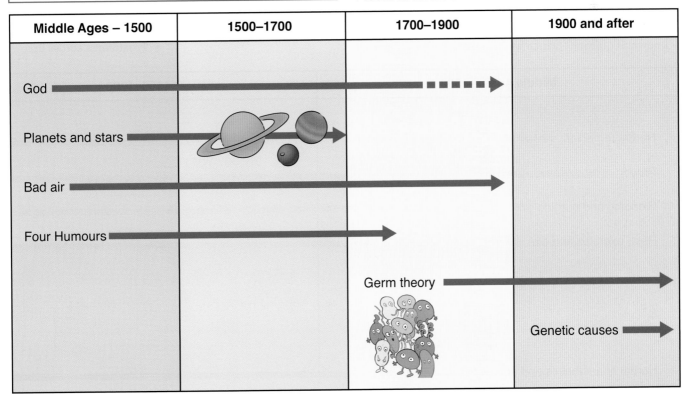

6.3 Methods of treatment

The pattern of continuities and changes in treatments has followed the pattern for ideas about the causes of disease and illness. The most significant changes have been the result of discoveries about causes, but treatments have not improved immediately after these discoveries. There has always been a time-lag as scientists and doctors have worked to find effective treatments based on the new ideas.

Medieval treatments c.1250–c.1500

The Theory of the four Humours led directly to **bleeding** and purging which were carried out to rebalance the Humours and so restore health. Physicians also recommended more exercise, changes in diet, and rest. They treated the wealthy who could afford to pay their fees, but these ideas did reach more people by the fourteenth century because they were written down in books summarising how to be healthy.

Most illnesses were treated by mothers, wives and local women with specialist knowledge. **Herbal remedies** were widely used and often contained ingredients such as honey and plantain that we now know do help cure infections. Many herbal ingredients are used in modern medicines. However, there were also many magical attempts at cures, and people prayed to God to help them recover or wore a carving of a saint who might help them. Simple surgery was carried out on the exterior of the body and some surgeons became very skilful.

Renaissance treatments c.1500–c.1700

Continuities in ideas about causes meant that there was a great deal of continuity in treatments. The discoveries of Vesalius (in **anatomy**) and Harvey (in **physiology**) did not lead to changes in treatments either. Physicians continued to bleed and purge, although, in the late 1600s, doctors such as Thomas Sydenham challenged the use of these treatments and were more likely to prescribe rest and good food, after taking great care over diagnosis. People continued to pray, wear charms, recite rhymes and, far more helpfully, use herbal remedies that they knew from experience did lead to recovery. Some new **remedies** were introduced as a result of overseas contacts. Some, such as tobacco, did more harm than good, but others proved helpful, such as the bark of the cinchona tree from South America – known as quinine – which was a good remedy for fevers.

▼ Treatments across time

Middle Ages – 1500	1500–1700
Herbal remedies	
Prayer	
Bleeding and purging	
Rest, exercise and diet	
Herbal anaesthetics and antiseptics	

Treatments in industrial England c.1700–c.1900

Treatments in this period were an incredible mix of improved new ideas and very unhelpful old methods! There were important breakthroughs in surgery with James Simpson's use of **chloroform** as an **anaesthetic** and Joseph Lister's use of carbolic acid to kill **infections**. These laid the basis for the wonders of modern surgery. Hospitals, influenced by Florence Nightingale, became cleaner and placed much more emphasis on the importance of good food and sanitation to help patients recover. However, at the same time, 'cure-all' tablets were sold in their millions, making fortunes for men such as Thomas Holloway. These tablets were at first made of lard, wax, turpentine and other items until the government in the 1880s introduced laws controlling the use of such ingredients. Herbal remedies continued and many continued to do good, such as the use of mashed turnips to ease the pain of chilblains, a remedy that had been used since the Romans.

Modern treatments c.1900–present

'Vinegar and brown paper' helped Jack mend his head when he tumbled down in the nursery rhyme but this wasn't a 'pretend cure'. As you read on page 76 this was still used to treat headaches in the 1930s. This example shows that treatments from earlier periods continued to be used during the 1900s, partly because people had to pay to see a doctor and have their illness diagnosed. However, changes in treatments have in many ways been truly revolutionary and miraculous from medicines such as aspirin, to 'magic bullets' which killed bacteria, to **antibiotics** such as **penicillin**. In surgery, improvements came with the identification of blood groups and the development of **transfusions**, followed by many technical developments, such as plastic, transplant and keyhole surgery. Other high-tech methods such as **radiotherapy** and **chemotherapy** became common treatments. More recently still, genetic medicine has created drugs to tackle illnesses created by particular genes. Changes in treatments have become so rapid that by the time this book is printed, just a few months after it was written, new treatments will have become available.

TREATMENTS ACROSS TIME

1. Explain one way in which medical treatments were:
   a) similar in 1400 and 1700
   b) similar in 1700 and 1900
   c) different in 1700 and 1900
   d) different in 1900 and 2000.

3. 'There was little change in methods of treating illnesses between 1250 and 1700.' How far do you agree? Explain your answer.

4. How rapidly did methods of treating the sick change between 1850 and 2000?

5. 'Simpson's use of chloroform has been the most important turning point in surgery.' How far do you agree? Explain your answer.

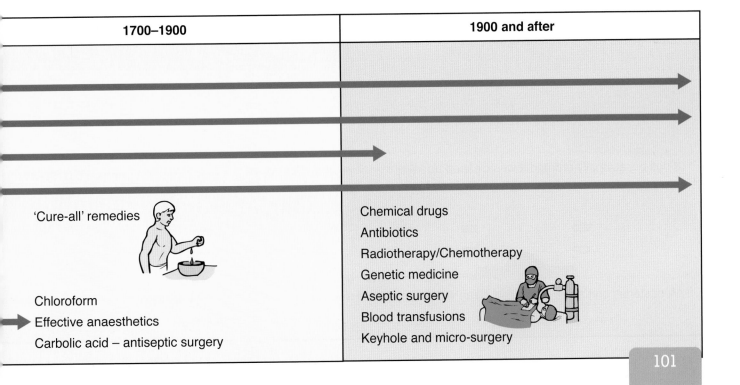

6.4 Preventing disease and illness

Methods of prevention were not instantly transformed by breakthroughs in understanding the causes of disease and illness. These breakthroughs were critical but they were the beginning. As with treatments, there have always been time-lags between the changes in ideas and improvements in prevention, usually because governments have needed time to take action or because new technologies have needed to be developed.

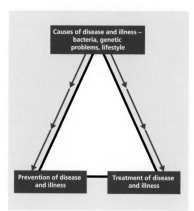

Medieval prevention c.1250–c.1500

Reactions to the Black Death exemplify most methods of preventing disease. People prayed for God to put an end to the pestilence, they went on pilgrimage and took part in religious processions. The king demanded that the streets of towns be cleaned to get rid of bad air and local town councils made great efforts to clean up, employing more people to cleanse the streets. People used herbs to try to keep away the bad air.

At other times great efforts were made to prevent illness or diseases. Physicians recommended regular bleeding and purging to prevent the Humours becoming unbalanced and causing illness. Town councils and many individuals spent money on ways of improving conditions – building public toilets, cleaning water supplies, cleaning the streets – but there was never enough money to deal with the many problems in towns.

Renaissance prevention c.1500–c.1700

We have more evidence about how people tried to prevent the spread of the plague in 1665 than we do about how they tried to prevent the Black Death in 1349, but essentially the methods were the same. People tried to keep bad air moving or to overcome it with other smells by creating bonfires in the streets or carrying bunches of herbs which they hoped would keep plague at bay. Victims of plague were **quarantined** in their homes and pesthouses although it was not possible to stop some escaping or to make sure all victims were quarantined. Prayer was still an important part of prevention for individuals and for the government which ordered special days of prayer for forgiveness.

▼ Prevention across time

Middle Ages – 1500	1500–1700
Individuals and town councils tried to keep towns clean – laws against litter and creating dirt	
Kings occasionally ordered towns cleaned up	
Monasteries and some towns had clean water supplies	

Prevention in industrial England c.1700–c.1900

The first breakthroughs came in the battle against **smallpox**. **Inoculation** was useful but Edward Jenner's development of **vaccination** was the first major triumph over an infectious disease, even if it took decades for governments to enforce the use of vaccination. Other vaccines were not developed until Pasteur had published his germ theory and even then it was several decades before effective vaccines for individual diseases were widely available. In the meantime governments were beginning to take action to clean up conditions in the industrial towns. The 1848 Public Health Act was a start, though a small one, permitting local councils to collect taxes to pay for cleaning water supplies and sewerage, but it was the 1875 Act that made such improvements compulsory. At the same time improvements in technology led to the building of much safer and more effective sewerage and water systems such as Bazalgette's immense scheme in London. A critical change had taken place in that governments were now beginning to become involved in protecting health and preventing disease, but this development remained a slow process.

Modern prevention c.1900–present

Pasteur's germ theory continued to have an impact on methods of prevention. New vaccines against infectious diseases continued to be discovered and made available. In the same week that this chapter was written in June 2015 it was announced that a vaccine against Meningitis B was to be offered to all babies from September 2015. Governments' involvement in prevention has increased through, for example, lifestyle campaigns to encourage people to live healthier lives and to use vaccines. This involvement has developed hugely since the creation of the NHS, which introduced free consultations with doctors and hospital treatment. Developments in science and technology have also played their part, most dramatically in the development of genetic screening to identify health problems of babies while still in the womb and to correct those problems.

PREVENTION ACROSS TIME

1. Explain one way in which methods of preventing disease and illness were:
   a) similar in 1350 and 1665
   b) similar in 1665 and 1850
   c) different in 1665 and 1900
   d) different in 1900 and 2000.

2. Why were there so few improvements in prevention before 1850?

3. How rapidly did methods of preventing disease and illness improve between 1800 and 2000?

4. 'Pasteur's germ theory has been the most significant turning point in preventing disease and illness.' How far do you agree? Explain your answer.

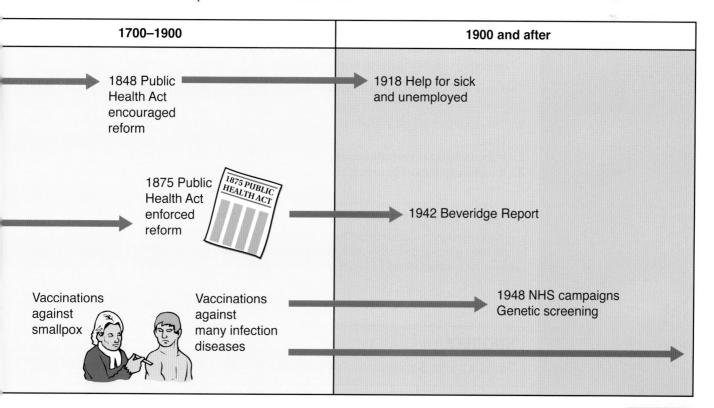

Part 2: The historic environment: The British sector of the Western Front 1914–18: injuries, treatment and the trenches

What is this historic environment unit about?

This unit counts for 10 per cent of your GCSE course. It is linked to the thematic unit on Medicine in Britain in two ways:

1. You will use your knowledge of medicine in the early twentieth century in this unit.
2. The enquiry approach you used to study 'Medicine in Britain' will help considerably because this historic environment unit is designed to develop your skills in historical enquiry – from asking questions to communicating your answer. We spent a lot of time on enquiry in 'Medicine in Britain' to prepare you for this.

There are also three major differences from your work on the thematic unit on Medicine in Britain:

1. This unit focuses on a single place, a historic site – the British sector of the Western Front.
2. It focuses on a very short period, the years 1914–18.
3. It looks much more closely at the contemporary sources and how we use them in an enquiry.

> This book does not provide all the material you will use for this unit. This is deliberate! We have given you the structure for your enquiry and plenty of information and sources but your teacher will add more sources, perhaps relating to the experiences of soldiers from your area.

ENQUIRY ?

Describe in your own words the enquiry process you use to investigate a new historical topic.

1.1 One man's war – questions and sources

I'd like to introduce my grandfather – that's him in the photograph on the right. This photograph was taken around 1928, ten years after the First World War ended. The little girl on his knee is my mother, sitting alongside her brother.

We're starting with one man, my grandfather, because history is about the experiences of individuals, real people like you and me who just happened to live in the past. We are going to investigate my grandfather's experiences during the First World War because those experiences overlap a great deal with the content of this unit, an enquiry into medicine on the Western Front during that war. His story reminds us that all the events and developments you investigate involved many, many real individual people with families, parents, children and friends.

What do I know about my grandfather? To be honest, not very much! He died in 1942, years before I was born. Fortunately my mother wrote a short account of her life (just a few pages, not a book!) and so I know his name – Arthur William Mansley – and that he was born in December 1896 and lived in Liverpool. My mother said that he was good looking, always well dressed, that he was a shoemaker and loved gardening. She also wrote:

> He lost a leg and was badly gassed in the war.

Unfortunately, that's all she said about his experiences in the war. So where do I start finding out more about him? The answer is with the census for 1911 – the detailed records (collected by the government every ten years since 1841) of who lived in every house in the country. According to the census (which I looked up online), in 1911 my grandfather lived at 43 Roscommon Street in Liverpool with his parents and eight brothers and sisters. His father was a shoemaker. Although Arthur was only 14 he had left school and was working as his father's assistant. Three years later, in August 1914, the war broke out. Arthur was 17 years old.

ASKING QUESTIONS

One of the skills you practised in the thematic unit on Medicine in Britain was asking good historical questions. Asking questions is an important part of this unit because it plays a part in your GCSE examination. So, we'll pause here, and ask you to ask some questions.

1. Make a list of questions you want to ask about medicine during the First World War. They could be about my grandfather's wartime experiences or about medicine in general. Use the question starters below to help you.

   When …?   What … ?   Why …?   How …?   What happened …?   Where …?

   What effects …?   How significant …?   Did it really …?   Who …?   Did they …?

2. When you have completed your list divide it into 'big' and 'little' questions – look back to page 13 to remind yourself of the differences between them.

Asking questions, identifying sources

This page shows you *some* of the questions you could ask about medical treatment and care during the First World War, together with some of the sources you might use to answer those questions. Both questions and sources are here because one aim of this unit is to work out which sources might be most helpful in answering individual questions. You know by now that sources are not 'useful' or 'useless' – their usefulness depends on what question you are trying to answer. For example, one source may be very useful for learning about surgical techniques, but completely unhelpful if you want to find out about how many soldiers recovered from wounds.

QUESTIONS AND SOURCES

Choose two of the questions below or from your list of questions from page 105. Which of the types of sources on the cards below do you think might be most useful for answering each of your two questions? Explain why you think each types of source might be useful.

We do not expect you to know the 'right' answers at this stage. This task is to get you thinking about what kinds of information *might* be in the sources and which questions they *may* help with. In the rest of this unit you will get to know most of these sources and find out which questions they are most useful for answering.

Some questions

What kinds of wounds did soldiers suffer from?

Did surgical techniques improve during wartime?

How were the injured moved to hospitals?

Did more soldiers suffer from illnesses than from wounds?

Where did my grandfather fight and what were conditions like?

How would his wounds have been treated?

How would he have been moved from the fighting to a hospital?

Would he have been well cared for?

Sources

National army records for individual soldiers

National newspaper reports

Government reports on aspects of the war

Medical articles by doctors and nurses who took part in the war

Personal accounts of medical treatments by soldiers, doctors, nurses or others who were involved

Photographs

Hospital records

Army statistics

Organising your understanding of the sources

Why did we set up the activity on the opposite page? It is because this unit is about how we undertake a historical enquiry and about the kinds of sources we use as well as being about medicine on the Western Front. Therefore you are going to use a variety of sources and learn different things from them. The first thing you will learn is the most obvious – the sources will:

- Increase your knowledge and understanding of the Western Front and the medical care received by soldiers.

However, other things you learn about the sources are just as important and will be tested in your examination. You will find out:

- What kinds of sources help us investigate medicine on the Western Front 1914–18.
- Which sources are most useful for investigating individual aspects of medicine and for answering particular questions.

To keep track of the sources and what we can learn from them we suggest you use a Knowledge Organiser such as the table below, perhaps on A3 paper or as a Word document. You may wish to keep additional, detailed notes to support the summary in your table. Completing the table is an important reminder that this unit is about enquiry and sources as well as about medical care on the Western Front.

Here is a guide to completing your table over the next few weeks:

1. After you have worked on a section of this unit identify which sources you have used and fill in a row of this table for each source. Decide which type of source each item is, e.g. is it a personal account, photograph, etc.? The text will remind you to do this.

2. Put the category in column 1 and the example (e.g. photograph of an operation taking place) in column 2.
3. Then complete columns 3–6 for the source.

You may use sources that fit more than one category of source or you may use other kinds of sources not listed below. Don't worry if sources do not fit neatly – historical research is unpredictable and you often find things that you don't expect. That's why it's enjoyable!

It is also important to remember that one source will not tell us everything we want to know. We should always try to use a combination of sources. This is because each source may add different information because different people created them, at different times, or because they are different types of source – a photograph and a diary perhaps. Using a variety of sources also allows us to check what each is saying, as we always need to ask whether the evidence in a source is typical of the evidence as a whole.

National records

- National army records for individual soldiers
- National newspaper reports
- Government reports on aspects of the war
- Medical articles by doctors and nurses who took part in the war

Local records

- Personal accounts of medical treatments by soldiers, doctors, nurses or others who were involved
- Photographs
- Hospital records
- Army statistics

Types of sources N – National L – Local	Examples of this type of source you have used	Which questions can this source help answer?	What information does it provide to help with those questions?	Which questions does this source NOT help answer or why do you have to use it cautiously?	Which other kind of source might you use in combination with this source?

Exploring Arthur's Service Record

When I began my investigation I was surprised that Service Records were kept for each soldier. Many Service Records were destroyed by bombing in World War Two but my grandfather's survived and can be downloaded from the National Archives website.

This document is far more detailed than I expected – and more puzzling. Arthur's rank is given as OS (Ordinary Seaman) and then AB (Able Seaman) and he joined the Royal Naval Division. He sounds like a sailor but no ships are mentioned and all the places listed are on land. So was Arthur a soldier or sailor?

The answer is – both! In 1914 the navy had too many men so the Royal Naval Division was created, using sailors as soldiers to fight on land. They kept their naval rank even though they fought on land.

The questions below get you started in understanding this document. You may not work out all the answers now but we will return to it and unravel its secrets. As you read, think back to what my mother said about Arthur's war experiences (see page 105).

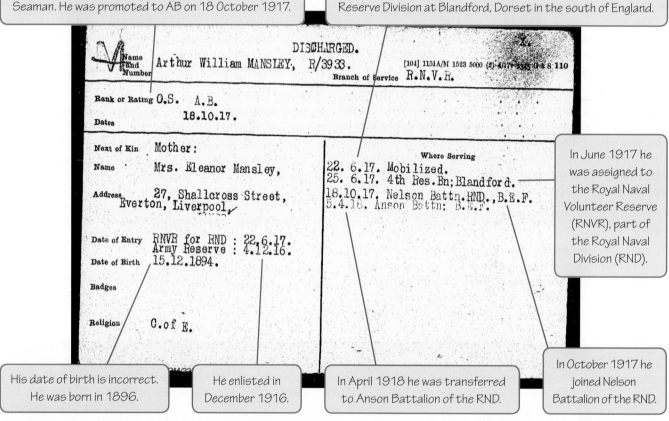

OS and AB stand for Ordinary Seaman and Able Seaman. He was promoted to AB on 18 October 1917.

On 22 June 1917 he received orders sending him to the 4th Reserve Division at Blandford, Dorset in the south of England.

In June 1917 he was assigned to the Royal Naval Volunteer Reserve (RNVR), part of the Royal Naval Division (RND).

His date of birth is incorrect. He was born in 1896.

He enlisted in December 1916.

In April 1918 he was transferred to Anson Battalion of the RND.

In October 1917 he joined Nelson Battalion of the RND.

ARTHUR'S WAR

1. What do you think these abbreviations on Arthur's Service Record mean?
   a) NOK   b) GSW

2. GH stands for General Hospital. How many hospitals did my grandfather spend time in?

3. What can you learn from the entries made on:
   a) 7 June 1918   b) 29 August 1918   c) 19 May 1919?

4. List three things you can learn from this document about Arthur's war experiences and identify the parts of the document you have used.

5. What other questions would this kind of document be useful for? Explain why it would be useful.

6. Fill in the first row of your table (page 107) for this document. Decide which category of source goes in column 1, then write 'Service Record for Arthur Mansley' in column 2. Fill in the rest of the columns in pencil so you can amend or add to them later.

Battalion
A battalion contained between 800 and 1000 men. The eight battalions in the RND were all named after famous British sailors.

28. 6.17. B'fd DO.179(4th Res)Reported & taken on strength 25.6.17(F/63)
18.10.17. Drafted to Nelson Battn.B.E.F.from 4th Res.Bn.B'ford.(RB).
19.10.17.DO/292.4th Res.Bn.:Rated A.B.18.10.17.(F/63)
30.10.17. BEF.D.O.71.From Base Depot,Calais, 24.10.17.to join Battn.
24.11.17. BEF.D.O.78. Joined Nelson Battn. from XIX Corps Rest Camp,13.11.17
17.1.18.HA/18354.Adm 9.GH.Rouen 7.1.18.PUO.Sev.AFB/104-80a.
12.1.18. BEF.D.O.6. To 150th Field Amb. 2.1.18.
18.3.18. HA/20535. Adm.2 Con.Dep.Rouen ex 9 GH. 11.3.18.
3.4.18. HA/21023.Dis to Reinf Rouen Class A ex 2 Con Dep 25.3.18.
16.4.18. HA/21782. Adm.54 GH Aubengue 10.4.18. NYD.N.Mld:AFB/104-80a.
12.4.18. (RECCH) 31. Cross-posted to Anson Battn.B.E.
10.4.18. Nelson 30. Joined L.Base Depot,Calais,29.3.18.S.
29.4.18. HA/22341. Adm.1 Con.Dep. Boulogne ex H. 22.4.18.
2.5.18. HA/22411. Trans.to 5 Rest Camp.Fit ex 1 Con.Dep. B'logne 23.4.18.
8.5.18. Anson 32. Joined L.Base,ex 54th G.H.,27.4.18.
25.4.18. Anson 29. To 148 FA.8.4.18.
4.6.18.C/1576."Wounded" 25.5.18.NOK.inf.5.6.18.FND.List No.1211. DO.37
7.6.18. HA/24288. Adm.16 GH Le Treport 30.5.18. Bay Wd.Scalp.Mld:NOK.infd.
17.6.18.HA/24730.Adm 3 Con Dep Le Treport 9.6.18.
27.5.18.ANSON 36.Rejoined Unit fm.BD.16.5.18.
15.7.18. HA/26062. Dis.to Base Dtls.ex 3 Con.Dep.Le Treport 7.7.18.
17.7.18. Anson. 46. Jnd. LIBD, 8.7.18.
6.8.18. Anson 50. Rejoined Battn.from Div.Wing,26.7.18.
29.8.18. Tele:mess.P.135816.OC 1 SAGH Abbeville tele:28.8.18 'Dang.ill.
GSW L.Leg amputation' NOK informed.FND List No:1270. (2nd occ)

Image Reference:8575

7.9.18.C/1674."Wounded" 26.8.18.- also Anson 56.
10.9.18.HW/2281.Ser.ill(impvd)in 1 SAGH Abbeville w/e 2.9.18.
10.9.18.P.137752.OC 1 SAGH Abbeville tele:5.9.18'No long.ser.ill'NOK infd:
13.9.18. HA/28604. Adm. 1 S.African GH Abbeville 26.8.18. GSW.L Leg R.Arm
Face
12.9.18. HB/14086 Adm: "ar Hos.Keighley, 8.9.18.SMO infd.17.9.18.
17.9.18. Anson 62. Invalided, 7.9.18. G.W.both legs.
7.10.18. Recd. AFB/103, 19.10.17,emb.Folkes.disemb.Boul; 20.10.17, jd.BD.Cal;
7.4.18, adm.148th FA; 3.5.18, jd. No.4 Med.Base; 4.5.18, to "L"IBD;
24.10.18. Form forw. to SCO.A'shot.
23.12.18. AFW.3016 recd. Furlough 20/31.12.18. Xmas leave under W.O.Wire
(6953(AMD.2/18.
5.2.19. AFW.3016 recd. Furlough 4.2.19. Pending admission to Roehampton.
25.3.19. Rep.recd. Transferred to Alder Hey Special Mil.Surgical Hos.
West Derby.Liverpool. Alnwick Informed 26.3.19.
19.5.19. Form D/145 recd. Passed to M.O.P. Surveyed at Haslar 8.5.19.
GSW.L.Leg;R.Little Finger;R.Foot & Hip; Head.Degree of disability
60%. Attributable to service. Recommended for discharge.
(17.6.19.W.G.Form to A.g. 9(b) Paid £11.0.0.
21.5.19.D.O/150 (Regt.Dept)"D"Coy.Discharged Invalided ex Anson Bn.
Disability Mul.GSW Addr.27,Shallcroft St,Everton,Liverpool.
23.7.19. Discharged List No.381.

Image Reference:8575

Visible learning: Planning my enquiry

You've seen a picture of my grandfather on page 105. Now this is me! I'm the person who's writing this book and planning this investigation. The key word is PLAN! I know a little. I want to know a lot – but just starting to read could leave me with a jumble of information that feels confusing and with no clear conclusions. Fortunately I have been studying history for many years so I know how to work my way through a new topic. This page shows you my plan for my enquiry.

I know a little about my grandfather and I have some questions. How do I plan my way from knowing a little and having lots of questions to finding the answers and knowing a lot more?

Stage 1 What do I know?

This is a summary of my main starting points:

- My grandfather fought in the First World War.
- My mother said he was gassed and had a leg amputated.
- His Service Record shows he spent time in several hospitals in France.
- The First World War was a different kind of war. Much of the fighting was in trenches.
- There was a very high casualty rate in some of the fighting.
- Medicine was changing rapidly in the late nineteenth and early twentieth centuries. Surgery was revolutionised by the use of anaesthetic and antiseptics, but blood loss was still a major problem.

Stage 2 What do I want to find out?

I need a set of questions as targets when I do my research so I know when I've completed my enquiry:

- What kind of conditions did my grandfather fight in?
- What kinds of treatment would he have received for his wounds?
- Who would have treated him?
- Were his wounds (and any illnesses) typical of those suffered by soldiers?
- Did the war change and improve medicine in any way? For example, did they solve the problem of blood loss? But I must be flexible and add to my questions if I find unexpected information.

Visible learning

Tackling new topics with confidence

I use this plan to help me explore any historical topic that is new to me. Starting to investigate a new topic can feel worrying, like starting completely from scratch, because dates, names and events are different BUT it's important to remember that HOW we study every topic is very similar. We use this same plan whether we're exploring Roman history or the First World War. We have shown you this approach very visibly so you feel more confident whenever you start to tackle a new topic. Look back to page 32 for more detail on how to carry out an enquiry.

Letting you into a secret

I have been writing history books as part of my job for the last 30 years. You might think I must know everything there is to know about history but that's not true. The 'secret' is that there are quite a few historical topics I don't know much about at all because I have never had to study or write about them. I taught the First World War many years ago but I have forgotten a lot of the detail so I'm not pretending in this enquiry that I do not know much at the start. I genuinely don't know much about the detail of the war and need to find out a lot more in order to understand what my grandfather's experiences might have been.

Stage 3 Where will I research and find the answers?

There are two kinds of sources I can use.

1. Books, articles and websites written by experts on the war and on the History of Medicine

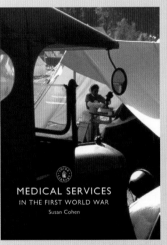

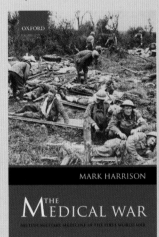

2. Sources from the war – photographs, accounts written by doctors, nurses or soldiers

Stage 4 How will I do this research?

I need to:

- Have my questions in mind so I always read with a purpose – to answer those questions.
- Keep careful notes, using my own Knowledge Organisers, so that I don't end up with a heap of disorganised information.
- Make sure the books I read and websites I use are really by experts. This means checking who wrote them and how they know what they're telling me.
- Ask questions about the sources I use. For example, is a photograph typical of conditions in the war, was the author present at the events he or she was describing, which are the most useful sources for each question?
- Remember that I may not be able to find exact and complete answers to all my questions so I need to use words such as 'probably',' in all likelihood' and 'possibly'.

- **There may be questions I can't answer at all! And I need to keep thinking! I might find unexpected information which prompts new questions or suggests I look in other books or records. I can't predict exactly what I'll find at the beginning of an enquiry. And I'm allowed to change my mind about my answer to a question as I find out more.**

1.2 The British sector of the Western Front

We will begin by exploring the site – the British sector of the Western Front. We need to know where it was, the main places where battles were fought and what the **terrain** was like where the fighting took place. Arthur's Service Record mentions several places in France, all linked to the Western Front. These places are among the towns shown on the map below.

> **Terrain**
> The type of ground – was it hilly, muddy, flat, easy to walk and run on?

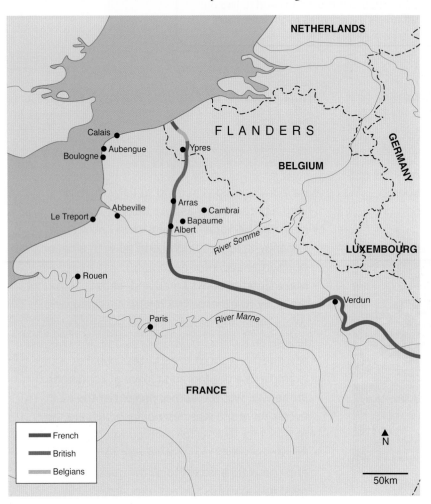

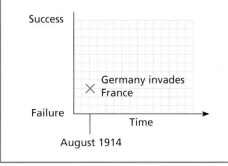

AN OUTLINE OF THE WAR

1. Use Arthur's Service Record (pages 108–109) to identify three places on the map where Arthur spent time.

2. Read a quick history of the First World War on these pages. Produce a living graph like the one below to record the successes and failures of Britain and her Allies between 1914 and 1918.

3. Which stages of the war did Arthur fight in? Check back to pages 108–109 to work this out.

◀ The Western Front, showing the British sector. As the fighting went on the size of the British sector changed depending on how successful the British and Allied armies were. This map shows the British sector in 1917. It stretched about 150km.

A quick history of the First World War

> The events shown on a purple background took place in the British sector of the Western Front

August 1914: War begins

Initially Austria-Hungary declared war on Serbia but alliances pulled other countries into war. Germany's invasion of France and Belgium led to Britain declaring war on 4 August 1914 on Germany in support of Belgium and France.

Germany, Austria-Hungary, Turkey **versus** Britain and her empire, Russia, France, Belgium, Serbia

August–September 1914: The first trenches

The German army planned to knock France out of the war quickly, but French and British troops halted the German advance at the battle of the Marne near Paris. Neither side retreated. Instead they dug in to defend the territory they had. Both sides built trenches defended with barbed wire and machine guns.

October–November 1914: First Battle of Ypres

In this battle, British troops stopped the German army from capturing ports such as Calais. This meant reinforcements and equipment could keep arriving by ship for the British army. By the end of 1914 trenches stretched from Switzerland to the English Channel. The trenches were so strongly defended that both sides found it very difficult to advance.

April–May 1915: Second Battle of Ypres

A German attack using chlorine gas for the first time in the war failed to capture Ypres. Allied casualties are estimated at 60,000, German at 35,000.

August 1915: Gallipoli Landings

British, Australian and New Zealand forces landed at Gallipoli in Turkey aiming to defeat Germany's ally, Turkey. The plan failed, leading to extremely high casualties.

February–December 1916: Battle of Verdun

German forces attacked the French army at Verdun. The French held out but 160,000 French soldiers were killed.

July–November 1916: Battle of the Somme

On 1 July the British and French launched a major attack, aiming to force Germany to move its troops away from Verdun to the Somme and so relieve the pressure on the French army. There were 60,000 British casualties on the first day alone and 400,000 by the time this battle ended. Germany did reduce the pressure on Verdun and the French army was not defeated. British forces gained just 5 miles of land during these months.

April–May 1917: Battle of Arras

In spring 1917 there was another large-scale Allied attack on German positions. Some ground was captured initially but casualties were very high.

July–November 1917: Third Battle of Ypres

In 1917 British and Allied troops launched a major attack to stop the German army breaking through weakened French defences. The aim was to capture Passchendaele ridge near the town of Ypres but the German defences were very strong and the ground turned to mud because of constant rain. The ridge was captured but at the cost of 245,000 casualties.

April 1917: United States enters the war

On 6 April 1917 the United States joined its allies – Britain, France and Russia – to fight in the war.

November–December 1917: Battle of Cambrai

For the first time the British army used a large number of tanks, massed together, to attack German trenches. After initial success the British were forced back. There were 40,000 British casualties.

October 1917: Revolution in Russia

By 1917 one and a half million Russian soldiers, badly led and poorly supplied, had been killed on the Eastern Front. This led to the overthrow of the Tsar of Russia. In November 1917 a Communist government took over and pulled Russia out of the war. This allowed Germany to move troops to the Western Front.

Spring 1918: The German Spring Offensive

The German army launched a major attack along a 50-mile front, aiming to bring the war to an end before American forces arrived and before Germany ran out of food supplies. At first this attack was very successful, making significant gains of territory, forcing British and Allied troops to retreat, and causing 200,000 British casualties. However, the German army could not make a complete breakthrough.

Summer and autumn 1918: The final months

The Allied army, reinforced by fresh US troops, broke through the German lines and pushed back the German army. Germany had no resources left to fight back. The war ended on 11 November 1918.

Four key places in the British sector of the Western Front

We all have a mental picture of the fighting on the Western Front. The picture in our minds probably contains trenches protected by barbed wire and an area of flat, muddy land known as 'No Man's Land' between the Allied and the German front lines. That is an accurate picture of parts of the Western Front at some times, but everywhere did not fit that generalisation. Some places on the Front saw very different fighting conditions and these two pages show some of that variety as well as telling you what was unusual about some of the major battles.

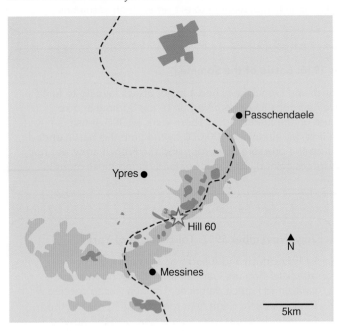

Ypres

The area surrounding the town of Ypres (called 'Wipers' by the British troops) was the scene of several major battles lasting months (see pages 112–13). Why did so much fighting take place around Ypres? There are two main reasons:

1. The town of Ypres stood on the most direct route to the Channel ports such as Calais and Dunkirk. If Germany captured those ports they would cut off most of the supplies to the British army – equipment, men and food. Therefore Ypres and the surrounding area had to be defended to keep the British war effort going.
2. The Ypres Salient (salient means 'bulge') was a vulnerable part of the Allied line. German forces occupied a ridge of high ground overlooking the Salient which meant they could fire down on British and Allied forces, and they could see the layout of defences and the movements of Allied troops. In addition, the higher German positions were well drained so were healthier and better for transport, and stronger defences could be

created. The British trenches were in low-lying ground with heavy soil which easily became water-logged and flooded, especially when churned up by shell-fire as this account shows:

> **Source A:** Bombardier J. W. Palmer, Royal Field Artillery, describing conditions in 1917 at the third Battle of Ypres
>
> It was mud, mud everywhere: mud in the trenches, mud in front of the trenches, mud behind the trenches. Every shell-hole was a sea of filthy, oozing mud. I suppose there's a limit to everything but the mud of Passchendaele – to see men sinking into the slime, dying in the slime – I think it absolutely finished me off.

The second Battle of Ypres in 1915 also saw the first extensive and effective use of poison gas by German troops. As Source B shows, gas attacks at this time took soldiers completely by surprise and without any defences, causing mass casualties.

> **Source B:** Private W. Hay, Royal Scots Regiment, recalling in a later interview his experience in 1915
>
> We started to march towards Ypres but we couldn't get past on the road with refugees coming down the road. We went along the railway line to Ypres and there were people, civilians and soldiers, lying along the roadside in a terrible state. We heard them say it was gas. We didn't know what the Hell gas was. When we got to Ypres we found a lot of Canadians lying there dead from gas the day before, poor devils, and it was quite a horrible sight for us young men.

The battle for Hill 60 near Ypres in April 1915 is an example of how German forces held the high ground around Ypres and of the methods used to try to capture this ground. Unlike other German positions, Hill 60 was actually a man-made hill, 60 metres above sea level, allowing German troops to fire directly down on Allied troops. In 1915 it was decided to attack Hill 60. Soldiers who had worked as coal miners in Wales and Northumberland dug tunnels into and under the hill. German soldiers dug counter-tunnels. If tunnels caved in or were blown in by the enemy, the soldiers who died underground were usually left where they were because of the difficulty of retrieving them.

On 17 April 1915, five mines were exploded under the German position; four mines went up in two pairs and the fifth mine as a single mine. The top of the hill was literally blown off. The British took the hill and over the following four days fought off fierce German counter-attacks. On 22 April the battle subsided with the British in control of the hill.

The Somme

The Battle of the Somme, which lasted from July to November 1916, is the best-known of all the battles. What made it stand out, even in 1916, was the huge casualty rate. British military planners had expected 10,000 casualties each day. In fact on the first day of the Battle, 1 July, the British army suffered nearly 60,000 casualties. Overall there were 400,000 Allied casualties and 450,000 German casualties. The medical consequences of this unexpectedly high number of casualties were enormous.

Visible learning

Warning! Generalisations can be bad for your marks

On pages 56–7 we gave you a warning about generalisations – big general statements that, for example, can make conditions everywhere on the Western Front sound the same. Trenches and No Man's Land were often very muddy but it's a mistake to think that the awful conditions at the third Battle of Ypres in 1917 were typical of all conditions all the time. Conditions at Ypres in 1917 were particularly bad because there had been record quantities of rainfall and the drainage system (which could have coped) had been destroyed by shell-fire. In contrast the ground at Arras (see below) was made up from chalky rock which drained easily and created dry conditions much of the time. Therefore, the experience of each soldier differed according to where he was and when he was there. Generalisations give us a 'general' picture but we must always ask of any description or photograph 'was this really typical of conditions all over the Western Front?'

A tank breaking through the wire at Cambrai. ▶

Arras

The Battle of Arras was fought in 1917, but what was really remarkable was what happened before the battle began. Soldiers from New Zealand and some from the north of England dug a network of tunnels in the ground underneath Arras. The chalky ground made tunnelling easy and the new tunnels joined up with ancient tunnels and quarries under the city, quarried out hundreds of years before. Rooms were created off the tunnels and fitted with running water and electricity supplies. This created accommodation for soldiers to live and sleep in and there was a hospital, large enough for 700 beds and operating theatres. The tunnels were also used as shelters against artillery fire and to convey troops to the Front in secrecy and safety.

Cambrai

The Battle of Cambrai late in 1917 saw the first large-scale attack by tanks although they had been used in smaller numbers since the Battle of the Somme in 1916. Over 450 tanks were used against the German front line. As there was no preliminary bombardment the assault was a surprise. The tanks proved effective and the German forces lost ground on the first day of the battle. However, the tanks did not have enough infantry support and, by themselves, could not defend and hold the ground captured. As a result the British lost almost all the ground they had taken.

THE TERRAIN ON THE WESTERN FRONT ❓

1. How did the Battle of the Somme put great pressure on medical resources?
2. Explain why there was so much fighting around Ypres.
3. What was so difficult about fighting conditions:
   a) in the Battles of Ypres
   b) at Hill 60?
4. Which new weapons were used at:
   a) Ypres in 1915
   b) Cambrai in 1917?
5. What was unusual about what took place beneath Arras?

The trench system of the Western Front

The trench system is the best-known, most important feature of the fighting. As the diagram opposite shows, there really was a trench *system*, not just a single front-line trench. In 1914 trenches were dug quickly and were very simple, but the system developed to create a highly effective defensive network.

The diagram at the bottom of the page opposite shows the ideal design for a British trench. However, many trenches at different stages of the war were far from ideal for reasons such as the impact of shell-fire or flooding after heavy or persistent rain. There were also times when trenches were less central to the war. Fighting was much more mobile in 1918 during the German Spring Offensive and later the British and Allied advance (see page 113).

It is easy to imagine my grandfather spending months at a time in the front line, but this did not happen. Men were rotated from the front line to the support and reserve trenches and then to their **billets** well behind the battle area. Rotation kept the men fresh, clean and well-fed and maintained morale. The information on the right of the diagram opposite shows roughly how much of a soldier's time was spent in the different parts of the system.

What would my grandfather's experience of a trench have been like? One way to begin answering this is to read descriptions by soldiers such as Source A. This description is by Lieutenant Charles Carrington of the Warwickshire Regiment who describes carrying equipment to the front-line trenches. His memories were recorded later for the Imperial War Museum. Before I can decide how useful this is as evidence I have to think about the questions shown below.

Source A

Although people talk about communication trenches and duckboards tracks they generally weren't there, and if they were, there was every probability that the enemy was going to shell them. So going along a trench [at night] meant stumbling along a dark wet ditch with an irregular floor and a right-angled turn every few yards so that you can't see where you're going. To manoeuvre these cursed things [bundles of barbed wire] round a corner was so fatiguing it can hardly be described.

So you'd go cursing and stumbling along in the dark, slipping into holes and stumbling over wires. Worst of all was the traffic problem, because there would be several parties of this kind going through the labyrinth of trenches, and you could have a jam as bad as a London traffic jam.

---

1. What valuable information does he give me?

For example: movement was difficult, with sharp corners and poor underfoot conditions. In the dark movement was far harder. Carrying equipment was difficult and trenches easily became blocked.

---

2. Is Lieutenant Carrington well informed and does his evidence agree with other sources?

For example: he was a soldier who knew the trenches; he could be exaggerating but there is no reason why he should.

---

3. Does my knowledge of the trench system suggest this is useful evidence?

For example: this is only one example. Not all sections of trench were the same but there are many other descriptions like this by soldiers.

Source B

▲ Stretcher bearers trying to help the wounded in a crowded trench

THE TRENCH SYSTEM ?

1. When a soldier was wounded in the front-line trench what route through the trench system would stretcher bearers take to evacuate him? Use the diagram opposite to work this out.

2. Look at Sources A, B and C. What problems were created by the trenches and the terrain surrounding them for medical treatment and transporting the wounded?

3. How useful do you think Source A is in helping me understand my grandfather's experience of the trenches? Remember the warning about generalisations on page 115.

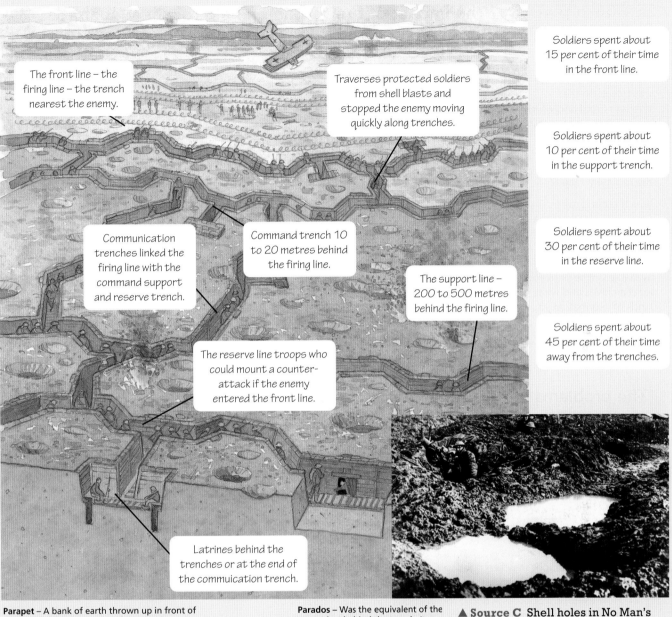

The front line – the firing line – the trench nearest the enemy.

Traverses protected soldiers from shell blasts and stopped the enemy moving quickly along trenches.

Communication trenches linked the firing line with the command support and reserve trench.

Command trench 10 to 20 metres behind the firing line.

The support line – 200 to 500 metres behind the firing line.

The reserve line troops who could mount a counter-attack if the enemy entered the front line.

Latrines behind the trenches or at the end of the commuication trench.

Soldiers spent about 15 per cent of their time in the front line.

Soldiers spent about 10 per cent of their time in the support trench.

Soldiers spent about 30 per cent of their time in the reserve line.

Soldiers spent about 45 per cent of their time away from the trenches.

▲ Source C Shell holes in No Man's Land.

Parapet – A bank of earth thrown up in front of the trench itself to allow a man to fire from the trench with a rest for his elbows and as much protection from incoming fire as possible. Parapets were required to stop a German rifle bullet. They were therefore four to five feet thick.

Parados – Was the equivalent of the parapet but behind the trench. It was designed to stop bullets carrying on to the next line of trenches and to shield men from the blast of a shell exploding behind them.

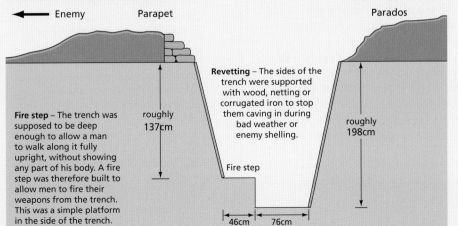

← Enemy   Parapet   Parados

Fire step – The trench was supposed to be deep enough to allow a man to walk along it fully upright, without showing any part of his body. A fire step was therefore built to allow men to fire their weapons from the trench. This was a simple platform in the side of the trench.

roughly 137cm

Revetting – The sides of the trench were supported with wood, netting or corrugated iron to stop them caving in during bad weather or enemy shelling.

Fire step

roughly 198cm

46cm   76cm

This illustration shows the main features of a trench but the reality of the war meant that the structure of trenches and conditions within them were often very different.

In the early stages of the First World War, soldiers dug trenches where and when they could. They used drainage ditches, banks, hedges and dips in the ground. Once the conflict settled down into siege warfare the trenches were improved with bunkers, dugouts, drains and fire steps.

The impact of the terrain on help for the wounded

Developing your enquiry

Can you find out where a regiment from your area was based on the Western Front and which major battles it fought in? What was typical or untypical of the conditions and battles the regiment faced?

Was there a local newspaper in your area that reported on developments in the war? Find out if it is available online or in your local archives and what kinds of information you can learn from it.

Over the last few pages I have built up a better idea of where my grandfather was based and what kinds of conditions he may have experienced. What these conditions were like depended on exactly where he was when he went to the Front in late 1917 and 1918. The trench system was well organised in theory, but was complicated and often hard to move around, especially at night. His Service Record shows he was wounded at least twice so whoever carried him or helped him back from the front for treatment would have encountered these problems with the terrain:

- Collecting the wounded from No Man's Land was dangerous. It might have to be undertaken under fire or at night.
- No Man's Land and the trenches could be deep in mud, making movement difficult and dangerous. Shell craters, many metres across and filled with water, made transporting the wounded extremely hazardous.
- The trench system could be clogged with equipment and men, moving in different directions. Carrying stretchers, which had to be manoeuvred round corners, often under fire, was extremely hard work.
- The number of wounded at any one time could be immense, slowing everyone down.

These problems meant that getting the wounded to a place where they could be treated often took a long time and cost many lives.

The problems of the terrain: exploring the sources

The questions below do two things. They help you consolidate your knowledge of this section on the terrain of the Western Front and they give you exam practice because they are the same form of questions you will answer in your exam. You can find more guidance on answering these examination questions on pages 148–162.

THE PROBLEMS OF THE TERRAIN

1. Describe two features of:
   a) the support trench system on the Western Front
   b) the conditions in which fighting took place in the Battles of Ypres
   c) two methods of warfare used first on the Western Front.

2. How useful are Sources A and B for an enquiry into the impact of the nature of the fighting on caring for the wounded on the Western Front? Explain your answer, using Sources A and B and your knowledge of the historical context.

3. How useful are Sources C and D for an enquiry into the impact of the terrain on caring for the wounded on the Western Front? Explain your answer, using Sources C and D and your knowledge of the historical context.

4. Use the BBC website (which has good information about the First World War – www.bbc.co.uk) and find two photographs which provide evidence about the topics covered on pages 116–17. Explain what we can learn from each photograph.

5. Choose two or three sources from this section to include in your table from page 107 and follow the instructions on page 107 for making notes on the usefulness of these sources.

Visible learning

Thinking carefully about sources

When you use a source there are three stages to think about:

a) What is it telling you about the subject of the enquiry – either directly or through what you can infer?

b) What does the information about the author or speaker and details such as the date suggest about how reliable or useful the source is for the enquiry?

c) How does your knowledge of the topic help you decide how useful the source is? For example, from your knowledge, does an account seem typical of other accounts of the same topic?

Source A: From the diary of Sapper J. Davey, Royal Engineers, for 10 May 1915

Not many hours went by before we were shelled out of this position and had to come farther back. I don't know how we have fared in the firing line. We went out at night to put some wire entanglements in front of the trenches. The sights were too awful for words. In our advanced trench when the flares went up we could see how things really were. Numbers of poor fellows lay in the bottom of the trench, the wounded amongst the dead crying for water and the stretcher bearers. Some had been waiting a day and a half to be brought in.

Source B: From the letters of Reverend John Walker, an army chaplain, who worked at a Casualty Clearing Station at the Battle of the Somme in 1916

1 July. We have 1500 in and still they come, 300–400 officers, it is a sight – chaps with fearful wounds lying in agony, many so patient, some make a noise, one goes to a stretcher, lays one's hand on the forehead, it is cold, strike a match, he is dead ...

2 July. Saddest place of all is the moribund ward, two large tents laced together, packed with dying officers and men, here they lie given up as hopeless, of course they do not know it.

3 July. Now I know something of the horrors of war, the staff is redoubled but what of that, imagine 1000 wounded each day. The surgeons are beginning to get sleep, because after working night and day they realise we may be at this for some months.

Source C: Gunner Sydney White. Royal Artillery. His memories were recorded later for the Imperial War Museum.

The only way up from Ypres was by a plank road fifteen to twenty feet wide. All munitions had to travel a considerable distance up this plank road, and the mud was so deep that on one occasion, with drag-ropes on the wheels and something like a hundred men on the drag-ropes, it was still impossible to pull the guns out of the mud. You saw fellows coming down from the trenches badly wounded, covered from head to foot in blood, and perhaps an arm missing. You saw some of the fellows drop off the duck-boards and literally die from exhaustion and loss of blood.

Source D

▲ A wounded Canadian soldier being carried back from the front at Passchendaele near Ypres in 1917

1.3 Illnesses and wounds

I now have a fairly good idea about the conditions my grandfather may have experienced during the war. Now it's time to move on to investigate a variety of aspects of medical care. By exploring my grandfather's record I hope to find out about the care of sick and wounded soldiers in general and about how typical his experiences were.

According to my mother, my grandfather lost his leg and was gassed. His record shows four occasions when he needed medical care. Therefore the questions around his picture are the ones I want to explore next. It's always vital for effective research to have questions to focus on.

Was he gassed?

Were these problems typical of the First World War?

Did he suffer other wounds and illnesses?

Were these problems new in the First World War?

Why did he lose his leg?

RECORDING YOUR RESEARCH

Use a table like this to record information about the illnesses and wounds suffered by soldiers, using the information on pages 120–6.

Type of illness or wound	What problems did it cause a soldier and the army in general?	How was it the result of conditions or weapons?	Methods of treatment or prevention
Trench fever			

A different kind of war

One important point before we begin is that a great deal of medical planning for a war had been done in the early 1900s, but no one could have predicted the kind of war that developed on the Western Front after 1914. The last war that the British had fought was the Boer War of 1899–1902 in South Africa. This had been fought on dry, hard ground by much smaller armies that were very mobile, and horses had played a large part for transport and carrying cavalry. In 1914 many army officers still expected this kind of fast-moving war with battles that lasted a day or perhaps two, and so medical planning was largely geared to this. The development of a very different kind of war meant that medical services had to adapt quickly to a very different environment.

Illnesses in the trenches

I will begin with the entry for 17 January 1918 shown below which says Arthur was admitted to the General Hospital in Rouen on 7 January and then the letters PUO.Sev. The lines below show he'd originally been sent sick to the Field Ambulance on 2 January. He stayed in Rouen until 11 March when he was admitted to the convalescent department and was discharged as fit on 25 March. So what does PUO.Sev. mean?

```
                      .  joined Nelson Battn. from XIX Corps Rest Camp,13.11.17.
   17.1.18.HA/18354.Adm 9.GH.Rouen 7.1.18.PUO.Sev.AFB/104-80a.
   12.1.18.   BEF.D.O.6. To 150th Field Amb. 2.1.18.
   18.3.18.   HA/20535. Adm.2 Con.Dep.Rouen ex 9 GH. 11.3.18.
    3.4.18.   HA/21023.Dis to Reinf Rouen Class A ex 2 Con Dep 25.3.18.
   16.4.18.   HA/21782. Adm.54 GH Aubengue 10.4.18. NYD.N.M18.AFB/104-80a
```

Trench fever

PUO stands for Pyrexia of Unknown Origin – Pyrexia is the medical name for the illness known as trench fever. The symptoms were severe headaches, shivering, pain in the bones and joints which lasted about five days but kept coming back. This is why the illness is also called 'relapsing fever'. It was certainly bad enough to make men unfit for fighting and for some to be invalided out of the army. Early diagnosis and effective nursing were crucial to recovery. Spells in hospitals of a month or more were common. Arthur spent two months in hospital and was away from the Front for three months. This fits with the letters 'Sev' on his record, which probably mean it was a severe case.

Trench fever was spread by lice, 'greybacks' as the soldiers called them. They lived in the seams of clothing and in blankets. Almost everyone had lice. Many men arrived at the Front already infested with lice from the crowded training camps. One **medical officer** on the Somme inspected 560 men and found 422 with lice. The link between lice and trench fever was not scientifically proved until 1918, but it was suspected by 1915 when serious efforts began to reduce its impact.

Efforts to reduce the number of cases focused on disinfecting clothing. When men came out of the front line their uniforms were fumigated, washed and ironed.

Bathhouses were built for them to use, and men were issued with a louse-repellent gel and other chemicals to put on their clothes and bodies; some even washed their underclothes in paraffin. Machines were sent to the Front which used steam to disinfect clothing and bedding. Some men, however, found the best way of dealing with lice was simply to pick them out of their clothing by hand.

All these efforts helped improved morale. However, the conditions in the trenches with men packed together and often sleeping wrapped in blankets close together in the cold meant that trench fever continued to be a problem, as Arthur's case in 1918 shows. The key point was that trench fever significantly reduced the number of men available to fight. Statistics from the British 2nd Army show that between July 1917 and July 1918 15 per cent of men were unfit for duty with trench fever, so it was a major cause of illness, second only to sexually transmitted diseases.

Lice were only one of the health problems men faced in over-crowded, damp or flooded trenches. Rats were often very unwelcome neighbours, feasting on bodies that could not be collected for burial because of constant gun and shell-fire. Private Thomas McIndoe of the Middlesex Regiment recalled seeing rats that 'if they were put in a harness they could have done a milk round, they were that big'.

Trench foot

Another major problem resulting from the conditions was trench foot. Standing in waterlogged trenches for hour after hour left men's feet numb, swollen, blistered and turning blue. Tight boots restricted blood flow which added to the problem and, while on duty, there was no chance to change wet boots and socks. Even more worrying, the condition developed and deteriorated rapidly and could lead to **gangrene**, the term for dead flesh and body tissue caused by insufficient blood flow. Gangrene spreads around the body and so often has to be treated with **amputation**.

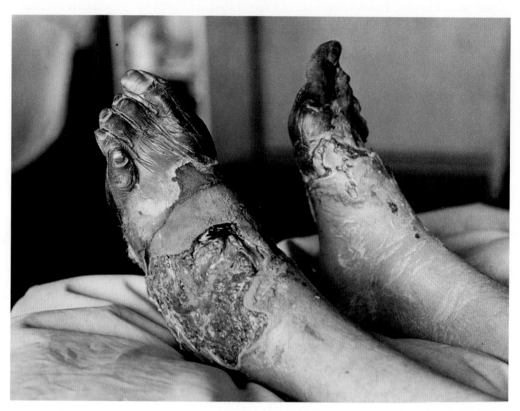

▲ Trench foot

It would have been difficult to predict cases of trench foot because no one had expected that the fighting would be dominated by trench warfare or the waterlogged conditions in some areas. The number of cases was greatly increased by the cold, wet winter of 1914–15. By January 1915 the 27th Division of the British Army had lost one-sixth of its 12,000 men to trench foot and the hospitals were full of men whose feet needed treatment.

Again, great efforts were made to reduce the drain on the number of fighting men. Senior medical officers ordered that every man should have three pairs of socks, change them twice a day and rub whale oil into their feet for protection. Men were split into pairs to look after each other's feet and high rubber waders were issued to wear in the worst conditions. Mechanical pumps were also sent to the trenches to reduce waterlogging and braziers were provided for heating.

These efforts did help reduce the number of cases but could not combat the day-to-day reality of fighting and the conditions men fought in. The terrain meant that waterlogging was common even before the drainage systems for many trenches were destroyed by shell-fire. Worse off were the men whose trenches were destroyed and who had to take shelter in flooded shell-holes for hours or days.

The puzzle of NYD.N.

One thing I have learned so far in this section is how common illnesses were among soldiers. I had assumed that soldiers would only have been in hospital as a result of wounds sustained in fighting, but that was obviously not the case. Trench fever, trench foot and many other illnesses such as **dysentery** weakened the army by taking men away from the front line.

```
                  ...D1s oo Reims Rouen Class A ex 2 Con Dep 25.3.18.
 16.4.18.    HA/21782. Adm.54 GH Aubengue 10.4.18. NYD.N.Mld:AFB/104-80a.
 1..4.18.  (NYDGH) 31. Cross-posted to Anson Bn.B.E.F.
 10.4.18.  Nelson 30. Joined L.Base Depot,Calais,29.3.18.S.
 29.4.18.  HA/22341. Adm.1 Con.Dep. Boulogne ex H. 22.4.18.
  2.5.18.  HA/22411. Trans.to 5 Rest Camp.Fit ex 1 Con.Dep. B'logne 23.4.18.
  8.5.18.  Anson 32. Joined L.Base,ex 54th G.H.,27.4.18.
 23.4.18.  Anson 29. To 1st ... .3.4.18.
```

Now I'll move onto something which was a puzzle when I first looked at it. The entry in Arthur's Service Record for 16 April 1918 says he was admitted to the General Hospital at Aubengue with NYD.N.Mld on 10 April, only two weeks after he returned to duty from having trench fever. The lines below show he was back with his battalion by the end of April.

NYD.N. was the army code for shell-shock. It means Not Yet Diagnosed. Nervous. Mld suggests it was a mild case. The term shell-shock was first used in 1914 to describe psychological reactions to danger, but as the war went on the number of cases grew until the army commanders feared an **epidemic** in late 1916 when there were 16,000 cases in six months. They feared shell-shock would be **contagious** with those affected spreading their fear to others.

This led to a change of policy. Instead of evacuating men to Britain they were treated in France, as close to the Front as possible. They were given rest, food and talks to calm them down and they kept in touch with their friends in their units. In 1917 orders were sent to medical officers that the words 'shell-shock' were not to be used in records and replaced by NYD.N. Medical officers made assessments of individuals and, if a man's condition was proved to be the result of an explosion, he was sent to hospital for treatment; some hospitals developed specialist centres for treating shell-shock.

Most men were returned to duty after a period of rest. It looks as if Arthur was one of these, though he did spend a short period in hospital. What is particularly interesting from my point of view is that there was no family talk of him having had shell-shock, but my mother said he was gassed – and there is no reference to gas poisoning in his record. I now wonder if he invented the story of being gassed as a cover story when he got home in case the symptoms of shell-shock reappeared. It would be much less shaming to say he'd been gassed than he'd suffered from shell-shock – but, of course, I cannot prove this.

Overall there were 80,000 recorded cases of shell-shock (1.28 per cent of overall casualties) although many more must have gone unrecorded. Some victims were treated, in our terms, very harshly, but in fact little differently from similar cases in the Second World War.

Loyalty before illness

One final point about illnesses – the number of illnesses actually fell during battles. Dr Charles Moran of the Royal Fusiliers wrote that 'During the battle of the Somme there were no sick' and quoted a man with an abscess on his hand and a fever who went back to the line after having the abscess lanced. When battles began, loyalty to friends meant very few men reported sick.

ILLNESS ON THE WESTERN FRONT

1. Describe two features of trench conditions that led to illness among soldiers.

2. **a)** Describe two features of the methods used to reduce the risk of trench fever.
   b) Describe two features of the methods used to reduce the risk of trench foot.

3. Why were plans changed to ensure many sick men were treated in France rather than being evacuated to Britain?

4. Why was the code NYD.N. used in medical records?

Weapons of war

One problem facing the medical services that we have already mentioned was the vast number of casualties. This is not surprising because this war was so much longer and the armies so much larger than in previous conflicts. In the Boer War of 1899–1902 the British army totalled 300,000 men, but in the First World War 40 million troops fought for Britain and her allies – to save you doing the maths that's over 130 times bigger than the Boer War army. However, the medical services did not simply face more casualties, but casualties with different and more severe wounds because of the nature and developments in weaponry, and because of the terrain the war was fought in.

Rifles

There was nothing new about rifles but they had become more efficient weapons. Soldiers no longer loaded them one bullet at a time. Since 1889 rifles had had a cartridge case which created automatic, rapid fire. Bullets were also designed with a more pointed shape which drove them deeper into the body from a longer distance.

Machine guns

Machine guns could fire 500 rounds per minute, the equivalent of the firepower of 100 rifles. They were a major part of trench defences and had a devastating impact against attacking forces approaching over No Man's Land. Like other weapons they were mass-produced by the industries of both sides.

Major weapons

Artillery

The successors of cannon grew bigger and more powerful throughout the war. For example, the British developed a howitzer which could send 900 kilogram shells a distance of over 12 miles. Bursts of shell-fire were no longer short-lived bursts lasting just a few hours at most. With factories churning out millions of shells, continuous bombardments could last weeks and months. Artillery fire was the greatest killer of all weapons, causing half of all casualties.

▲ A major reason for this was that guns were improved so that the recoil when fired did not change their position. This meant they could be fired more rapidly and did not have to be re-aimed.

Shrapnel

Shrapnel consisted of a hollow shell which was packed with steel balls or lead, together with gunpowder and a timer fuse. Shrapnel was designed to explode in mid-air above the enemy, causing maximum casualties. It was most effective against troops advancing across open land. High-explosive shells which broke into many fragments upon detonation were generally most effective against soldiers in trenches.

The nature of wounds

My grandfather suffered two wounds. The first, recorded on 7 June 1918, was, if I am interpreting the abbreviations correctly, a 'mild' bayonet wound to the scalp which put him out of action for just over a month. Statistics gathered from hospital records suggest that bayonet wounds, along with hand grenades and pistols, account for just 5 per cent of all wounds.

```
29.8.18. Tele:mess.P.135816.OC 1 SAGH Abbeville tele:28.8.18 'Dang.ill.
         GSW L.Leg amputation' NOK informed.RND List No: 1270. (2nd occ)
```

```
 7.9.18.C/1674"Wounded" 26.8.18.- also Anson 56.
10.9.18.HW/2281.Ser.ill(impvd)in 1 SAGH Abbeville w/e 2.9.18.
10.9.18.P.137752.OC 1 SAGH Abbeville tele:5.9.18'No long.ser.ill'NOK infd:
13.9.18. HA/28604. Adm. 1 S.African GH Abbeville 26.8.18. GSW.L Leg R.Arm
                                                                    Face
```

The second and far more significant injury came in late August when he suffered gunshot wounds to the left leg, arm and face, leading to his left leg being amputated. The photograph of him on page 105 also reveals that two of the fingers on his hand are either missing or shortened; I assume as a result of this incident. How typical was this kind of wound and why was it so devastating?

These kinds of devastating wounds were the product of increasingly powerful weapons. Artillery shells removed limbs or inflicted major internal damage to the body and head, often causing rapid blood loss. Machine gun and rifle bullets had the power to break major bones as well as piercing vital organs such as the liver and kidneys. A broken bone may not sound too severe today, but soldiers who suffered gunshot wounds to the leg in the early stages of the war had only a 20 per cent survival rate because of blood loss and the impact on the body of the shock of the wound. Over 41,000 men had limbs amputated.

What was just as damaging was the secondary effect – the 'blast impact' from bullets, shrapnel and shells. These objects first hit bones, muscle or organs but set off a blast effect which destroyed or damaged tissue and even bone for inches around the initial impact; and in the human body 'inches' includes a lot of vital human tissue.

The nature of the weapons also led to some very specific problems that were new in quantity if not entirely new in the type of wound. Many men suffered major blood loss from the impact of shell fragments and bullets. Those shell fragments and shrapnel could also be extremely small and so very hard to find within the body, although their tiny size did not stop them having the potential for being deadly.

The widespread use of shrapnel and the devastation caused by shell fragments also led to unexpectedly high numbers of head injuries early in the war when (it's now hard to believe) men went into battle wearing cloth or leather headgear. As a result steel helmets were designed and manufactured, being used by British troops from the autumn of 1915, but were only available in sufficient numbers to be widely used in the summer of 1916.

The use of steel helmets made a significant difference, but still over 60,000 British and Allied soldiers suffered wounds to the head and eyes, some leaving men alive but without noses, eyes, mouths, jaws. Head wounds were also made worse by the blast impact, as the original impact of the bullet or shrapnel was followed by the shock waves rattling the brain around within the skull.

Infection

The more powerful bullets and shell fragments went deeper into the body than those of previous wars. What added considerably to their danger was the material they carried deep into the body – fragments of muddy clothing and soil which led to **infection**. Many men could have recovered from the initial injury, but died when infection developed.

The impact of infection on death rates was a major difference from previous wars. Doctors who had served in South Africa where the ground was hard and dry, not farmland, had used simple **antiseptic** dressings on wounds, and victims had not developed infections. However, the Western Front battlefields had been farmland for centuries and had been manured year in, year out. This meant soil carried into wounds took microscopic amounts of manure with it, leading to the infections which killed many soldiers. The length of time some casualties had to lie in No Man's Land or trenches before being rescued also gave time for infection to develop in wounds before there was any opportunity for treatment.

The particular infection that caused so many deaths and amputations was gas gangrene. This was carried by **bacteria** in soil and was a particularly fast-developing infection. Gas gangrene had been rare in previous wars and so few military surgeons had experience of dealing with it, hence the many deaths it caused early in the war. In its early stages it has a sweet smell which nurses were looking out for, as the smell might be the first sign of infection. Medical accounts describe wounds which became hugely swollen with gas, turned white, then green and made a bubbling sound or sensation when pressed.

The impact of gas

Gas was used by both France and Germany in 1914. They used tear gas to disable the enemy but with no success. The first use of gas capable of killing the enemy came in 1915 at the second battle of Ypres when the German army used chlorine gas as a weapon. The gas suffocated hundreds of unprotected soldiers in a surprise attack. Their only protection came from urinating on their handkerchiefs and holding them over their noses. Other forms of gas were used later, notably phosgene and mustard gas. However, gas did not develop into a war-winning weapon as it was hard to target a particular place and, once gas masks were developed, it was easy to defend against. Fewer than 5 per cent of British soldiers died in gas attacks and, bad though that was, it was far fewer than many expected.

Gas was a horrific weapon but in most cases its effects – blindness, loss of taste and smell and coughing – were short-lived and disappeared after two weeks of treatment. Doctors near the Front (rather than in hospitals well behind the lines) gave sufferers oxygen to reduce breathing problems and washed the skin thoroughly to remove traces of poison gas. Most of those who feared they had been blinded recovered their sight. However, the large numbers of gas casualties, even if only affected temporarily, clogged up the treatment areas and made it harder for doctors to identify and treat those more in need of help.

◀ Both soldiers and horses needed protection from gas. Hundreds of thousands of horses were used by cavalry regiments; most often to haul supplies, ambulances and guns, and in many other tasks, as they were less likely to get bogged down in mud than motor vehicles. The experience of horses inspired Michael Morpurgo's book and play *War Horse*.

Visible learning

Changing my mind

In the section on shell-shock on page 123 I came to the conclusion that my grandfather was probably not gassed because there was no reference to being gassed in his Service Record. However, reading about the impact of gas has led to me rethinking this conclusion. Until now I had seen gas as a particularly dangerous weapon which led to death or major health problems in most cases. I thought that if Arthur had been gassed he would have been in hospital and that would have appeared on his record. Yet the evidence I have read suggests that many men affected by gas were never admitted to hospitals. So perhaps I need to revise my conclusion that Arthur was not gassed. It's quite possible he may have been gassed but that it doesn't appear in his record because he was treated close to the front line without hospitalisation. To find out more, I would need to find out more about the battles he took part in, but I'll say more about that later on page 145.

WOUNDS ON THE WESTERN FRONT **?**

1. Describe two features of the weapons used on the Western Front that caused severe wounds to soldiers.

2. Describe two reasons why wounded soldiers on the Western Front were so likely to develop life-threatening infections.

3. What new problems with wounds did doctors face on the Western Front in comparison with earlier wars?

4. 'Soldiers were not well cared for medically and little improvement took place in treatment during the war.' To what extent do you agree with this statement based on what you have read so far? What evidence best supports your view?

5. What is important about the Visible learning box above for understanding how to carry out an enquiry?

How would I follow up this part of my enquiry?

In this section I've explored the kinds of illnesses and wounds suffered by soldiers and whether my grandfather's illnesses and wounds were typical of the overall pattern. Certainly trench fever and gunshot wounds were typical. One other thing that seems to be emerging is that he was lucky to be wounded in 1918, not 1914 or 1915, as treatments seem to have improved rapidly during the war (I will come back to this in detail in the section on surgery and treatment on pages 138–43). There are two things I can do to follow up this initial stage of this enquiry:

1. I could find out more about the impact of particular weapons and about the nature of wounds and illnesses, perhaps by reading more history books on the medical history of the war or by reading accounts by soldiers, doctors and nurses who served in the war. These two kinds of sources would give me very different but equally valuable information.

2. The obvious thing I do not know about my grandfather is which battles he took part in and where exactly he was when he was wounded. Was he injured when his unit was attacking or defending or even retreating? The way to find out would be to establish whether his battalion's war diary exists (probably at the National Archives) and to see if I can get a copy to read.

Developing your enquiry

1. Different kinds of poison gas were used as weapons. Find out what they were and how their effects differed.

2. What other questions do you want to explore after reading this section?

3. The BBC website (www.bbc.co.uk) will help you build up your knowledge of the war and medicine on the Western Front. Explore the site and identify which sections will be useful for your enquiry.

Illnesses and wounds – exploring the sources

Source A

Soldiers of the East Yorkshire Regiment having their feet inspected by their medical officer near Rodincourt on 9 January 1918. This trench looks to be in good condition with duckboards above the mud to help keep soldiers' feet dry.

Source B: From 'A report on Gas Gangrene' by Anthony Bowlby, Consulting Surgeon to the British Army, October 1914

The gangrene found amongst our wounded soldiers is directly due to infection introduced at the time of the wound, and this is likely to occur if muddy clothing has been carried by the projectile, or if earth has been carried by the explosion.

Source C: From the diary of Sister Katherine Luard of the Queen Alexandra Nursing Sisters, 15 April 1915. ADMS stands for Assistant Director, Medical Services.

This afternoon the medical staff of both divisions have been trying experiments in a barn with chlorine gas, with and without different masks soaked with some antidote, such as lime. All were busy coughing and choking when they found the ADMS of the 5th Division getting blue and suffocated. He's had too much chlorine and was brought here looking very bad, and for an hour we had to give him fumes of ammonia til he could breathe properly. He will probably have bronchitis. But they found out what they wanted to know – that if you put on this mask, you can go to the assistance of men overpowered by the gas, with less chance of finding yourself dead too when you get there.

Source D: From the memories of Private Harry Patch of the Duke of Cornwall's Light Infantry, describing events in 1917

The shelling was bad. You could hear the big shells coming, although if you could hear them that was alright, they'd just gone over. You never heard the whizz-bangs coming, they were just there. And you never heard the shell or the bullet that hit you. Of course whizz-bangs were shrapnel and that was worse than a bullet. A bullet wound was clean, shrapnel would tear you to pieces. It was a whizz-bang that killed my three friends and wounded me, it was just bad luck. They had those four magazines over their shoulders, fully loaded. That's why they all got blown to pieces.

ILLNESSES AND WOUNDS

1. Which of Sources A–D is useful for an enquiry into each of the topics listed below?
   a) Gas attacks   **b)** Health problems in the trenches   **c)** The dangers from artillery
   d) The dangers from infections in wounds

2. Choose two of the sources and explain how useful they are for the chosen enquiries.

3. How would you follow up one of the sources to find out more about the topic? Think about what question or questions you would ask next and what types of source you could use.

4. Choose two of the sources above to include in your table from page 107 and follow the instructions on page 107 for making notes on the usefulness of these sources.

How have I been finding out about the war?

On pages 110–11 I set out my plan for how I was going to learn more about the war and my grandfather's experiences. In the pages since then information and sources have been appearing, almost as if by magic. Where has all this information and the sources come from?

I have been following the plan I set out in stage 3 on page 111 'Where will I research and find the answers?' I started with my grandfather's Service Record but I have been using books, websites and sources. Here are some of them:

Books and websites

I have been reading general histories of the war to find out about the main battles but I have concentrated more on books which focus on the medical history of the war. Two books in particular have been useful:

1. Susan Cohen, *Medical Services in the First World War* – this was published in 2014 so should be up to date with the latest research into the war. The list of reading and archives at the back suggests the author has a very good knowledge of the topic. It's also a short book – only 64 pages – so it gives me the main details quickly. It's also got plenty of photographs, some of which I may use in this book.

2. Mark Harrison, *The Medical War: British Military Medicine in the First World War* – published in 2010. This is much longer (346 pages) and so far more detailed. It is written by a historian at Oxford University who is one of the leading experts on medicine in wartime so I feel confident I can rely on the information he provides as being accurate. When he quotes from a soldier's letter or official documents he always provides the details of where this has come from.

I have been careful using websites because it can be harder to know if their information is accurate. One site I have found helpful is *The Long, Long Trail* (www.1914-1918.net) which has a section on the medical treatment of casualties.

Photographs and memories

In these books and others I have found a range of photographs and also the memories of soldiers, nurses and doctors. These were often written down or recorded long after the war by historians wanting to make sure these memories of the war were not lost when people died. One very good collection is *Forgotten Memories of the Great War* by Max Arthur, published in 2002, which uses extracts from recordings made by the Imperial War Museum.

The photographs and personal memories have been the most immediately interesting items. They give an insight into people's emotions and reactions to the things they saw, but they do only give one person's view of events or a snapshot of what was happening at one particular place or time in the war. That's why the books by historians are important to read as well – they can give the 'bigger picture', such as how medical care changed over the four years of the war, or whether one person's experience was typical or unusual. For example, the statistics collected and used by historians show how widespread illnesses such as trench foot and trench fever were – something I would not have expected before I started reading, when I assumed that almost everyone who needed treatment had been wounded. I can see from this that Arthur's long period in hospital with trench fever was very typical.

Moving on

So I have been learning a lot and I have changed my mind as I found out more – I was feeling very clever that I'd 'proved' that he wasn't gassed and then realised he might have been after all. Now for the next part of this enquiry – how did the wounded reach the places where they were treated and was the evacuation of the wounded well organised?

1.4 Helping the wounded

I now know about the wounds and illnesses Arthur suffered and I've found out how typical they were on the Western Front. My next mini-enquiry investigates how, when he was wounded in August 1918, he got from the Front to the hospital in Abbeville. The source below sent a shiver up my spine when I read it. It's about a different soldier but I think it tells me quite a lot about the kinds of experiences Arthur might have had.

Source A: H. P. Cotton was a signaller in the Royal Artillery who enlisted in 1909 and served throughout the war until wounded at the Battle of Arras in 1917. He wrote this account after the war and it is part of the Liddle Collection of records from both World Wars at the University of Leeds. He was awarded the Military Medal for bravery at Arras. Back in Britain he underwent more operations on his legs and was then discharged from the Army as 'Physically unfit for further service' and awarded 80 per cent disability pension. The 100 per cent (Total Disablement) pension was then 28 shillings per week which would be worth between £35 and £40 a week today.

… regaining consciousness after this further injury, I – and many others lying around in similar circumstances – shouted as loud and for as long as we were able to attract attention. Eventually I was located by a party of 8th Lincolns making their way to a sunken road to collect rations. Stretcher bearers arrived and conveyed me in 'fits and starts' under heavy shell fire to the Regimental Aid Post – a dugout excavated in the side of a hill. There, clothing – or remains of clothing – and boots were cut away from affected parts with an open razor, one was examined by a medical officer, a yellowish liquid poured over wounds and copious bandages applied. Various particulars – rank, name, regimental number etc. – were taken whilst awaiting to be taken rearward by ambulance – often horse drawn to a Casualty Clearing Station which was equipped with a mobile operating theatre. I was informed that I had received multiple gunshot wounds in both legs, right foot and right hand and had lost a quantity of blood due to lying out on the battlefield without attention … Some time after my first surgical operation for the removal of the largest pieces of metal (mostly shrapnel bullets), I with many others was taken to a nearby hospital train by stretcher bearers … After a long railway journey – or so it seemed – we were transferred to ambulances and taken to a Base Hospital at Camiers. Later I learned it was a tent hospital … I soon discovered that I was in the Danger Ward and my parents visited me for 3 days (I think). One or two operations were performed on me at this hospital and I spent about two months there before I was fit enough to be transferred to Blighty [Britain]. Thence I was taken by ambulance to Calais. Lady drivers were then operating ambulances at the bases and I well recall lying on a very narrow stretcher with 16 tubes in my numerous wounds and the changing of gears by a not too efficient driver on very indifferent roads … We were unloaded and the casualties transferred to a hospital ship …

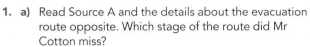

THE EVACUATION ROUTE

1. **a)** Read Source A and the details about the evacuation route opposite. Which stage of the route did Mr Cotton miss?
   b) What can you learn from his account about each stage of the route?
2. How useful is Source A for understanding the evacuation route described opposite?
3. What are the strengths and weaknesses of Source A for understanding Arthur's experience?
4. Draw your own diagram showing the stages of the evacuation route and add notes recording the main features of each stage.

Visible learning

Mnemonics

On page 23 we explained about using mnemonics to help remember parts of a topic. Work out a mnemonic to help you remember the stages of the evacuation route.

The evacuation route

The aim was to treat the wounded as quickly as possible because survival depended on the speed of treatment. Few soldiers went through every stage. Some could walk to the Regimental Aid Post or Dressing Station and did not need a stretcher. Some were taken straight from the Aid Post to a Casualty Clearing Station, because of their wounds or the availability of transport.

1 Stretcher bearers

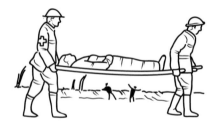

Stretcher bearers recovered the dead and wounded, sometimes during a break in fighting, often under fire. Stretcher bearers had to deal with mud, shell-craters and crowded, twisting trenches. They carried basic medical supplies – bandages and morphine for pain relief. There were only 16 bearers per battalion of up to a thousand soldiers, and it took four men to carry a stretcher, sometimes six or even eight in the thick mud of the Ypres battlefields, so often there were not enough bearers.

2 Regimental Aid Post (RAP)

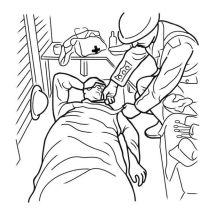

The RAP was very close to the front line, sometimes in the firing trench, but at most a couple of hundred metres behind it. It was moved forward when casualties were expected in an attack. It could be in a dug-out in the trenches, inside a ruined building or simply behind a wall. In the RAP was the battalion regimental medical officer whose job was to distinguish between the lightly wounded and those needing more medical attention. He would bandage very light wounds with dressings and send men back into action. The rest were sent to Dressings Stations for treatment, sometimes after being given pain relief. The Aid Post was often poorly lit and under fire. There was just one medical officer and a team of up to 30 orderlies and stretcher bearers for each battalion.

3 Field Ambulance and Dressing Stations

A Field Ambulance was not a vehicle but a large, mobile medical unit with medical officers, support staff and, from 1915, some nurses. The staff of the Field Ambulance set up Dressing Stations in tents or derelict buildings to receive the wounded sent from the RAP and sort them into more or less serious cases, a system known as **triage**. These Dressing Stations were between a quarter of a mile and a mile behind the front line. All serious cases were sent to Casualty Clearing Stations by motorised or horse-drawn ambulances or by lorry.

Triage
The system of splitting the wounded into groups according to who needed the most urgent attention.

---

4 Casualty Clearing Station (CCS)

The CCS was the first large, well-equipped medical facility the wounded would see. They were seven to twelve miles from the fighting, usually in a series of large tents or huts, though some were in schools and factories. There were usually around seven doctors with nursing and other staff. By 1917 they were performing more operations than the hospitals, including many amputations. They contained operating theatres, mobile X-ray machines, wards with beds for around fifty men, kitchens, toilet blocks and accommodation for the medical staff. The CCS could deal with a thousand casualties at a time, but often had far more in the first two years of the war.

5 Base Hospitals

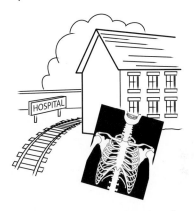

The Base Hospitals (also known as General or Stationary Hospitals) were usually civilian hospitals or large converted buildings near railways so patients could be moved quickly. Many soldiers arrived by train, motor ambulance or even by barge along canals because the journey was less bumpy. By 1918 some hospitals could take as many as 2500 patients. They had operating theatres, laboratories for identifying infections, X-ray departments and some had specialist centres for treating, for example, victims of gas poisoning. My grandfather was in four hospitals – Rouen, Le Treport, Abbeville and Aubengue.

From the Base Hospital most patients were sent back to England in hospital trains. Others, like Arthur in early 1918, would be sent to convalescent wards before returning to the fighting units.

The effectiveness of the evacuation route

One of the most important things I have learned is how much medical care changed during the war. Arthur had a higher chance of better treatment in 1918 than 1914. In 1914 the speed of events and the numbers of casualties were greater than predicted. One example was that no motor ambulances were sent to France in 1914, and the horse ambulances could not cope with the numbers of wounded. Miss M. Peterkin, a nursing sister at Rouen wrote in her diary on 18 September 1914:

> They say that wounded lie for days up at the front, with no-one taking any notice of them, and it is a notorious fact that we only get relatively slight cases here, for the simple reason that the bad ones either die on the battlefield, or on the train on the way down here.

The army greatly improved the evacuation and treatment of the wounded once the nature of the war was understood. By November 1914 there were 250 motor ambulances in France with more arriving daily. Horse ambulances continued to be valuable, however, in muddy and cratered ground, even if they needed six horses rather than two in such conditions. Ambulance trains were another important development, able to carry up to 800 casualties. There had been four ambulance trains in 1914, but by July 1916 there were 28. Barges were used too, with a fleet of ambulance barges carrying wounded along the River Somme.

The Battle of Arras which began in April 1917 and lasted 39 days shows the progress made in evacuation efficiency. During the battle, 160,000 British and Australian forces were killed and, in the first three days alone, over 7000 wounded and sick soldiers needed treatment. Despite these demands the evacuation route worked smoothly, though many doctors and support staff worked under fire and some Dressing Stations and CCSs had to move because of shell-fire. The CCSs never became too full because planning had made sure that there was enough staff and equipment – including 28 ambulance trains to move the wounded on to hospitals. The historian Mark Harrison concluded:

> The efficiency of casualty disposal at Arras stands as a testament to the managerial competence of the senior medical staff but it also demonstrates the high priority which the general staff now attached to such matters.

Medical care was so important because it got fit men back into the line quickly and so kept the army as efficient as possible. In 1914 it was assumed that most of the wounded would be sent to Britain for treatment. However, the nature of the fighting demanded more and more soldiers and evacuation to Britain slowed down the wounded returning to fighting. The solution was to treat as many men as possible close to the front line. Surgeons at CCSs did far more operations than originally planned and the hospitals in France grew far larger. As a result 67 per cent of the wounded returned to the Front and did so more quickly than if they had been evacuated to Britain.

▲ The army was creative in finding effective places for medical care. One outstanding example is the underground hospital at Arras. Existing tunnels and quarries were extended by miners in 1916 to create an underground town for soldiers to live in, fitted with running water and electricity. This included a large hospital with 700 beds and operating theatres. The underground space was so large that a horse-drawn railway was used to move supplies.

Nurses and doctors

All medical officers and men in 1914 belonged to the RAMC – Royal Army Medical Corps – which organised and provided medical care. It consisted of all ranks – from doctors to ambulance drivers and stretcher bearers – and it was responsible for keeping men healthy through good sanitation as well as treating the wounded and sick. The RAMC rapidly expanded to cope with the scale of the war and the numbers of wounded. It had 9000 men in 1914 but increased over 12 times to 113,000 by 1918. More doctors were recruited by raising the age at which doctors could serve abroad to 45. These doctors had to learn quickly about wounds they had never seen before in conditions completely different from any they had experienced.

▲ Nurses at a war hospital in 1916.

The main body of military nurses in 1914 were the well-trained Queen Alexandra's nurses, of whom there were 300 in 1914 but 10,000 by the end of the war. These numbers reveal a shift in attitudes to nurses serving near the front line. In 1914 the British army only accepted the Queen Alexandra nurses and turned away volunteer nurses who then found work with the French and Belgian armies. However, the numbers of casualties changed attitudes and soon thousands of women were at work supporting the British army. Their work varied hugely, from professional nursing in operating theatres to scrubbing floors, cooking and washing clothes. The best known group of volunteers was the VADs (Volunteer Aid Detachment), mainly middle – and upper-class women with little experience of work before the war, who found themselves doing a lot of the scrubbing and cleaning. Though, by 1917, they were doing more nursing, changing dressings and giving painkillers.

The work of the FANY – First Aid Nursing Yeomanry – reveals the changes brought by the nature and site of the war. The FANY were founded in 1907 by a soldier who had been wounded in the Sudan in Africa. He hoped they would be a kind of nursing cavalry, women on horseback galloping to the aid of the wounded. Nearly 500 women of the FANY did help the wounded but as ambulance drivers and nurses, not on horseback. They also worked for the Belgian army until the British changed their policy towards women and recruited them in 1916. One FANY unit ran the Calais ambulance convoy for two years with 22 drivers and 12 ambulances. Others carried supplies to the front, drove motorised kitchens to supply food and they even had a mobile bath vehicle which could give baths to 40 men an hour!

THE EFFECTIVENESS OF THE EVACUATION ROUTE

1. I think my grandfather had a higher chance of better medical care in 1918 than in 1914. What evidence can you find on these pages to support that argument?

2. Describe two features of:
   a) The Regimental Aid Posts
   b) The Casualty Clearing Stations
   c) Methods of transporting the wounded on the Western Front
   d) The work of nursing units such as the FANY.

Developing your enquiry

There are some excellent websites which provide sources about the war or deal with particular aspects of the war. Explore one of these sites and explain why it is a valuable site for an enquiry into the topic of this section 'Helping the wounded'.

- Imperial War Museum
  http://www.iwm.org.uk/
- The RAMC in the Great War
  http://www.ramc-ww1.com/
- FANY
  http://www.fanyarchive.org.uk/

Helping the wounded – exploring the sources

Pages 130-3 have introduced the main features of the system of evacuation and the medical care received by the wounded. The sources here help deepen your knowledge and provide a range of insights, sometimes more immediate and human reactions to dealing with men in agony, shock and close to death. With a little imagination I can also use these sources to build up my picture of my grandfather's experiences.

Source A: From the recorded memories of William Easton, East Anglian Field Ambulance. He was 18 in 1916. Here he described conditions near Ypres in 1917.

Up at Ypres we used to go up the line and we'd be waist deep in mud. We were carrying the wounded down near a place called Hooge, where had been a terrific amount of fighting. One trip down a trench in those conditions and you would be all in – exhausted. If you got two or three wounded men down in a day, that was all you could expect to do. We had to carry men in fours there and we had to be very careful because you could do more damage to a man than the shell if you jolted him too much or he fell off the stretcher. To make carrying easier we had slings which we put round our shoulders and over the stretcher's handles.

Source B: Captain Maberley Esler, Royal Army Medical Corps, speaking in an interview for the Imperial War Museum about his work at a Regimental Aid Post

In our front-line dugout we had first aid dressing and morphia and that was all. Several [wounded] got tetanus from an infection in the ground which was carried in shelled areas – very much like it was carried in farmland in the Fens. But it was all first aid work. The only value of a medical officer being in a front-line trench was to help the morale of the men. I remember going in the first night we were in the trenches and one fellow who thought I couldn't hear said to another chap 'Good God, the MOs come up with us – that makes you feel better, chum, doesn't it?' Then I realised I was doing some good by being there. Medically I felt no good at all.

Source C: Number of casualties passed through 76th Field Ambulance Advanced Dressing Station at Hooge Chateau from 2 August 1917 to 14 August 1917 – details recorded by staff at the Advanced Dressing Station.

Dates	Lying	Sitting
2.8.17	88	50
3.8.17	69	300
4.8.17	35	452
5.8.17	31	66
6.8.17	94	178
7.8.17	48	109
8.8.17	28	125
9.8.17	34	157
10.8.17	53	86
11.8.17	113	841
12.8.17	88	120
13.8.17	36	112
14.8.17	22	60
Totals	**739**	**2656**
Grand Total	**3395**	

▲ **Source D:** An ambulance wagon photographed at Ovillers, Somme in December 1916. It would have been heading from a Dressing Station to a Casualty Clearing Station.

Source E: An extract from the *London Gazette*, 30 July 1918, recording awards of the Military Medal to members of the FANY

Miss Muriel Thompson, FANY

Miss Winifred Millicent Elwes, FANY

Miss Elsie Agnes Courtis, FANY

Miss Mary Richardson, FANY

Miss Mollie O'Connell-Bianconi, FANY

Miss Hilda May Dickinson, FANY

Miss Elizabeth Beveridge Callander, FANY

For conspicuous devotion to duty during a hostile air raid. All these lady drivers were out with their cars during the raid, picking up and in every way assisting the wounded and injured. They showed great bravery and coolness, and were an example to all ranks.

Source F: From orders sent by Surgeon-General W. Pike (Director of Medical Services, 1st Army) to officers commanding Casualty Clearing Stations, 19 April 1916. Non-Commissioned Officers (NCOs) were soldiers who had been promoted to ranks such as Corporal or Sergeant.

Owing to the fact that modern battles as a rule last several days, care must be taken that NCOs and men of your Clearing Station should be divided into day and night parties, of which of course, the day party will be the larger. As far as possible, some Officers and Sisters should be also off-duty for at least six hours in the 24.

▲ **Source G:** A ward in the British Red Cross Hospital in Le Touquet, France in April 1914.

Source H: An extract from an article in the *Journal of the Royal Army Medical Corps*, 1915

Admirable as was the organization of the large base hospitals, the transport of the wounded from the fighting line seems to have been very badly managed during the advance of the Germans through Belgium and northern France. The supply of motor ambulances proved totally inadequate and the slightly wounded had to shift for themselves and squeeze into goods trains.

GETTING THE WOUNDED TO HOSPITAL

1 a) Which of sources A–H is useful for an enquiry into each of the topics listed below:
    i) The work of Regimental Aid Posts
    ii) The work of Dressing Stations
    iii) Operating theatres in hospitals
    iv) The work of Casualty Clearing Stations
    v) Transportation of the wounded
   b) Choose two of the sources and explain how useful each one is for the chosen enquiry.

2. How would you follow up one of the sources to find out more about the topic? Think about what question or questions you would ask next and what types of source you could use.

3. Which of these sources do you think have been useful for understanding my grandfather's experiences after being wounded? Explain your choices.

4. Choose two of the sources above to include in your table from page 107 and follow the instructions on page 107 for making notes on the usefulness of these sources.

Thinking carefully about sources

Look back to page 118 for a brief reminder about thinking about sources and use pages 148–162 when writing answers to questions.

1.5 Medicine in the early 1900s

So far I have built up a picture of the kinds of wounds and illnesses my grandfather and other soldiers suffered from and how the wounded men were rescued and transported to be treated. The next and final part of my enquiry will therefore be an exploration of what kinds of treatment they received, especially what new methods were being developed which made a real difference to saving lives. First, however, this page provides a reminder of how medicine had developed by the early years of the twentieth century. It seems likely that before 1914 young men like Arthur knew little or nothing about these scientific developments that would play a big part in saving their lives during the war.

MEDICINE IN THE EARLY 1900S

1. This doubles as the chance for a little revision. Try answering the questions below without reading this page and page 137, then use these pages to check how many you got right.

a) Which discovery was made by Wilhelm Röntgen?	**b)** Which surgeon pioneered the use of antiseptics such as carbolic acid?	**c)** In which decade did the pioneer of antiseptics publish the results of his work?
d) Which major surgical problem was still unsolved by 1900?	**e)** What is the difference between antiseptic and aseptic surgery?	**f)** When did Röntgen make his discovery?
g) What was Karl Landsteiner's important discovery?	**h)** Which breakthrough by a French scientist inspired the breakthrough in antiseptic surgery?	

2. Describe two features of:
   a) Aseptic surgery in use around 1900
   b) Landsteiner's discoveries about blood

3. These questions require you to use the knowledge you have about the Western Front to think about problems facing surgeons during the war.
   a) Why would aseptic surgery be both important and very difficult to achieve on the Western Front?
   b) Why would X-ray machines be vital pieces of equipment for surgeons on the Western Front?
   c) Why would blood **transfusions** be so important, and what problems would need to be solved to make them even more valuable?

Infection and aseptic surgery

Antiseptic surgery – killing germs in wounds

There are **germs** in the operating theatre but surgeons use methods, e.g. carbolic spray, to stop open wounds being infected.

Aseptic surgery – preventing germs reaching wounds

Cleaning and **sterilising** methods prevent there being any germs in the operating theatre to infect wounds.

Joseph Lister's use of antiseptic surgery was one of the great turning points in the history of surgery. In 1867 he published his ideas and the results of his use of carbolic acid as an antiseptic to kill bacteria in wounds (see page 65 for more detail). His methods reduced the death rate in his surgical patients from 46 per cent to 15 per cent.

By the 1890s surgeons were moving a significant step further, from antiseptic to aseptic surgery, which means from killing germs already in wounds to stopping them getting into wounds at all. To ensure operating theatres were aseptic:

- Operating theatres and hospitals were rigorously cleaned.
- From 1887 all instruments were steam-sterilised. Robert Koch had discovered that steam was even better at killing bacteria than carbolic acid.
- Surgeons stopped operating in ordinary clothes and wore surgical gowns and face masks.
- In 1894, sterilised rubber gloves were used for the first time – for however well surgeons' hands were scrubbed, they could still hold bacteria in the folds of skin and under the nails.

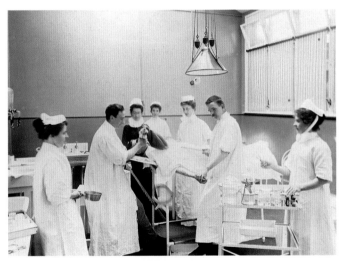

▲ An operating theatre at the Royal Hospital, Portsmouth, 1902.

X-rays

X-rays had been in use for less than twenty years when the war began. A German scientist, Wilhelm Röntgen, was carrying out experiments in 1895 when he noticed something remarkable – cathode rays in a test tube were lighting up a far wall even though he had covered the test tube in black paper. These rays could pass through the paper. Röntgen did more experiments and discovered that they could also pass through wood, rubber and human flesh but not metal or bone.

Röntgen called these rays X-rays because they were so mysterious and published his findings in December 1895. The impact was immediate. Within six months hospitals, including the London Royal Hospital, were using the first X-ray machines to identify, for example, if a bone was broken and where it was broken.

The problems of blood loss

Blood loss had always been a major cause of death and scientists and doctors had been trying for centuries to find a way to give people blood to make up for blood lost. In the 1600s the members of the Royal Society had attempted a blood transfusion from a sheep to a man (see page 40) and other experiments continued throughout the nineteenth century. The really puzzling thing was that some worked but others did not. Why?

The first breakthrough came with the discovery of the different blood groups in 1900. Karl Landsteiner (an Austrian doctor) identified the blood groups and demonstrated that some blood groups are incompatible with others – you cannot give a person blood from someone whose blood group is incompatible. This showed why some transfusions had succeeded – by chance the two people involved had had the same blood group. Landsteiner also explained in more detail why this happened – each blood **cell** has **antibodies** which react against those from a different blood group. Blood transfusions only work if there is no reaction.

This discovery meant that blood transfusions were now possible so long as the patient and the donor were in the same room. However, it was not possible to collect and store blood for later use. When doctors tried to store blood it clotted, forming a semi-solid mass. This meant it did not flow, so could not flow into the veins of someone needing blood. This was not too great a problem when there was time and space to put a donor in the same room as the patient and the demand for blood was not huge.

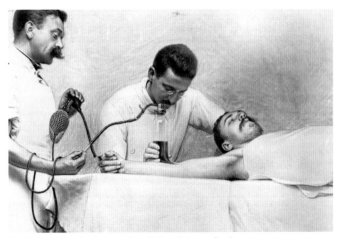

▲ An early photograph of blood transfusion.

1.6 The impact of the Western Front on medicine and surgery

The more I have learned about the war on the Western Front, the more I have realised that Arthur was fortunate to be at the Front in 1917 and 1918, not in 1914 and 1915. The system for evacuating the wounded had become much more efficient and methods for protecting soldiers from illnesses had improved. Doctors had learned a great deal about the kinds of wounds inflicted by the much more powerful and explosive weapons being used. This final section explores the improvements in treating those wounds. It seems highly likely that these improvements helped Arthur when he suffered severe wounds in August 1918 (see page 125).

Before looking at the improved methods used by doctors, it is important to understand why so much improvement took place in medicine and surgery during the First World War. The diagram below shows how the particular combination of circumstances created the opportunity and need for rapid improvements.

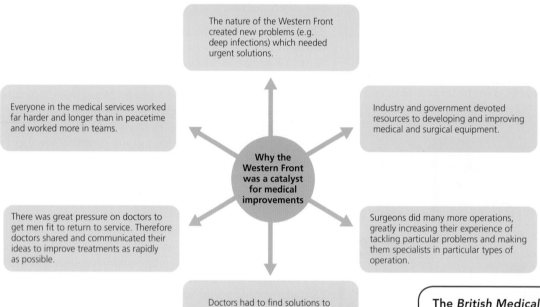

The nature of the Western Front created new problems (e.g. deep infections) which needed urgent solutions.

Everyone in the medical services worked far harder and longer than in peacetime and worked more in teams.

Industry and government devoted resources to developing and improving medical and surgical equipment.

Why the Western Front was a catalyst for medical improvements

There was great pressure on doctors to get men fit to return to service. Therefore doctors shared and communicated their ideas to improve treatments as rapidly as possible.

Surgeons did many more operations, greatly increasing their experience of tackling particular problems and making them specialists in particular types of operation.

Doctors had to find solutions to the new problems created by the more powerful weapons.

MEDICAL DEVELOPMENTS ON THE WESTERN FRONT

1. Which two factors in the diagram above do you think played the biggest part in improving surgical and medical techniques?

2. Use this table as a Knowledge Organiser to make notes on the main developments described on pages 139–143.

Medical development	What problem did it tackle?	What was the improvement or method?	What were the benefits of this development?

3. Read pages 139–143. Describe two features of:
   a) new surgical approaches on the Western Front
   b) new equipment used in surgery on the Western Front.

The *British Medical Journal*

One valuable source for wartime medicine is the *British Medical Journal*, although you have to be medically trained to really understand it. Its past editions can be seen online and just reading the titles of articles shows how much work was being done to improve medical care for soldiers. Here is a selection of articles from July 1916:

'Some of the Principles and Problems relating to the treatment of Gunshot Fractures'

'A method of treating "Shell Shock"'

'Head Injuries in War'

'Gunshot Wound of Spinal Column and Trachea: Recovery'

'The treatment of chlorine gas poisoning by venesection'

'Some notes on trench fever'

Treating wounds and infection

Joseph Lister had begun to solve the problem of infection in surgical wounds that caused so many deaths in the mid-1800s. His use of antiseptic surgery killed the bacteria that developed in wounds. By the early 1900s surgeons had developed aseptic surgery which meant that operating theatres were bacteria-free zones. However, the conditions on the Western Front threw surgeons back forty years. Many wounds were already infected when the soldiers reached the operating theatre as a result of fragments of muddy clothing or soil getting into the wound. Aseptic operating theatres were therefore not enough to stop infections. Wartime wounds were causing new problems that needed new solutions.

Surgeons therefore went back to the kinds of antiseptic methods used by Lister forty years earlier. They used chemicals such as carbolic acid and hydrogen peroxide to kill the bacteria already in soldiers' wounds. However, this was not enough to stop the spread of gas gangrene. A more effective solution was worked out by two doctors, Alexis Carrel and Henry Dakin, who used a system of tubes (the Carrel–Dakin method) which kept a chemical solution flowing through the wound and fought the infection or stopped it developing. This was more effective because it was continuous, not a one-off treatment, and did reduce the number of amputations that resulted from infection.

The second major development in dealing with infections was to carry out deeper surgery, cutting away more tissue around the wound. The problem was that many wounds were very deep with bacteria deep inside the body. In 1914 surgeons still used Boer War methods of limited surgery, removing a bullet and sewing up the wound but not taking away the tissue around the bullet-wound. The result was that infection remained in the body and killed many patients who were expected to recover from the wound itself. Therefore by 1915 more extensive surgery was used. Surgeons:

- made sure all shell and bullet fragments and shrapnel were removed, however small
- cut out all tissue and dead muscle surrounding the wound that might become infected
- did not sew up wounds immediately, but kept them open for the use of antiseptics – immediate sewing up had trapped bacteria inside.

This type of surgery created larger wounds but much reduced the chances of gas gangrene and **tetanus** (the major cause of amputations and deaths) developing.

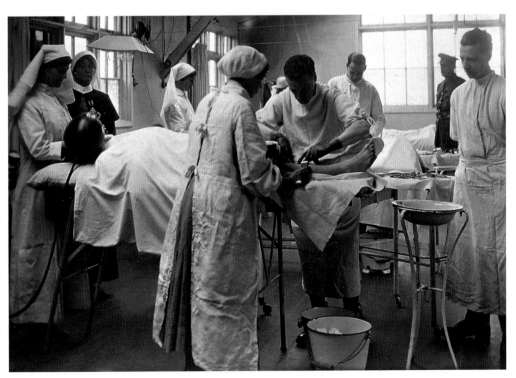

◀ Development of surgical teams who worked together smoothly and efficiently – a surgeon, anaesthetist, nursing sister and two orderlies. Another way of increasing efficiency and effectiveness was in the Casualty Clearing Stations where surgical teams worked on particular types of wound.

The Thomas splint

A splint to help fractured bones heal does not sound like a dramatic development but the Thomas splint saved many thousands of lives. It may even have saved my grandfather! Early in the war soldiers who had their femur, the thigh bone (the longest and strongest bone in the body), broken by gunfire died in huge numbers. Henry Gray, the Consulting Surgeon to the British 3rd Army said that about 80 per cent of soldiers shot in this way in 1914 and 1915 died.

The reason was that doctors had only very simple splints to fix to the wounded leg. This did not stop the broken ends of the bone causing considerable blood loss which weakened the wounded soldiers so much that many died before they could be treated.

The solution was the Thomas splint, invented by Hugh Owen Thomas, a Liverpool surgeon. This splint pulled the leg lengthways, stopping the bones grinding on each other and so greatly reduced blood loss. By coincidence, Thomas's nephew, Robert Jones, became the army's Director of Military Orthopaedics in 1916, and he made sure the Thomas splint was used from 1916 onwards. All regimental medical officers were taught how to use it so that it was used as near the front line as possible, in Aid Posts and Dressing Stations. This meant that when soldiers reached the Casualty Clearing Stations they were fit enough to be operated on because they had not lost too much blood. The Thomas splint reduced the death rate for this type of wound from 80 per cent to 20 per cent or lower, and far fewer amputations were needed. As a result the Thomas splint was described by Ambrose Lockwood, a surgeon in the RAMC, in the *British Medical Journal* in 1940 as:

> the most important agent of all … in combatting shock and in saving life and limbs.

I do not know which part of my grandfather's leg was damaged by gunfire, but if it was his thigh bone then there is a very high chance that a Thomas splint was used to keep him alive for the operation.

▼ Thomas splint in use

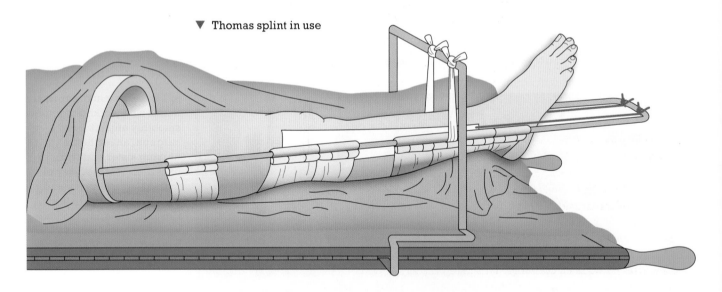

Mobile X-ray machines

Doctors had quickly realised the potential of X-rays as soon as Röntgen had publicised his discovery, but it was their use in the First World War which really demonstrated how important they could be. Many casualties had been wounded by bullets, shrapnel and, worse, tiny fragments of these objects, all of which needed to be located to make surgery faster and more effective. X-rays made rapid location of these objects possible, enabling surgeons to remove them more easily and completely, reducing the chances of infection. The increased use of X-rays therefore reduced the death rate from infections.

This was another aspect of medical care that was not as effective early in the war as it became later, because the scale of the war took planners by surprise. In January 1915 there were only two mobile X-ray vehicles in the British army. However, the government ordered many more X-ray machines to be manufactured. By early 1916 most Casualty Clearing Stations, as well as all hospitals, had X-ray equipment with additional X-ray lorries attached to groups of Casualty Clearing Stations.

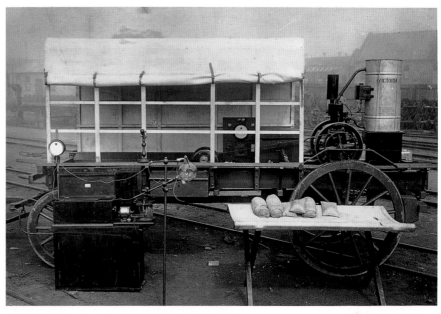

▲ A portable X-ray machine developed during the First World War.

Blood transfusions and the storage of blood

The work of Landsteiner (see page 137) had shown that blood could be transfused safely from one person to another, but the problem remained of how to store blood without it clotting. Until this problem was solved the donor and the patient had to be directly connected to avoid clotting. The huge wartime need for blood made solving this problem even more urgent. The impact of high explosives and machine gun bullets led to many men dying from blood loss when the wounds themselves need not have been fatal.

A series of linked discoveries solved the problem of storing blood and increasing the number of transfusions.

1. An American scientist, Richard Lewisohn, discovered that sodium citrate could be added to blood to prevent it clotting. This meant that blood could be stored and so the donor did not have to be present when a transfusion was carried out. This increased the number of transfusions considerably, saving many lives. However, this stored blood deteriorated quickly and had to be used soon after being donated.
2. Scientists first found that blood could be stored in refrigerated conditions and then that adding a citrate glucose solution to the blood allowed it to be stored for several days after it had been collected. This led to the first blood banks being created ahead of a major attack, so blood would be available for use with the wounded.
3. A British surgeon, Geoffrey Keynes, created a portable machine for storing blood which could be used to take blood closer to the front line of fighting. This meant that soldiers could receive blood sooner, stopping their bodies going into shock and so saving more lives.

As a result of all these developments the first blood depot was created before the Battle of Cambrai in 1917. Stocks of blood group O were collected and held ready for use as soon as the battle began. Group O had been chosen because it can be given to everyone safely, even if a person has a different blood group.

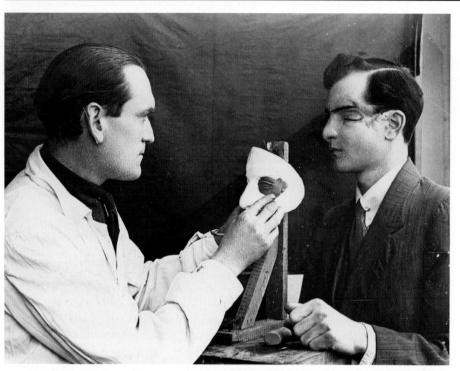

▲ Captain Wood, an artist before he joined the Army, painting an artificial face plate fixed over the cavity made in the soldier's face by a bullet wound near or in the eye.

Plastic surgery had been carried out centuries earlier in India but its use had always been limited by the danger of infection and the absence of effective **anaesthetics**. The solving of both these problems in the nineteenth century paved the way for surgeons to make considerable progress in plastic surgery to solve the problems created by so many terrible wounds caused by bullet and shell damage, especially to the face. One major improvement in techniques was the use of skin grafts, taking skin from another part of the patient's body and grafting it onto the area of the wound.

Surgeons carried out over 11,000 plastic surgery operations, increasing their experience and learning from each other. By November 1915 seven hospitals in France had specialist areas for dealing with wounds needing plastic surgery, particularly to the head. Surgeons developed new techniques using jaw splints and wiring and metal plates as 'replacement' cheeks.

Harold Gillies was a New Zealand surgeon who served with the RAMC through the war and became known as the 'father of plastic surgery'. In France he worked with French surgeons, learning from their techniques, and then persuaded the army's chief surgeon that a specialist facial injury care was needed in England for the wounded. In 1917 The Queen's Hospital was opened in Kent, specialising in repairing facial injuries.

Brain surgery

The number of serious head injuries was another unusual feature of the early part of the war. One major reason was that for soldiers standing in trenches, their heads were the most vulnerable part of their bodies. However, there had been little surgery carried out on the brain before 1914 – relatively little was known about how the brain worked and this made surgery on the brain extremely risky. Therefore, in 1914, many head injuries were not operated on, with wounds being bandaged but little surgery carried out. Another reason was the amount of time needed to tackle a single head wound – time that could be used more effectively by operating on several men with simpler wounds.

However, the number of head and brain injuries from 1914 pushed surgeons to try new ideas, even if some of them were as simple as putting rubber bands round the head to put pressure on wounds and so reduce bleeding. Two developments changed the approach to head wounds and particularly brain surgery:

1. More soldiers were kept alive and fit enough to cope with operations because they were given blood transfusions and also saline solutions to reduce shock.
2. Surgeons developed new techniques and improved their skills through dealing with large numbers of head wounds. The use of X-rays meant that surgeons were able to locate, identify and remove bullet and shell fragments and the surgeon Harvey Cushing invented a surgical magnet to extract bullets from head wounds.

Medicine and surgery – exploring the sources

By now you will have realised that we keeping asking you the same questions about sources – the types of question you will answer in your exam. There is more guidance on answering these questions on pages 153–54. The task this time is slightly different, but again it is designed to help you do well in your exam by making sure you understand the nature of the questions you will face.

1. Read pages 153–54. Now design questions which follow the models on those pages and use the sources on this page.

> **Source A:** Captain Geoffrey Keynes describing the development of blood transfusions in 1915. Keynes was a young RAMC doctor who later became a consultant surgeon and was knighted for his pioneering work on blood transfusions. He wrote an autobiography *The Gates of Memory* published in 1981.
>
> The first thing to do was get the [blood] group of the donor and the patient matching, and we had the serum for doing that. It had just been discovered as well as the method by which we could prevent the blood from clotting. It turned out to be very simple. You simply put sodium nitrate solution in the flask, a certain amount, then ran in the pint of blood, shook it around, and gave it to the patient through a pipe. You took it from a donor into a flask and then from the flask to a patient. I spent two weeks with the Harvard Unit [an American unit based at a hospital in France] and during the time I contributed something by devising an improved apparatus ... After a fortnight studying this technique I went back to the casualty clearing station where I was working and introduced the method there. It saved countless lives of men who would otherwise have died from shock and loss of blood.

> **Source B:** From 'The Development of British Surgery at the Front' by Surgeon-General Sir Anthony Bowlby, published in the *British Medical Journal* in June 1917. This extract comes from the section on head injuries.
>
> By careful individual observation [by doctors], and by the comparison of results, a method of treatment has been evolved which is applicable to all cranial wounds, and capable of modification in individual cases. It may be summarised as follows:
>
> A primary cleansing of the wound. The transmission of the patient as soon as possible to the hospital where he will convalesce. The taking of x-ray pictures. The excision of the scalp and bone wound. A limited and careful removal of foreign bodies. The covering the exposed brain. The closure of the wound, with superficial drainage, and prolonged rest in bed.

> **Cranium**
> The skull, especially the parts enclosing the brain.
>
> **Excision**
> Cutting out

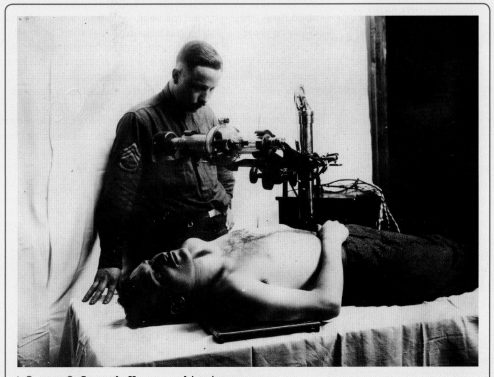

▲ **Source C:** An early X-ray machine in use

1.7 Conclusions: What have you learned about medicine in the First World War?

I began this enquiry with an *outline* knowledge of the events of the war, the weapons and the conditions in the trenches and the terrible human death toll. Quite often, however, I have shied away from reading or watching TV programmes about the war because it was too emotional to think about all those young men marching to their deaths. Writing this book has forced me to read more and having very specific questions to explore has guided me very effectively. So, what have I learned?

1. People expected a very different war so the scale of the casualties and the conditions on the Western Front took everyone – doctors, generals, the government – by surprise. This war was nothing like previous wars such as the Boer War in South Africa.

2. Doctors and military leaders had to find solutions to the new problems very rapidly in order to get as many wounded men back into action as soon as possible. They needed vast amounts of money and resources and they needed to be inventive and to be better organised with strong teamwork to share and communicate ideas. Throughout the war everyone worked extremely hard to improve medical care.

3. Illnesses such as trench fever were extremely common and required a great deal of medical care. Huge efforts were made to prevent men falling ill.

4. The war had a very significant impact on medical and surgical techniques for dealing with severe wounds and these methods continued to be used and improved after the war.

The nature of medical prevention and treatment therefore changed a great deal across the years of the war. This was one major influence in keeping men's morale high because they trusted their regimental medical officers and believed they would receive good medical care.

You will recognise this triangle from work on the thematic unit ▶ on Medicine in Britain. As I wrote this conclusion I realised the impact of the war created a slightly different medical triangle from the one we used earlier in the book.

▲ In the week I wrote these pages I visited York Minster, somewhere I've often visited before. This time I realised I was paying much closer attention to First World War memorials to individual soldiers and to regiments. In my mind I was asking questions such as 'Where was he on the Western Front?', 'Did he get help at a Casualty Clearing Station or Aid Post?' This unit has created the 'scenery' in which I can imagine the people in the memorials. Tucked away, sadly hidden in a corner, is the memorial in this photograph, to all the women who were killed in the war. The lists of names on the boards begin with Queen Alexandra nurses but there are many others too. I feel very pleased that I'm now so much more aware of the work these women did during the war.

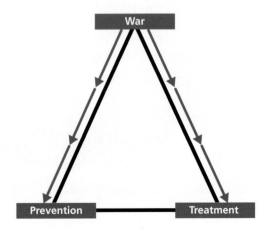

What have I learned about my grandfather?

I never knew my grandfather. I wondered whether this enquiry would make me feel closer to him, to feel a stronger link after exploring his medical record and how he might have been treated. However, my honest reaction is that he still feels like someone from history to me – someone I am interested in but the 'blood connection' doesn't feel any closer. I've studied many other individuals from the past, especially from the Wars of the Roses and I don't feel any closer to Arthur than I do those people in the 1400s. If you're surprised – well, I am too!

However, following one man's experience had provided a strong core to this enquiry. It has given a focus to the questions I've been exploring and I feel as if I'm finding out about real individuals, not just a group of people called 'soldiers'. Here's what I have learned:

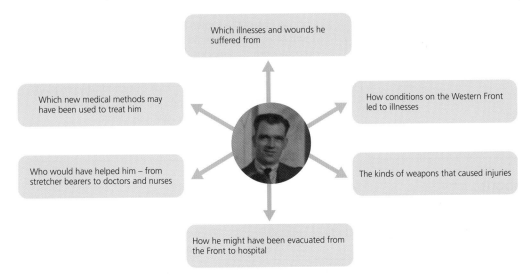

Which illnesses and wounds he suffered from

How conditions on the Western Front led to illnesses

Which new medical methods may have been used to treat him

Who would have helped him – from stretcher bearers to doctors and nurses

The kinds of weapons that caused injuries

How he might have been evacuated from the Front to hospital

One conclusion I have reached is that if Arthur had to be wounded then he had a far better chance of survival in 1918 than if he had been wounded in 1914. Blood transfusions, methods of preventing infection and, as he had a leg wound, the Thomas splint, may all have played a part in his recovery.

The key point to remember is that every enquiry needs different sources. You have to think carefully about which sources will be most helpful for answering particular questions.

What next?

Historical enquiries are rarely finished. You begin with questions and you do research to find answers but there's always more detail to find out, more sources to look at. I now have more questions I could explore:

1. Where exactly was he fighting and which military actions did he take part in? For example, was he wounded as part of an Allied advance or was he wounded when the German army was pushing forward?
2. Can I find out more about the hospitals he was in?

To find the answers I need to think about what kinds of sources will help me. Here are some possibilities:

> Soldiers' diaries
> Descriptions by doctors of operations during the war
>
> Photographs of particular hospitals
> Photographs of trench conditions
>
> The diary kept by his battalion or regiment
> Statistics of admissions to hospitals

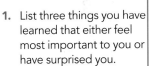

WHAT HAVE YOU LEARNED?

1. List three things you have learned that either feel most important to you or have surprised you.

2. Compare what you have learned about the war in this unit with what you learned at KS3. What are the similarities and differences?

3. What else would you now like to find out about the war?

4. Which sources do you think will be most useful for answering my two questions above about my grandfather?

1.8 Visible learning: Review and revise

Thinking about sources

We have done a lot of work already in this unit to prepare you for questions 1 and 2 in paper 1 of your exam. You can also find more guidance on the specifics of tackling these questions on pages 152–54. This page is designed to help you with question 2b in paper 1 of your exam. Question 2b will look like this:

2(b) How could you follow up Source B to find out more about the problems involved in (a topic will be identified)? In your answer, you must give the question you would ask and the type of source you could use. Complete the table below. (4 marks)

> Detail in Source B that I would follow up:
>
> Question I would ask:
>
> What type of source I could use:
>
> How this might help answer my question:

The focus is therefore on asking questions, identifying sources that would be relevant to the topic and would help you answer the questions you ask, and on using your knowledge of the topic. You can find more guidance on this question on page 154 but this activity will help you practise asking questions and choosing sources. This is a good activity to do with a partner so you can share ideas.

> 1. Choose one of the topics in the *pink box* below. Write down at least two questions you want to ask about it to deepen your knowledge.
> 2. Look at the sources in the *blue box*. Select one source that would help you answer your questions and explain how it might help answer the questions. You could choose different sources for each question.
> 3. Repeat questions 1 and 2 for at least one more topic.

Topics to find out more about

1. The evacuation route	2. The types of wounds caused by weapons	3. The work of Casualty Clearing Stations
4. The medical work in hospitals	5. The treatment of soldiers affected by gas	6. The work of stretcher bearers
7. Methods of dealing with infected wounds	8. Conditions in the trenches	9. The work of Regimental Aid Posts
10. The use of blood transfusions	11. New surgical techniques	12. Medical problems caused by the Battle of the Somme
13. The work done by nurses	14. Changing attitudes to women working near the Front	15. The use of X-ray machinery

Sources you could use

A. Diaries and letters written at the time by medical staff	B. Medical articles by doctors published during the war in the *British Medical Journal* and other specialist journals	C. Recollections by soldiers written or recorded after the war ended
D. The records of Casualty Clearing Stations about admissions and cases	E. Photographs	F. Diaries and letters written by soldiers during the war
G. Newspaper accounts of fighting during the war	H. Statistics of different types of injuries and operations collected by the army command	I. Orders and instructions issued by the Chief Surgeons in overall charge of medical care for the British army
J. Recollections by medical staff written or recorded after the war ended	K. The records of individual hospitals, listing admissions and types of operations	L. The Service Records of individual soldiers

Cementing your knowledge

In your examination you will be asked three questions (see page 148). These questions will be about the sources we use to find out about medicine on the Western Front and will also test your skills in enquiry, such as asking questions. To do well in all the questions you also need a good level of knowledge about the topics you have studied in this unit. Examiners will be looking to see how much you know and how you use that knowledge in your answers. Therefore it is important that you make that knowledge stick to your brain. We did a lot of work on this in the thematic unit on Medicine in Britain, so you can use those techniques again.

1 Test yourself!

The more you identify what you're not sure about, the more chance you have of succeeding in your exam. How many of these can you get right?

1. What was shrapnel?	2. Why were there so many infected wounds on the Western Front?	3. Name two groups of nurses working on the Western Front.
4. What was sodium citrate used for?	5. When were steel helmets in common use?	6. What does 'triage' mean?
7. Which problem did 'greybacks' cause?	8. Which is the odd one out? Ypres Cambrai Verdun The Somme	9. Name two types of gas used as weapons.
10. What percentage of thigh-bone fractures led to death in 1914?	11. Put in order: Aid Post Hospital Clearing Station Dressing Station	12. What was unusual about the hospital at Arras?

2 Asking questions

We have provided some answers below but it is your job to come up with suitable matching questions. Try to make each question as detailed as possible so you are using your knowledge to help you word it. This is a valuable way of revising because you have to think carefully about topics from a different angle.

1. Regimental Aid Post	2. Ypres	3. The Thomas splint	4. Gas gangrene	5. Blood transfusions
6. Trench foot	7. FANY	8. Often six, sometimes even eight	9. Casualty Clearing Stations	10. Aseptic surgery

3 Telling the stories

The tasks in 1 and 2 above focus on individual pieces of information but you also need to have an understanding of the 'stories' at the heart of this unit. Take each of these questions in turn and prepare an answer that will take you a minute to explain aloud. Explaining it aloud will help 'cement' it in your brain.

1. How was the trench system designed to create effective defence?
2. How did the terrain on the Western Front lead to illnesses and infected wounds?
3. Why did weaponry create more damaging wounds?
4. How were the wounded evacuated from No Man's Land to hospitals?
5. What had been the main developments in medicine and surgery in the early 1900s?
6. What were the key new developments in medical and surgical treatments during the war?
7. 'Soldiers received better care in 1918 than in 1914.' How far do you agree with this statement?

Introducing the exam

Simply knowing a lot of content is not enough to achieve a good grade in your GCSE History exam. You need to know how to write effective answers to the questions. Pages 151–62 give you an insight into the exam and provide guidance on how to approach the different questions. This page and the next introduce the structure of Paper 1 of your

exam. The guidance on page 150 helps you approach your exam with confidence.

Paper 1 is divided into two sections. Section A covers the **study of a historic environment** on the British sector of the Western Front. Section B covers the **thematic study** of Medicine in Britain c.1250–present.

Paper 1: Thematic study and historic environment

Option 11: Medicine through time, c.1250–present

Time: 1 hour 15 minutes
You must have:

① Source Booklet (enclosed)

Instructions

② • Answer Questions 1 and 2 from Section A.
③ • From Section B, answer Questions 3 and 4 and then **EITHER** Question 5 **OR** Question 6.

Information

• The total mark for this paper is 52.
④ • The marks for each question are shown in brackets.

SECTION A: The British Sector of the Western Front, 1914–18:
injuries, treatment and the trenches

Answer Questions 1 and 2.

⑤ 1. Describe **two** features of the methods used to reduce the risk of trench foot on the Western Front.

Feature 1

Feature 2
(Total for Question 1 = 4 marks)

⑥ 2. (a) Study Sources A and B in the Source Booklet.
How useful are Sources A and B for an enquiry into the problems the medical service faced transporting injured soldiers?

Explain your answer, using Sources A and B and your own knowledge of the historical context.
(8 marks)

⑦ (b) **Study Source B**

How would you follow up Source B to find out more about the problems the medical service faced transporting injured soldiers?

In your answer, you must give the question you would ask and the type of source you could use.

Complete the table below: (4 marks)

Detail in Source B that I would follow up: _____
Question I would ask: _____
What type of source I could use: _____
How this might help answer my question: _____

(Total for Question 2 = 12 marks)
TOTAL FOR SECTION A = 16 MARKS

SECTION B: Medicine in Britain, c.1250–present

Answer Questions 3 and 4. Then answer EITHER Question 5 OR 6.

(8) → **3.** Explain one way in which people's responses to the 1665 Great Plague in London were similar to the way that people reacted to the Black Death in Britain. (4 marks)

(9) → **4.** Explain why there was rapid progress in approaches to preventing illness in Britain during the period c.1750–c.1900. (12 marks)

(10) →
> You may use the following in your answer:
> * the 1875 Public Health Act   •   the work of John Snow
>
> You **must** also use information of your own.

Answer **EITHER** Question 5 OR Question 6.

Spelling, punctuation, grammar and the use of specialist terminology will be assessed in this question.

EITHER

(11) → **5.** 'There was little progress in medicine in Britain during the medieval period (c.1250–c.1500).'
How far do you agree? Explain your answer. (16 marks)

> You may use the following in your answer:
> * St Bartholomew's Hospital   •   the Theory of the four Humours
>
> You **must** also use information of your own.

OR

6. 'Jenner's vaccination against smallpox was a major breakthrough in the prevention of disease in Britain during the period c.1700–c.1900.'
How far do you agree? Explain your answer. (16 marks)

> You may use the following in your answer:
> * cowpox   •   cholera
>
> You **must** also use information of your own.

(12) →
(Total for spelling, punctuation, grammar and the use of specialist terminology = 4 marks)

(Total for Question 5 or 6 = 20 marks)

Timing tip

It is important to time yourself carefully. One hour and fifteen minutes sounds a long time but it goes very quickly! Some students run out of time because they spend too long on Section A, thinking that it is worth spending half their time on this Section. However, Section A is worth 16 marks whereas Section B is worth 36 marks. The final two questions of Section B are worth more marks than all the other questions put together. This shows the importance of having a time plan and sticking to it.

Look at the plan on the sticky note to the right. You could use this plan or develop your own and check it with your teacher.

Questions 1 and 2 approx. 25 minutes

Questions 3 and 4 approx. 25 minutes

Either Question 5 or 6 approx. 25 minutes

Planning for success

① THE SOURCE BOOKLET

The exam paper on pages 148 and 149 gives you an idea what your exam will look like. We have not included the Source Booklet. For practice use the sources and activities in Part 2 of this book (pages 104–47). Make sure you spend time reading and annotating the sources before you attempt Question 2 in the exam.

② FOLLOW INSTRUCTIONS CAREFULLY

Read the instructions very carefully. Some students miss questions they need to answer while others waste time answering more questions than they need to answer. Remember to answer **both** parts of Question 2 and to choose between EITHER Question 5 OR 6. You will also see that for Question 1 you need to describe **two** key features whereas with Question 3 you only need to explain **one** way in which people's reactions were similar.

③ THINK CAREFULLY ABOUT WHICH QUESTION YOU CHOOSE

After Questions 1, 2, 3 and 4, you need to decide whether to answer Question 5 or Question 6. Do not rush your decision. Think carefully about which question you will perform best on. Plan your answer – it is worth 16 marks, nearly a third of the total marks for the paper.

④ SPEND TIME DE-CODING QUESTIONS

The marks for each question are shown in brackets. This gives you an idea of how much you need to write, as does the space for your answer on the exam paper. However, do not panic if you do not fill all the space. There will probably be more space than you need and the quality of your answer is more important than how much you write. The most important thing is to keep focused on the question. If you include information that is not relevant to the question you will not gain any marks, no matter how much you write!

Read each question carefully before you to start to answer it. Use the advice on de-coding questions on page 151 to make sure you focus on the question.

⑤ DESCRIBING KEY FEATURES

The first question asks you to describe two features of an aspect of the historic environment you have studied. Headings on the exam paper help you write about each feature separately. Advice on how to gain high marks is on page 155.

⑥ EVALUATING THE USEFULNESS OF A SOURCE

This question asks you to evaluate how useful two sources are for a specific enquiry. Use the Source Booklet to annotate the sources. Make sure you use your own knowledge to place

the source in its historical context. This is a challenging task. Page 153 explains how to approach this question.

⑦ FOLLOWING UP A SOURCE

This question has four parts. You need to fill in the table on the exam paper. Page 154 provides advice on this question.

⑧ EXPLORING SIMILARITIES OR DIFFERENCES BETWEEN TWO PERIODS

This is the first question that tests you on your knowledge and understanding of Medicine from 1250 to the present. It will usually ask you to explain a similarity or a difference between the key features of two different periods. Page 155 explains how to answer this question.

⑨ EXPLAINING WHY MEDICINE CHANGED (OR STAYED THE SAME)

Questions such as this test your ability to write effective explanations. You may be asked to explain why medicine progressed so quickly or why there was little change during a period. Pages 156–57 help you write a good answer to this question.

⑩ USING THE STIMULUS MATERIAL

When you attempt Question 4 and either Question 5 or 6 you will have bullet points as stimulus material to help plan your answer. You do not have to include them but try to use them to get you thinking and to support your arguments. You must bring in your own knowledge too. If you only use the stimulus material you will not gain high marks for your answer.

⑪ MAKING JUDGEMENTS

This question carries the most marks and requires a longer answer that needs careful planning. You will be provided with a statement. It may be about the pace of change in a period (for example Question 5) or the significance of an individual or a discovery (for example Question 6). Pages 158–159 provide advice on answering this question.

⑫ CHECKING THE QUALITY OF YOUR WRITING

Make sure you leave five minutes at the end of the exam to check your answers. If you are short of time check your answer to the final question first as spelling, punctuation, grammar and use of specialist terminology are assessed in this question. You can gain 4 additional marks on this question – page 161 provides advice on what to focus on. However, remember that the accuracy of your spelling, punctuation and grammar is important in all questions as it affects the clarity of your answer.

De-coding exam questions

The examiners are not trying to catch you out: they are giving you a chance to show what you know – and what you can do with what you know. However, you must stick to the question on the exam paper. Staying focused on the question is crucial. Including information that is not relevant or misreading a question and writing about the wrong topic wastes time and gains you no marks.

To stay focused on the question you will need to practise how to 'de-code' questions. This is particularly important for Section B of the exam paper. Follow these **five steps to success**:

Step 1 Read the question a couple of times. Then look at **how many marks** the question is worth. This tells you how much you are expected to write. Do not spend too long on questions only worth a few marks. Remember it is worth planning the 12- and 16-mark questions.

Step 2 Identify the **conceptual focus** of the question. What is the key concept that the question focuses on? Is it asking you to look at:

- the **significance** of a discovery or individual
- **causation** – the reasons why an event or development happened
- **similarities** – between the key features of different periods
- **change** – the extent of change or continuity, progress or stagnation during a period?

Step 3 Spot the **question type**. Are you being asked to:

- **describe** the key features of a period
- **explain** similarities between periods or why something happened
- **evaluate** how useful a source or collection of sources is
- reach a **judgement** as to how far you agree with a particular statement.

Each question type requires a different approach. Look for key words or phrases that help you work out which approach is needed. The phrase 'How far do you agree?' means you need to weigh the evidence for and against a statement before reaching a balanced judgement. 'Explain why' means that you need to explore a range of reasons why an event happened or why the pace of change during a period was fast or slow.

Step 4 Identify the **content focus**. What is the area of content or topic the examiner wants you to focus on?

Step 5 Look carefully at the **date boundaries** of the question. What time period should you cover in your answer? Stick to this carefully or you will waste time writing about events that are not relevant to the question.

Look at the exam question below. At first glance it appears this question is just about Jenner's vaccination against smallpox. This shows the danger of not de-coding a question carefully. If you simply describe what Jenner did you will not get many marks as you are still not focusing on the actual question.

The conceptual focus is significance – you need to reach a judgement on how far Jenner's work was a 'major breakthrough' in the prevention of disease.

The date boundaries for the question are c.1700 and c.1900. If you include references to events in the twentieth century you will waste time and not pick up any additional marks.

> 6. 'Jenner's vaccination against smallpox was a major breakthrough in the prevention of disease in Britain during the period c.1700–c.1900.' How far do you agree? Explain your answer.
>
> (16 marks)

16 marks are available – this means the question requires an extended answer. It is definitely worth planning this answer!

The content focus is more than just Jenner. It is exploring a wider theme – the prevention of disease in Britain.

The phrase 'How far do you agree?' means that this question requires you to reach a judgement about the statement in quotation marks. This means analysing the impact of Jenner's work and its limitations. It also means weighing its significance against other important breakthroughs (such as Snow's work on preventing cholera).

PRACTICE QUESTIONS

Look at the other questions in Section B of the exam paper on page 149.

Break each question down into the five steps and check you have de-coded the question effectively.

Describing key features of a period

'Describe' questions only carry 4 marks so it is important to get to the point quickly so you do not waste precious time that is needed for questions that carry 12 or 16 marks.

Look at the question below.

> **1.** Describe **two** features of the method used to reduce the risk of trench foot on the Western Front. (4 marks)
>
> Feature 1: _____
>
> Feature 2: _____

Tip 1: Stay relevant to the question

One major problem with 'Describe' questions is that students write too much! They include details that are not relevant to the question. Make sure you stick to the question – describe two key features of the methods used to reduce trench foot.

You do not need to:

■ include more than two features (extra features will gain you no more marks)
■ evaluate and reach a judgement as to how successful the methods used to reduce the risk of trench foot were.

If you write too much you could run out of time later in the exam when you are answering questions that are worth a lot more marks and need longer answers.

Tip 2: Keep it short and simple

You can get 2 marks by simply identifying two features of the methods used to reduce the risk of trench foot.

For each feature you identify add a sentence that adds further detail and develops your answer.

Look at the example below. Then practise your technique by tackling the examples in the practice question box.

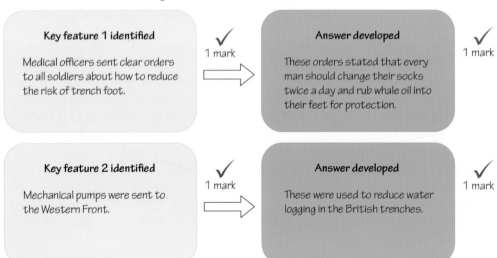

Key feature 1 identified

Medical officers sent clear orders to all soldiers about how to reduce the risk of trench foot.

✓ 1 mark

Answer developed

These orders stated that every man should change their socks twice a day and rub whale oil into their feet for protection.

✓ 1 mark

Key feature 2 identified

Mechanical pumps were sent to the Western Front.

✓ 1 mark

Answer developed

These were used to reduce water logging in the British trenches.

✓ 1 mark

> ## Practice questions
>
> 1. Describe two features of trench conditions that led to illness among soldiers.
> 2. Describe two features of the methods used to reduce the risk of trench fever.
> 3. Describe two features of the support trench system on the Western Front.
> 4. Describe two features of Regimental Aid Posts.
> 5. Describe two features of the Casualty Clearing Stations.
> 6. Describe two features of the methods of transporting the wounded on the Western Front.
> 7. Describe two features of the work of nursing units such as the FANY.

> ### REMEMBER
>
> Stay focused and keep it short and simple. Four sentences are enough for four marks.

Evaluating the usefulness of sources

In Section A of the exam you will be asked to evaluate the value of a source for a specific enquiry. Look at the example below.

> **2.** (a) Study Sources A and B. How useful are Sources A and B for an enquiry into the problems the medical service faced transporting injured soldiers? Explain your answer, using Sources A and B and your own knowledge of the historical context. (8 marks)

You should annotate the sources in the booklet before you start to write your answer. Also, to evaluate effectively we need to use criteria. Use the criteria opposite to help you.

> **Source A:** From the recorded memories of William Easton, East Anglian Field Ambulance. He was 18 in 1916. Here he described conditions near Ypres in 1917.
>
> Up at Ypres we used to go up the line and we'd be waist deep in mud. We were carrying the wounded down near a place called Hooge, where had been a terrific amount of fighting. One trip down a trench in those conditions and you would be all in – exhausted. If you got two or three wounded men down in a day, that was all you could expect to do. We had to carry men in fours there and we had to be very careful because you could do more damage to a man than the shell if you jolted him too much or he fell off the stretcher. To make carrying easier we had slings which we put round our shoulders and over the stretcher's handles.

> **Source B:** An extract from an article in the *Journal of the Royal Army Medical Corps*, 1915.
>
> Admirable as was the organization of the large base hospitals, the transport of the wounded from the fighting line seems to have been very badly managed during the advance of the Germans through Belgium and northern France. The supply of motor ambulances proved totally inadequate and the slightly wounded had to shift for themselves and squeeze into goods trains.

REMEMBER

The question is asking you how useful the sources are, not how useless they are. There will not be any sources that are completely useless. Try not to get bogged down telling the examiner just what is wrong with a source. Look at the strengths of each source as well as considering any limitations. Try to begin and end your answer positively. Start your answer by highlighting how each source *helps* us with this enquiry.

☐ Criteria 1: Consider the content of the source

Highlight or underline useful information for the enquiry in both sources. Make sure you judge how useful it is for the enquiry specified in the question. For this question the sources need to help us understand the problems involved in performing operations on the Western Front. Start your answer by highlighting how each source helps us with this enquiry.

☐ Criteria 2: Consider the provenance of each source

Look at the captions provided above the sources. Think carefully about the following key questions and the impact that this might have on how useful the source is.

■ **What is the nature of the source?**

What type of source is it? How does this affect its utility? For example, a private letter or diary can be useful because the person usually gives his or her honest view.

■ **What are the origins of the source?**

Who produced it? Are they likely to have a good knowledge of the events they talk about? Are they likely to give a one-sided view?

■ **What is the purpose of the source?**

Why was it produced? How might this affect the reliability of the source? For example, a politician's speech or a newspaper report might be produced for propaganda purposes – to encourage people to support the war.

☐ Criteria 3: Use your own knowledge of the historical context to evaluate the source

Compare the information and key messages contained in the source with your own knowledge of the enquiry topic. Do the **CAT test**. Ask yourself these three key questions:

■ How **comprehensive** is the source? Does it have any limitations? What does it miss out?

■ How **accurate** is the source? Does it 'match' what you know about the topic?

■ How **typical** is the source? Did the events described happen regularly on the Western Front or are they unusual and untypical of what went on for the majority of the time?

Practice questions

You can find sources with practice questions on pages 118, 128 and 135.

Following up sources

One of the key aims of this book is to help you understand how we use the enquiry process to research history. As we said on page 105, asking the right historical questions is a crucial part of enquiry and historical research. Exam questions like the one below provide you with the opportunity to show the enquiry skills you have been developing throughout the book.

> 2. (b) How could you follow up Source B (page 153) to find out more about the problems the medical service faced transporting injured soldiers? In your answer, you must give the question you would ask and the type of source you could use. Complete the table below.
>
> (4 marks)
>
> - Detail in Source B that I would follow up: _____
> - Question I would ask: _____
> - What type of source I could use: _____
> - How this might help answer my question: _____

The key tip with this question is to make sure that the four different parts of your answer link together.

Step 1: Link the detail to the enquiry

Start by identifying the focus for the enquiry – in this case the problems the medical service faced transporting injured soldiers. Make sure that the detail you say that you would follow up is linked to this enquiry. For example, if Source B mentions that the supply of motor ambulances was inadequate, you could identify this as a detail that you would follow up as this is linked to the main enquiry.

Step 2: Link the question to the detail

The question you choose must be linked to the detail you are following up from the source. Do not simply choose an interesting question unrelated to the enquiry! If we were following up the detail about motor ambulances we could use 'Why was there a lack of motor ambulances on the Western Front?' as our question.

Step 3: Link the type of source to the question

You now need to choose a type of source that would be useful for following up that question. Look at the list in the box opposite. Make sure you choose a source that would help with the question. For example, in this case Government reports would provide a useful insight into the problems faced by the medical service in providing adequate numbers of motor ambulances.

Step 4: Link this with your own knowledge

Do not forget to explain the advantages of using this type of source and link it to the enquiry. The source type mentioned above would be particularly useful as these reports were produced for use within the government and the aim was to keep people accurately informed of the situation on the Western Front. The reports were not produced for propaganda purposes (in contrast, newspaper accounts might try to paint a positive picture).

REMEMBER

This question is only worth 4 marks. Do not go into detailed explanations of why you chose to follow up with a particular type of source – you do not have time. One or two sentences will be fine.

Practice questions

You can find sources with practice questions on pages 128 and 135.

Different types of sources

National records

- National army records for individual soldiers
- National newspaper reports
- Government reports on aspects of the war
- Medical articles by doctors and nurses who took part in the war

Local records

- Personal accounts of medical treatments by soldiers, doctors, nurses or others who were involved
- Photographs
- Hospital records
- Army statistics

Exploring similarities or differences between the key features of two different periods

Question 3 is the first question that tests your knowledge and understanding of the thematic study on Medicine in Britain, c.1250–present. Remember this is where de-coding questions comes in useful. Look at the question below.

This is an 'explain' question. However, as it is only worth 4 marks, you only have to explain one similarity.

This question has a very specific content focus. To save time make sure you stay relevant – only write about people's responses. There is no need to go into the background of each plague.

The date boundaries are crucial. You must focus on the right case studies, from the specified centuries – the Black Death (fourteenth century) and the great plague that hit London in 1665 (seventeenth century).

> 3. Explain **one** way in which people's responses to the 1665 Great Plague in London were similar to the way that people reacted to the Black Death in Britain. (4 marks)

The conceptual focus of this question is 'similarities' – the ability to be able to compare different periods of history and spot similarities.

The first thing to notice is that the question is only worth 4 marks. It is important that you are clear on the focus of the question so that you can keep your answer short and to the point.

Explaining similarities between time periods

As this is an 'explain' question you must do more than simply identify a similarity. You will need to support your answer with specific details – a good motto is 'prove' don't 'say'. Would your explanation convince the reader that there was a similarity between the ways that people reacted to plagues that were over 300 years apart?

For example you might 'say' that one similarity between reactions to the two plagues was that people's reactions were based on religion. However, this would not get you high marks. Instead you need to prove your big point about religion by providing supporting information **and** 'killer evidence'.

Practice questions

You can find further practice questions on pages 47, 72 and 94.

- **BIG POINT** – With a question only worth 4 marks do not spend time on an introduction. Start your answer with your 'big point' – in this case that reactions were based on religion.

- **SUPPORTING INFORMATION** – You need to develop your initial 'big point' or argument. You could explain how in both centuries people responded to the plague by praying and asking God for help.

- **KILLER EVIDENCE** – You now need to prove that this was the case by providing specific examples from each time period. For the fourteenth century you could refer to the Flagellants while for the seventeenth century you could explain how people put red crosses on their doors and wrote 'God have mercy on us'.

REMEMBER

You should only be spending around five minutes on this question. Keep your answer focused on explaining **one** way in which people behaved or reacted in a similar way. Do not list lots of similarities.

Tackling 12-mark explain questions

Look at the question below.

> **4.** Explain why there was rapid progress in approaches to preventing illness in Britain during the period c.1750–c.1900. (12 marks)
>
> **You may use the following in your answer:**
> - the 1875 Public Health Act
> - the work of John Snow
>
> **You must also use information of your own.**

This question is different in two ways from Question 3 on page 155. Firstly, the conceptual focus is different – in this case the key concept is causation (explaining **why** an event took place or explaining the pace of change). Secondly, this question is worth 12 marks. The examiner will expect you to give a range of reasons **why** there was rapid progress in approaches to preventing illness in Britain between 1750 and 1900. The question also supplies stimulus material (see page 150, Point 10).

It is important to spend time planning this question during your exam. Follow the steps below to help you plan effectively and produce a good answer.

Step 1: Get focused on the question

Make sure you de-code the question carefully. Note that the content focus is on 'approaches to preventing illness' so do not go into medical treatments or what people believed caused disease.

Step 2: Identify a range of factors

Try to cover more than one cause. If your mind goes blank always go back to the key factors that influence change in medicine (see page 8). The stimulus bullet points can also help you. For example, in the question above, the reference to 'the 1875 Public Health Act' shows how the government played a key role in improving methods of prevention.

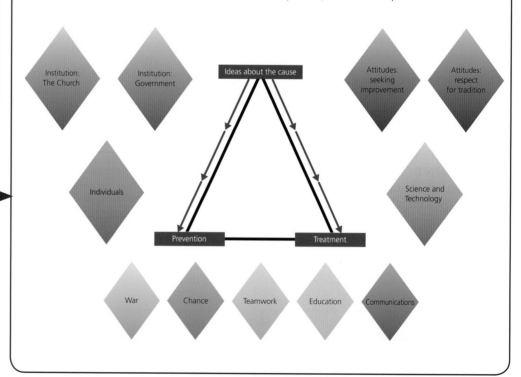

Step 3: Organise your answer using paragraphs

Do not worry about a long introduction. One or two sentences are more than enough and you can use words from the question. Look at the example below. Note how the student has built a short introduction into the first paragraph which focuses on the role played by government.

The period 1750–1900 saw a real improvement in approaches to preventing the spread of disease. One important reason for this was that the government started to take responsibility for improving methods of prevention.

Aim to start a new paragraph each time you move onto a new factor that caused change. Signpost your argument at the start of the paragraph. For example, you could start your next paragraph like this:

Developments in science and technology also played a crucial role in improving methods of prevention.

Step 4: Do not 'say' that a factor was important – 'prove' it was

Remember that a list of reasons why treatment of illness improved will not get you a high-level mark. You need to **prove** your case for each factor. This means developing your explanation by adding supporting information and specific examples (killer evidence).

This is where your work on connectives will come in useful. Look again at the advice on page 25 and remember to tie what you know to the question by using connectives such as 'this meant that', 'this led to' and 'this resulted in'. For example, you may want to build on the opening to your first paragraph by using the example of the 1875 Public Health Act as a way that the government helped to improve methods of prevention. Look at how the student below starts to prove a point.

In 1875 the government introduced a new Public Health Act. This meant that local councils had to improve sewers and drainage, provide fresh water supplies and appoint Medical Officers to inspect facilities.

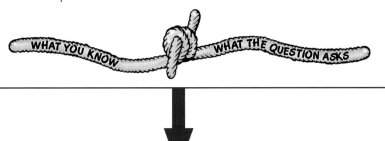

Step 5: End your answer with a thoughtful conclusion

Keep your conclusion short. A good conclusion makes the overall argument clear – it is not a detailed summary of everything you have already written! Make it clear which factor played the most important role. You may want to show how it links to other factors.

Practice questions

You can find further practice questions on pages 47, 72 and 94.

REMEMBER

Do not try to cover too many factors that led to change. Select which factors you can make the strongest argument for. Remember in the exam you would have approximately 15 minutes to answer this question.

Making judgements – tackling the 16-mark question

The last question on the exam paper carries the most marks and requires a carefully planned, detailed answer. You will be provided with a statement in quotation marks and be asked to reach a judgement about **how far you agree** with it. The phrase 'how far' is important as it is unlikely that you will totally agree or disagree with the statement. The examiner will be looking for you to show that you can weigh the evidence for and against the statement.

Look at the example below.

5. 'There was little progress in medicine during the medieval period (c.1250–c.1500).' How far do you agree? Explain your answer. (16 marks)

You may use the following in your answer:
• St Bartholomew's Hospital
• The Theory of the four Humours

You must also use information of your own.

(Total for spelling, punctuation, grammar and the use of specialist terminology = 4 marks)

(Total for Question 5 = 20 marks)

Step 1: Focus

The content focus is important – you have to reach a judgement on medicine, as a whole, in Medieval Britain. This includes ideas about the cause of disease as well as methods of treatment and prevention. The conceptual focus is on change and continuity. You have to evaluate the extent to which medicine progressed or stayed the same, and may do so using the stimulus points (see page 150, Point 10). Focus on the phrase in the question – do you think there was 'little progress' in medicine?

Step 2: Identify

In 16-mark questions you are required to reach a judgement on a statement. In order to do this effectively you need to identify **clear criteria** for reaching that judgement. Just as you need to cover a range of factors in 'explain' questions, you need to **cover a range of criteria** in 'judgement' questions.

Possible criteria for reaching a judgement:

■ If you are judging the importance of an individual or discovery you could analyse and evaluate the immediate impact, the short-term impact and the long-term impact.

■ If you are judging the extent of change you could analyse and evaluate how many people benefited (Did everyone benefit or was it just the rich or those living in a certain area?) or how quickly medicine or an area of medicine progressed (Were there immediate benefits? Were they long lasting and permanent?).

In this example, you are being asked to reach a judgement on 'medicine' in Medieval Britain, so you could explore our three main **themes** and use the following three criteria:

■ Was there 'little progress' in ideas about the cause of disease and the way the body worked?

■ Was there 'little progress' in ways of preventing illness and disease?

■ Was there 'little progress' in ways of treating illness?

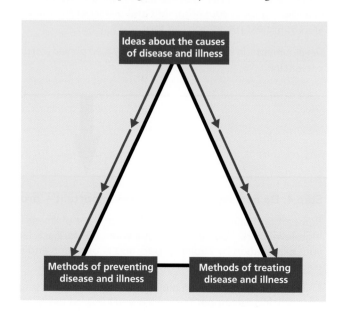

Step 3: Organise

There are two ways of organising your answer.

Approach 1: Write about one criterion in each paragraph:

■ Paragraph 1 – Evaluate the extent to which ideas about the cause of disease and the way the body worked progressed (weigh the evidence for and against).

■ Paragraph 2 – Evaluate the extent to which methods of prevention progressed (weigh the evidence for and against).

■ Paragraph 3 – Evaluate the extent to which treatments progressed (weigh the evidence for and against).

■ Paragraph 4 – Your final conclusion – weigh the evidence – how far do you agree with the statement?

Approach 2: The simplest is to plan 'for' and 'against' paragraphs:

■ Paragraph 1 – Evidence to **support** the statement (make sure that you use the criteria – little progress in ideas about cause, prevention and treatments)

■ Paragraph 2 – Evidence to **counter** the statement (once again use the criteria)

■ Paragraph 3 – Your final conclusion – weigh the evidence – how far do you agree with the statement?

Step 4: Prove

Remember to tie what you know to the question. Do not include information and think that it will speak for itself. Some students think that simply dropping in examples to the right paragraphs is enough. One of the stimulus points refers to St Bartholomew's Hospital. The following statement from a student could be further developed and gain more marks.

In the medieval period many hospitals were set up. For example, St Bartholomew's in London was founded in 1123.

This does not **prove** that the way people were treated improved in the medieval period. To gain more marks, the student would need to go on to explain that hospitals such as St Bartholomew's cared for older people who could no longer look after themselves. Also, it is important to show that St Bartholomew's was not the only hospital to be set up during this period. 'Killer evidence' could be introduced to strengthen the argument – remember that by 1400 there were over 500 hospitals in England.

Step 5: Conclude

Your conclusion is a crucial part of your answer. You have been asked to reach a judgement on a statement. You need to clearly state how far you agree with it and your reason why. It would be easy to sit on the fence and avoid reaching a final conclusion. But sitting on the fence is a dangerous position. Your answer collapses and you lose marks.

Instead of sitting on the fence, you need to be confident and reach an overall judgement. Imagine that you have placed the evidence on a set of scales. How far do they tip in favour of the statement or against it?

You can then move on in your conclusion to explain your judgement. Do not repeat everything you have already written. Think of the scales – what are the heaviest pieces of evidence on each side? Build these into your conclusion in the following way:

JUDGEMENT – Start with your judgement – try to incorporate words from thequestion into this sentence.

↓

COUNTER – Show that you are aware that there is some evidence to counter this andgive the best example.

↓

SUPPORT – Explain why, overall, you have reached the judgement you have. Give yourkey reason or reasons why.

To a large extent, I agree that medicine was slow to progress in Britain during the medieval period.

↓

Many new hospitals were established that provided care for people within local communities.

↓

However, there were not significant improvements in the way that illnesses were treated. Life expectancy stayed the same and there was little progress in methods of preventing the spread of disease.

Practice questions

You can find further practice questions on pages 47, 72, 94, 99, 101 and 103.

REMEMBER

Leave enough time to **check your answer** carefully for spelling, punctuation and grammar.

Four crucial marks are available (this is as much as your answer to Question 1, 2b or 3).

- You will be marked for the accuracy of your spelling and punctuation.
- You will also be marked for your grammar – does your work make sense? Are your arguments clear?
- Finally, the examiner will consider your use of 'specialist terms' – have you used a wide range of historical terms?

What are the key ingredients of effective writing in GCSE history?

The language you use to express your ideas is very important. One of the ways to get better at history is to be more precise with your use of language. For example, rather than simply saying that you *agree* or *disagree* with a statement you can use language that shows whether you agree to *a large extent* or only *to some extent*. Look at the different shades of argument below and experiment with using some of the phrases. Use them when you are debating or discussing in class.

Thinking carefully about the language you use

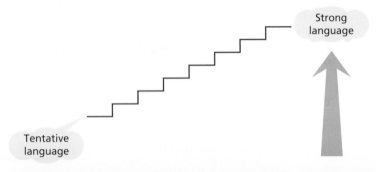

Varying your language to show how far you agree with a statement:	Varying your language to show how important a factor/cause is:
I totally/entirely/completely/absolutely agree with …	… was by far the most important reason why …
I substantially/fundamentally/strongly agree with …	The key/crucial/essential factor was …
I agree to a large extent with …	… was the main cause of …
I mainly/mostly agree with …	The most influential cause was …
I agree to some extent with …	… played a significant/important/major role in …
I partially/partly agree with …	… was of some importance in …
I only agree with … to a limited/slight extent	
Varying your language to show the significance or importance of an individual, discovery, event or development:	**Varying your language to show the extent of change:**
… made the most important/significant contribution to …	… was revolutionised in …
… had a crucial/major/highly significant impact on …	… totally changed during …
… had an important/influential impact on …	… was transformed during …
… was of some importance/significance	… there was fundamental change in …
… only made a limited/partial/slight/minimal contribution to …	The period saw significant/important progress in …
	… saw some changes in … … saw some progress in …
	… saw limited/slight/minimal progress in …

Helpful phrases and sentence starters			
When you want to explore the other side of an argument: On the other hand … However … Alternatively, it could be argued that …	**When you want to highlight similarities:** In the same way … Similarly … This is similar to the way that … Likewise …	**When you want to make an additional point to support an argument:** Also … Additionally … In addition … Moreover … Furthermore …	**When you want to show that an individual, event or discovery was important:** … was a crucial turning point in … … acted as an important catalyst for … Without this event/ development/ discovery … would not have happened. This had an immediate impact on … In the short term this transformed/revolutionised … In the long term this had a lasting impact on …
When you want to link points or show that one thing led to another: Therefore … Due to … Consequently … One consequence of this was … This caused … This led to … This resulted in … This meant that …	**When you want to refer to evidence in a source:** Source A suggests/implies/ indicates that … According to Source B … Source A shows/illustrates/ demonstrates that …	**When you want to give examples to support a point:** For example … For instance … This can be seen when … This is clearly shown by … This is supported by … This is proven by …	

You can use the **progression grid** below to get an idea of what getting better at history looks like. This is designed to give you a general idea of what you need to do to produce good answers in the exam. It focuses on the four key things in the coloured squares on the bingo card (page 162).

The History progression grid

		Question focus	Organisation	Line of argument	Supporting information
High level ↑		The answer is consistently focused on the question.	The answer is structured very carefully and explanations are coherent throughout the answer.	The line of argument is very clear and convincing. It flows throughout the answer.	Supporting information has been precisely selected, and shows wide-ranging knowledge and understanding.
		The answer is mainly focused on the question.	The answer is well organised but some parts lack coherence.	The line of argument is clear, convincing and generally maintained through the answer.	Supporting information is accurate and relevant, and shows good knowledge and understanding.
		The answer has weak or limited links to the question.	Some statements are developed. There is some attempt to organise the material.	The line of argument is partly convincing but not maintained through the answer.	Supporting information is mainly accurate and relevant, and shows some knowledge and understanding.
		The answer has no real links to the question.	The answer lacks organisation.	The line of argument is unclear or missing.	Supporting information is limited or not relevant.

Self-assessing and peer assessing your work

It is important that you check your own work before you hand it to your teacher to be marked. Sometimes you may be asked to assess the work of someone else in your class. In both cases you need to know what you are looking for. What are the key ingredients of great writing in history?

You can use the **bingo card** as a checklist – get competitive and try and show that you have covered all the squares and got a full house of ingredients!

The answer starts with a **clear focus on the question** (there is no long introduction). Key words from the question are used during the answer. For longer answers, each paragraph is linked to the question.	Statements and arguments are fully developed and explained – showing good knowledge and understanding. Arguments are **well supported** by accurate, relevant and well-selected evidence.	**Connectives** are used to help prove arguments and show significance/impact. Look for phrases like: *this led to …* *this resulted in …* *this meant that …*
There is a **clear line of argument** at the start of each paragraph – think of it as a signpost for what follows. The rest of the paragraph supports this argument. The line of argument flows throughout the answer building up to a clear conclusion.	Paragraphs have been used to provide a **clear structure**. Each paragraph starts with a different cause/factor (12-mark explain questions) or a different theme/criteria (16-mark judgement questions).	The answer shows **wide-ranging** knowledge and understanding. It considers a range of factors/causes (explain questions) or explores the evidence for **and** against a statement (judgement questions).
The language used helps to construct very precise arguments – showing how important the writer thinks a cause/factor, event or individual is. A good range of specialist **historical vocabulary** has been used.	There is a **clear conclusion**. For explain questions factors/causes are prioritised or linked. For judgement questions there is a focus on 'how far' the writer agrees with the statement.	The answer has been **carefully checked** for spelling, punctuation and grammar. The meaning is always clear throughout the answer.

Glossary

Amputation   The removal of a limb by surgery

Anaesthetics   A drug or drugs given to produce unconsciousness before and during surgery

Anatomy   The science of understanding the structure and make-up of the body

Anthrax   An infectious disease mostly affecting animals but occasionally people

Antibiotic   A drug made from bacteria that kill other bacteria and so cure an infection or illness

Antibodies   A substance produced in the body to counter infections

Antiseptics   Chemicals used to destroy bacteria and prevent infection

Apothecary   A pharmacist or chemist

Astrology   The study of planets and how they might influence the lives of people

Bacteria/bacterium   A tiny living organism, too small to be seen by the naked eye, which causes disease

Battalion   A battalion contained between 800 and 1000 men

Billets   Accommodation for soldiers

Biochemistry   The study of the chemical processes that occur in living things

Bleed/Bleeding   The treatment of opening a vein or applying leeches to draw blood from the patient. Also means the loss of blood caused by damage to the blood vessels

Cell   The basic unit of life that makes up the bodies of plants, animals and humans. Billions of cells are contained in the human body

Cesspit   A place for collecting and storing sewage

Chemotherapy   Treatment of a disease, such as cancer, by the use of chemicals

Chloroform   A liquid whose vapour acts as an anaesthetic and produces unconsciousness

Contagion   The passing of disease from one person to another

Cranium   The skull, especially the parts enclosing the brain

Dispensary   A place where medicines are given out

Dissection   The cutting up and examination of the body

DNA   Deoxyribonucleic acid, the molecule that genes are made of

Dysentery   A severe infection causing frequent, fluid bowel movements

Epidemic   A widespread outbreak of disease

Excision   Cutting out

Faeces   Waste material from the stomach and digestive system

Four Humours   The Ancient Greeks believed the body contained four Humours of liquids – blood, phlegm, black bile and yellow bile

Gangrene (gas gangrene)   The infection of dead tissue causing, in the case of gas gangrene, foul-smelling gas

Gene   Part of a cell that determines how our bodies look and work. Genes are passed from parents to children

Germ   A micro-organism that causes disease

Germ theory   The theory that germs cause disease, often by infection through the air

Gene therapy   Medical treatment using normal genes to replace defective ones

Herbal remedy   A medicine made up from a mixture of plants, often containing beneficial ingredients

Immune system   The body's defence system against infections, bacteria, etc.

Immunotherapy   A method of treating disease by stimulating the body's immune system to work more effectively

Infection   The formation of disease-causing germs or micro-organisms

Inoculation   Putting a low dose of a disease into the body to help it fight against a more serious attack of the disease

Leeches   Blood-sucking worms used to drain blood from a wound

Ligature   A thread used to tie a blood vessel during an operation

Malaria   A fever spread by mosquitos

Medical officer   A person appointed to look after the public health of an area

Miasma   Smells from decomposing material were believed to cause disease

Microbe   Another name for a bacterium or micro-organism

Passive smoking   The involuntary inhaling of smoke

Patent medicines   A medicine usually sold for a profit. In the nineteenth century patent medicines were often made from a mix of ingredients that had no medical benefits. They were also known as 'cure-alls'

Penicillin   The first antibiotic drug produced from the mould of penicillium to treat infections

Physician   A doctor of medicine who has trained at university

Physiology   The study of how the body works

Plague   A serious infectious disease spread to humans by fleas from rats and mice

Pneumonia   The inflammation of the lungs due to an infection

Polio   A contagious illness that can cause paralysis and death

Poor Law Unions   Local organisations set up to take care of the poor and unemployed

Privies   Toilets, usually public toilets outside houses

Public health   Refers to the well-being of the whole community

Pus   A pale yellow or green fluid found where there is infection in the body

Quarantined   Separated from the rest of the local population because of illness

Radiotherapy   Treatment of a disease, such as cancer, by the use of radium

Radium   A metallic chemical element discovered by Marie Curie in 1898

Remedy   A drug or treatment that cures or controls the symptoms of disease

Scarlet fever   An infectious disease mostly affecting children

Scrofula   Tuberculosis of a gland in the neck. Sometimes known as the King's Evil, as it was believed that being touched by the king could cure the disease

Septicaemia   Blood poisoning caused by the spread of bacteria from an infected area

Smallpox   A dangerous disease causing fever that was a major cause of death until it was beaten by vaccination

Staphylococci bacteria   Bacteria found on the skin that can cause infection if the bacteria become trapped

Sterilise   To destroy all living micro-organisms from surfaces and surgical instruments, e.g. on a scalpel before an operation

Streptococci   A bacterium that causes infections such as scarlet fever and pneumonia

Sulphonamide   An antibacterial drug used to treat bronchitis and pneumonia

Superbugs   Bacteria that have developed immunity to treatment of antibiotics or methods of destroying them by cleaning

Superstition   An unreasonable belief based on ignorance and sometimes fear

Syphilis   A sexually transmitted disease that was common from the late fifteenth century until the introduction of penicillin

Tetanus   A disease in which muscles go rigid or into spasm and which can lead to death

Transfusion   The transfer of blood from one person to another

Triage   The system of splitting the wounded into groups according to who needs the most urgent attention

Tumour   A swelling caused by cells reproducing at an increased rate or an abnormal growth of cells that may or may not be cancerous

Ulcer   An open sore on the skin

Vaccination   The injection into the body of killed or weakened organisms to give the body resistance against disease

Virus   A tiny micro-organism, smaller than bacteria, responsible for infections such as colds, flu, polio and chicken pox

Voluntary hospitals   Hospitals supported by charitable donations

Wise woman   A woman believed to be skilled in magic or local customs

Workhouses   Accommodation for the poor who could no longer pay for or look after themselves. The poor had to work and families were split up in workhouses

---

Answers to decisions on page 33

1. a) – 3 points   b) – 0 points   c) – 0 points
   [The doctors did a]

2. a) 2 points   b) – 0 points   c) – 3 points
   [The doctors did a and c]

3. a) 2 points   b) – 0 points   c) – 3 points
   [The doctors did a and c]

4. a) 3 points   b) – 3 points   c) – 3 points
   [The doctors did all three]

5. Yes – 3 points   No – 0 points
   [The doctors did use the stone]

Index

The Publishers would like to thank the following for permission to reproduce copyright material.